HOW TO BE
A DICTATOR

HOW TO BE
A DICTATOR

The Cult of Personality in the Twentieth Century

FRANK DIKÖTTER

BLOOMSBURY PUBLISHING

NEW YORK · LONDON · OXFORD · NEW DELHI · SYDNEY

BLOOMSBURY PUBLISHING
Bloomsbury Publishing Inc.
1385 Broadway, New York, NY 10018, USA

BLOOMSBURY, BLOOMSBURY PUBLISHING, and the Diana logo
are trademarks of Bloomsbury Publishing Plc

First published in 2019 in Great Britain
First published in the United States 2019

ISBN: HB: 978-1-63557-379-4; EBOOK: 978-1-63557-380-0

Library of Congress Cataloging-in-Publication Data is available

2 4 6 8 10 9 7 5 3 1

Typeset by Newgen Knowledge Works Pvt. Ltd., Chennai, India
Printed and bound in the U.S.A. by Berryville Graphics Inc., Berryville, Virginia

Contents

'So that in the first place I put for a general inclination of all mankind a perpetual and restless desire of power after power that ceases only in death. The cause of this is not always that a man hopes for a more intensive delight than he has already attained or that he cannot be content with moderate power, but because he cannot assure the power and means to live well which he has present without the acquisition of more.'

THOMAS HOBBES,
The Essential Leviathan: A Modernised Edition

'Is it better to be loved rather than feared, or vice versa? The answer is that one would prefer to be both but, since they don't go together easily, if you have to choose, it's much safer to be feared than loved... Men are less worried about letting down someone who has made himself loved than someone who makes himself feared. Love binds when someone recognises he should be grateful to you, but, since men are a sad lot, gratitude is forgotten the moment it's inconvenient. Fear means fear of punishment, and that's something people never forget.'

NICCOLO MACHIAVELLI,
The Prince, a modern translation by Tim Parks

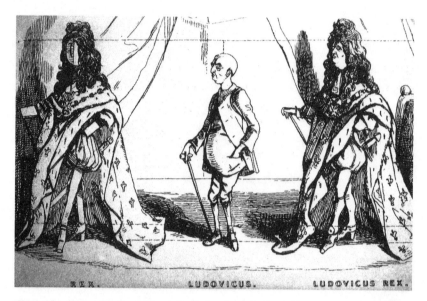

W.M. Thackeray, *The Paris Sketch Book*, London: Collins' Clear-Type Press, 1840.

Preface

In 1840 the satirical novelist William Makepeace Thackeray, famous for lampooning the high and mighty, published a caricature of Louis XIV. To the left stands a clothes horse, displaying the king's sword, his ermine and fleur-de-lis robe, his wig with tumbling curls of hair, his shoes with their aristocratic heels. In the centre the man himself, a poor Ludovicus in underwear, with spindly legs, a protruding stomach, bald, bare and toothless. But on the left he emerges fully dressed, a proud Ludovicus Rex in full regalia. Thackeray had undressed the King of Kings to show the man, frail and pitiful without the trimmings of power: 'Thus do barbers and cobblers make the gods that we worship.'[1]

'L'État, c'est moi,' the seventeenth-century king allegedly pronounced: 'I am the state.' As Louis saw it, he was answerable to God alone. He was an absolute monarch, who for more than seventy years used his autocratic power to weaken the nobility, centralise the state and expand his country by force of arms. He also projected himself as an infallible Sun King around whom everything revolved. He made sure he was glorified by all, with medals, paintings, busts, statues, obelisks and triumphal arches appearing throughout the realm. Poets, philosophers and official historians celebrated his achievements, acclaiming him as omniscient and omnipotent. He transformed a royal hunting lodge south-west of Paris into the Chateau of Versailles, a monumental, 700-room palace with a sprawling estate where he held court, obliging his noble courtiers to compete for favours.[2]

Louis XIV was a master of political theatre, but all politicians, to some extent, rely on image. Louis XVI, a descendant of the Sun King, was sent to the guillotine after the 1789 revolution, and the notion of divine right was buried with him. The revolutionaries held that sovereign rights were vested in the people, not in God. In the democracies that gradually emerged over the next two centuries, leaders understood that they had to appeal to voters, who could remove them at the ballot box.

There were, of course, other ways of achieving power, besides elections. One could organise a coup, or rig the system. In 1917 Lenin and the Bolsheviks stormed the Winter Palace, proclaiming a new government. Later they referred to their coup as a 'revolution' inspired by 1789. A few years later, in 1922, Mussolini marched on Rome, forcing parliament to hand over power. Yet as they and other dictators found out, naked power has an expiry date. Power seized through violence must be maintained by violence, although violence can be a blunt instrument. A dictator must rely on military forces, a secret police, a praetorian guard, spies, informants, interrogators, torturers. But it is best to pretend that coercion is actually consent. A dictator must instil fear in his people, but if he can compel them to acclaim him he will probably survive longer. The paradox of the modern dictator, in short, is that he must create the illusion of popular support.

Throughout the twentieth century hundreds of millions of people cheered their own dictators, even as they were herded down the road to serfdom. Across large swathes of the planet, the face of a dictator appeared on hoardings and buildings, with portraits in every school, office and factory. Ordinary people had to bow to his likeness, pass by his statue, recite his work, praise his name, extol his genius. Modern technologies, from radio and television to the industrial production of posters, badges and busts, made dictators ubiquitous to an extent that would have been unimaginable in the time of Louis XIV. Even in relatively small countries like Haiti, thousands were regularly obliged to hail their leader, marching in front of the presidential palace, dwarfing the festivities organised at Versailles.

In 1956 Nikita Khrushchev denounced Joseph Stalin, detailing his reign of fear and terror. He gave a name to what he viewed as his erstwhile master's 'loathsome adulation' and 'mania for greatness', calling it the 'cult of the individual'. It was translated as 'cult of personality' in English. It may not be a rigorously developed concept proposed by a great social scientist, but most historians find it quite adequate.[3]

When Louis XIV was still a minor, France was rocked by a series of rebellions, as aristocrats attempted to limit the power of the crown. They failed, but left a deep impression on the young king, who developed a lifelong fear of rebellion. He moved the centre of power from Paris to Versailles, and obliged the nobles to spend time at court, where he could observe them as they were made to win royal favour.

Dictators, likewise, were afraid of their own people, but even more fearful of their entourage at court. They were weak. Had they been strong, they would have been elected by majority. Instead, they decided to take a shortcut, often over the bodies of their opponents. But if they could seize power, others could too, raising the prospect of a stab in the back. There were rivals, often just as ruthless. Mussolini was merely one of several established fascist leaders and had faced a rebellion within the ranks before he marched on Rome in 1922. Stalin paled in comparison to Trotsky. Mao was repeatedly stripped of his positions by more powerful rivals in the 1930s. Kim Il-sung was imposed on an unwilling population by the Soviet Union in 1945, and was surrounded by communist leaders with a far more distinguished pedigree of underground work.

There were many strategies for a dictator to claw his way to power and get rid of his rivals. There were bloody purges, there was manipulation, there was divide and rule, to name only a few. But in the long run the cult of personality was the most efficient. The cult debased allies and rivals alike, forcing them to collaborate through common subordination. Most of all, by compelling them to acclaim him before the others, a dictator turned everyone into a liar. When everyone lied, no one knew who was lying, making it more difficult to find accomplices and organise a coup.

Who built up the cult? There were hagiographers, photographers, playwrights, composers, poets, editors and choreographers. There were powerful ministers of propaganda, and sometimes entire branches of industry. But the ultimate responsibility lay with the dictators themselves. 'Politics in a dictatorship begins in the personality of the dictator,' wrote Mao Zedong's doctor in a classic memoir.[4] The eight dictators in this book had widely differing personalities, but every one made all the key decisions that led to his own glorification. Some intervened more often than others. Mussolini, by one account, spent half of his time projecting himself as the omniscient, omnipotent and indispensable ruler of Italy – on top of running half a dozen ministries. Stalin constantly pruned his own cult, cutting back what he thought was excessive praise only to allow it to reappear a few years later when he judged the time was ripe. Ceaușescu compulsively promoted his own person. Hitler, too, attended to every detail of his image in the early years, although later in his career he delegated more than usual when compared with other dictators. All of them used the full resources of the state to promote themselves. They were the state.

Not all historians would give a dictator centre stage. Ian Kershaw famously described Hitler as a 'non-person', a mediocre man whose personal characteristics could not explain his popular appeal. The spotlight, he believed, had to be turned on 'the German people' and their perception of him.[5] But how would one know what people thought of their leader, since freedom of speech is always the first casualty of a dictatorship? Hitler was not elected by a majority, and within a year of coming to power the Nazis threw some 100,000 ordinary people into concentration camps. The Gestapo, the Brown Shirts and the courts alike did not hesitate to lock up those who failed to acclaim their leader properly.

At times expressions of devotion to a dictator appeared so spontaneous that outside observers – as well as later historians – assumed that they were genuine. The Stalin cult, one historian of the Soviet Union tells us, 'was widely accepted and deeply believed by millions of Soviet people of all classes, ages and occupations, especially in the cities'.[6] It is a vague and unsubstantiated statement, no more true or false than its opposite, namely that millions of Soviet people of all backgrounds did not believe in the Stalin cult, especially in the countryside. Even keen supporters found it impossible to read the mind of their leader, to say nothing of probing the thoughts of millions of people regimented by their own regime.

Dictators who lasted possessed many skills. Many excelled at hiding their feelings. Mussolini saw himself as Italy's finest actor. In an unguarded moment Hitler, too, called himself Europe's greatest performer. But in a dictatorship many ordinary people also learned how to act. They had to smile on command, parrot the party line, shout the slogans and salute their leader. In short, they were required to create the illusion of consent. Those who failed to play along were fined, imprisoned, occasionally shot.

The point was not so much that few subjects adored their dictators, but that no one knew quite who believed what. The purpose of the cult was not to convince or persuade, but to sow confusion, to destroy common sense, to enforce obedience, to isolate individuals and crush their dignity. People had to self-censor, and in turn they monitored others, denouncing those who failed to appear sufficiently sincere in their professions of devotion to the leader. Underneath the appearance of widespread uniformity, there was a broad spectrum, ranging from those who genuinely idealised their leader – true believers, opportunists, thugs – to those who were indifferent, apathetic or even hostile.

Dictators were popular at home, but also admired by foreigners, including distinguished intellectuals and eminent politicians. Some of the greatest minds of the twentieth century were willing to ignore or even justify tyranny in the name of the greater good, and helped to shore up the credentials of their favourite dictators. They appear only fleetingly in these pages, since they have been the subject of several excellent studies, not least the work of Paul Hollander.[7]

Since a cult had to appear genuinely popular, welling up from the hearts of the people, it was invariably tinged with superstition and magic. In some countries the religious overtones were so striking that one might be tempted to see it as a peculiar form of secular worship. But in every case this impression was deliberately cultivated from above. Hitler presented himself as a messiah united with the masses in a mystical, quasi-religious bond. François Duvalier went to great lengths to assume the air of a Voodoo priest, encouraging rumours about his otherworldly powers.

In communist regimes in particular there was an added need for some sort of traditional resonance. The reason for this was simple: few people in predominantly rural countries like Russia, China, Korea or Ethiopia understood Marxism-Leninism. Appeals to the leader as some sort of holy figure were more successful than the abstract political philosophy of dialectical materialism that a largely illiterate population in the countryside found hard to comprehend.

Loyalty to one person mattered most in a dictatorship, more so than loyalty to one creed. Ideology, after all, can be divisive. A body of work can be interpreted in different ways, potentially leading to different factions. The greatest enemies of the Bolsheviks were the Mensheviks, and they both swore by Marx. Mussolini spurned ideology and kept fascism deliberately vague. He was not one to be hemmed in by a rigid set of ideas. He prided himself on being intuitive, following his instinct rather than espousing a consistent worldview. Hitler, like Mussolini, had little to offer except himself, beyond an appeal to nationalism and anti-Semitism.

The issue is more complicated in the case of communist regimes, since they were supposed to be Marxist. Yet here too it would have been imprudent for ordinary people and party members alike to spend too much time dwelling on the writings of Karl Marx. One was a Stalinist under Stalin, a Maoist under Mao, a Kimist under Kim.

In the case of Mengistu, commitment to the tenets of socialism, beyond the obligatory red stars and flags, was shallow. Across Ethiopia there were posters of the holy trinity, namely Marx, Engels and Lenin. But it was Lenin, not Marx, who appealed to Mengistu. Marx had offered a vision of equality, but Lenin came up with a tool to seize power: the revolutionary vanguard. Instead of waiting for the workers to gain class consciousness and overthrow capitalism, as Marx had suggested, a group of professional revolutionaries, organised along strict military lines, would lead the revolution and establish a dictatorship of the proletariat to engineer the transition from capitalism to communism from above, ruthlessly eliminating all enemies of progress. For Mengistu the collectivisation of the countryside may have been Marxist, but most of all it was a means to extract more grain from the countryside, allowing him to build up his troops.

Communist dictators transformed Marxism beyond recognition. Marx had proposed that the workers of the world should unite in a proletarian revolution, but Stalin instead advanced the notion of 'socialism in one country', holding that the Soviet Union should strengthen itself before exporting revolution abroad. Mao read Marx, but turned him on his head by making peasants rather than workers the spearhead of the revolution. Instead of maintaining that material conditions were the primary force of historical change, Kim Il-sung proposed the exact opposite, claiming that people could achieve true socialism by relying on the spirit of self-reliance. In 1972 the Great Leader's thought was enshrined in the constitution, as Marxism vanished altogether from North Korea. Yet in all these cases the Leninist concept of the revolutionary vanguard remained virtually unchanged.

More often than not ideology was an act of faith, a test of loyalty. This is not to suggest that dictators lacked any worldview, or a set of beliefs. Mussolini believed in economic self-sufficiency and invoked it like an incantation. Mengistu was fixated on Eritrea as a rebel province and was certain that relentless war was the only solution. But ultimately ideology was what the dictator said it was, and what the dictator decreed could change over time. He personalised power, making his word the law.

Dictators lied to their people, but they also lied to themselves. A few became wrapped up in their own world, convinced of their own genius. Others developed a pathological distrust of their own entourage. All were surrounded by sycophants. They teetered between hubris and paranoia, and as a result took major decisions on their own, with devastating consequences that cost the lives of millions of people. A few became unmoored from reality altogether, as with Hitler in his final years, not to mention Ceaușescu. But many prevailed. Stalin and Mao died of natural causes, having made themselves the objects of adoration for many decades. Duvalier managed to pass on power to his son, prolonging his cult by twelve years. And in the case of the most extravagant cult ever seen, the Kim clan in North Korea has now reached generation three.

The list of leaders commonly regarded as modern dictators reaches well beyond a hundred. Some were in power for a few months, others for decades. Among those who could easily have been included in this book are, in no particular order, Franco, Tito, Hoxha, Sukarno, Castro, Mobutu, Bokassa, Gaddafi, Saddam, Assad (father and son), Khomeini and Mugabe.

Most had a cult of personality in one form or another, creating variations on a common theme. A few did not, for instance Pol Pot. For two years after he took power, even his exact identity was in dispute. In Cambodia people deferred to Angkar, or 'The Organisation'. But as the historian Henri Locard has noted, the decision not to build a cult of personality had disastrous consequences for the Khmer Rouge. Concealment behind an anonymous organisation that nipped in the bud any and all opposition soon backfired. 'Failing to induce adulation and submissiveness, the Angkar could only generate hatred.'[8] Even Big Brother, in George Orwell's *1984*, had a face that stared out at people from every street corner.

Dictators who survived often relied on two instruments of power: the cult and terror. Yet all too often the cult has been treated as a mere aberration, a repellent but marginal phenomenon. This book places the cult of personality where it belongs, at the very heart of tyranny.

Mussolini

Located on the edge of the historic centre, EUR is one of Rome's most austere districts, criss-crossed by wide, linear avenues and imposing buildings covered in gleaming white travertine marble – the same material used to build the Colosseum. EUR stands for Esposizione Universale Roma, a gigantic world fair designed by Benito Mussolini to mark the twentieth anniversary of the March on Rome in 1942. As its master architect Marcello Piacentini put it, the project would showcase a new, eternal civilisation, a 'Fascist civilisation'. Although the exposition never took place, interrupted by the Second World War, many of the buildings were completed in the 1950s. One of the most iconic structures of the EUR, built on an elevated podium like an ancient Roman temple, surrounded by majestic umbrella pines, contains the state archives.[1]

In a majestic reading room with towering columns one can read through the dusty and yellowing correspondence addressed to the Duce. At the height of his glory he received up to 1,500 letters a day. All of these went through a personal secretariat employing some fifty people, who selected several hundred items for his personal attention. By the time Mussolini fell from power in the summer of 1943, the archive contained half a million files.[2]

On 28 October 1940, celebrated as Day One of the fascist calendar, telegrams came from all corners of the realm. There were odes to 'His Supreme and Glorious Excellence', with Salustri Giobbe exalting 'the supreme genius who has prevailed over all the storms of the world'. The prefect from Trieste, to take another example, sent word that the entire population praised his genius, while the city of Alessandria formally hailed him as the Creator of Greatness.[3]

Most of all, however, admirers of the Duce wanted signed photographs. They were requested by people from every walk of life, from schoolchildren who wrote to offer Christmas greetings to mothers mourning the deaths of their soldier sons. Mussolini often obliged. When Francesca Corner, a ninety-five-year-old pensioner from Venice, received a reply, she was overcome by the 'greatest outpouring of emotion', according to the local prefect who dutifully witnessed and reported the occasion.[4]

Like most dictators, Mussolini fostered the idea that he was a man of the people, accessible to all. In March 1929, in front of the assembled leadership, he boasted that he had responded to 1,887,112 individual cases brought to his attention by his personal secretariat. 'Every time that individual citizens, even from the most remote villages, have applied to me, they have received a reply'.[5] It was a bold claim, but, as the archives testify, one not entirely without merit. By one account, Mussolini spent more than half of his time curating his own image.[6] He was the ultimate master of propaganda, at once actor, stage manager, orator and brilliant self-publicist.

Few could have predicted his rise to power. The young Mussolini tried his luck at journalism for the Italian Socialist Party, but fell out of favour with his comrades for advocating Italy's entry into the First World War. He was drafted into the army and wounded when a mortar bomb accidentally exploded in 1917.

As elsewhere in Europe, the end of the war brought a period of industrial unrest. After years of slaughter on the battlefield and regimentation on the factory floor, workers began taking part in strikes that paralysed the economy. Inspired by Lenin's seizure of power in Russia in 1917, entire municipalities became socialist and started flying the red flag, declaring themselves in favour of a dictatorship of the proletariat. These were the Red Years, as Socialist Party membership grew to more than 200,000 by 1920, while the General Confederation of Labour boasted over two million adherents.[7]

In 1919 Mussolini launched a movement that would become the Fascist Party. Its programme was vaguely libertarian, patriotic and anti-clerical, and was stridently promoted in the pages of Mussolini's *Popolo d'Italia*. But fascism failed to win over enough voters in the general elections to secure even a single seat in parliament. Party members left in droves, with fewer than 4,000 committed followers remaining nationwide. Derided by his political opponents, Mussolini bitterly pronounced that 'fascism has come to a dead end', openly speculating that he might leave politics altogether for a career in the theatre.[8]

His loss of nerve was momentary. In September 1919 the poet Gabriele d'Annunzio led 186 mutineers in a raid on Fiume, a city to which Italy had made a claim in the wake of the collapse of the Austro-Hungarian monarchy a year earlier. Mussolini realised that the power he had failed to obtain through free elections could be seized through brute force. But d'Annunzio also inspired Mussolini in other ways. In Fiume the flamboyant poet pronounced himself Duce, a term derived from the Latin word *dux*, meaning leader. For fifteen months, until he was dislodged by the army, d'Annunzio held the Istrian port city in thrall, appearing regularly on a balcony to address his followers, who were dressed in black shirts and greeted their leader with a straight-armed salute. There were daily parades, fanfares, distributions of medals and endless sloganeering. As one historian has put it, fascism took from d'Annunzio not so much a political creed as a way of doing politics. Mussolini realised that pomp and pageantry appealed far more to the crowd than incendiary editorials.[9]

Fascism as an ideology remained vague, but Mussolini now realised the shape it would take: he would be the leader, the one sent by destiny to revive the fortunes of his nation. He started taking flying lessons in 1920, posing as the new man with the vision and drive to carry through a revolution. He was already an accomplished journalist who knew how to use a terse, direct, unadorned style to convey sincerity and resolution; now he practised as an actor, using staccato sentences and sparse but imperious gestures to present himself as an indomitable leader: head tilted back, chin pushed forward, hands on hips.[10]

In 1921 the government began to court the fascists openly, hoping to use them to weaken opposition parties on the left. The army, too, was sympathetic. Fascist squads, in some cases protected by the local authorities, roamed the streets beating up their opponents and assaulting hundreds of trade union headquarters and socialist party centres. As the country moved towards civil war, Mussolini conjured up a Bolshevik peril, turning fascism into a party devoted to the destruction of socialism. Italy, he wrote, needed a dictator to save it from a communist uprising. In the autumn of 1922, by which time fascist squads had grown powerful enough to control large parts of the country, Mussolini threatened to send some 300,000 armed fascists to the capital, even though in reality fewer than 30,000 blackshirts were ready, most of them so poorly equipped that they were no match for the garrison troops in Rome. But the bluff worked. As fascists began occupying government offices in Milan and elsewhere during the night of 27/28 October, King Victor Emmanuel, mindful of the fate of the Romanovs after 1917, summoned Mussolini to Rome and appointed him prime minister.[11]

A royal appointment was one thing, a popular image another. Mussolini, still in Milan, wanted to develop the myth of a March on Rome, one in which he entered the capital on horseback, leading his legions across the Rubicon to impose his will on a feeble parliament. But even after he had been asked to form a government, there were only a few thousand fascists in the capital. A counterfeit march was hurriedly organised. Blackshirts made their way to the capital, their first order of business being the destruction of the printing machines of opposition newspapers to make sure that the fascist version of events prevailed. Mussolini arrived by train in the morning of 30 October. His victorious troops were reviewed by the king and sent back home the following day. Seven years later, to celebrate the anniversary of the march on Rome, an equestrian statue was inaugurated in Bologna, standing five metres tall, the Duce peering into the future, holding the reins in one hand, a banner in the other.[12]

Mussolini was only thirty-nine. He was small in stature, but created an impression of greater height by maintaining a straight back and stiff torso. 'His face was sallow, his black hair was fast receding from a lofty brow, the mouth was large, his features mobile, the jaw massive and in the centre of his head two large, very black piercing eyes which seemed almost to protrude from his face.' Most of all, his manner of speech and his theatrical gestures – head leaning halfway back, chin jutting sharply forward, rolling eyes – were calculated to give an impression of power and vitality. In private he could be courteous and perfectly charming. The English journalist George Slocombe, who met him in 1922, observed that his public persona changed dramatically in one-to-one encounters, as his muscles lost their tension, his tense jaw softened and his voice became cordial. Slocombe noted that Mussolini had been on the defensive his entire life. 'Now that he had assumed the role of aggressor, he could not shake off his instinctive distrust of strangers lightly.'[13]

His wariness of other people, including his own ministers and party leaders, remained with him to the end of his life. As Ivone Kirkpatrick, a sharp observer posted at the British Embassy put it, 'He was sensitive to the emergence of any possible rival and he viewed all men with a peasant's suspicion'.[14]

There were plenty of rivals to worry about. While he projected an image of iron leadership, fascism was not so much a united movement as a loose amalgamation of local squad leaders. Only a year earlier, Mussolini had faced rebellion within the ranks from some of the most established fascists, including Italo Balbo, Roberto Farinacci and Dino Grandi. They had accused him of being too close to the parliamentarians in Rome. Grandi, a fascist leader in Bologna with a reputation for violence, had tried to bring about Mussolini's fall. Balbo, a thin young man with dishevelled hair, was an extremely popular figure who would remain a serious rival for decades to come. Mussolini's response was to form a coalition government that excluded all prominent fascists from office. In his first appearance as prime minister he intimidated the Chamber of Deputies, which was hostile, and flattered the Senate, which was friendly. Most of all, he assured them that he would respect the constitution. Relieved, a majority gave him full powers, a few speakers even begging Mussolini to impose a dictatorship.[15]

Mussolini appeared briefly on the international scene, travelling to Lausanne and London to be courted by potential allies. At Victoria Station he and his entourage were given a triumphant welcome, having to move through a 'screaming mass of humanity, blinded by the flashes of the photographers' cameras'. Still basking in the glory of his March on Rome, he was acclaimed by the press as the Cromwell of Italy, the Italian Napoleon, the new Garibaldi in a black shirt. While his international image would go from strength to strength, it would be sixteen years before he crossed the Italian border again.[16]

At home, few people had ever seen the Duce. Mussolini was keen to bring the population under his spell, with whirlwind tours around the country, endless unannounced visits to villages, mass meetings with workers and inaugurations of public projects. He soon had his own train and demanded that it slow down when there was a large crowd, always making sure to stand by the window: 'All of them should be able to see me,' he explained to his valet, who was tasked with finding out on which side of the tracks the masses were gathered. What was at first a political necessity would over time become an obsession.[17]

While Mussolini was wary of his rivals, he immediately put one of his most reliable collaborators in charge of the press at the Ministry of the Interior, an institution the Duce ran himself. Cesare Rossi's task was to promote fascism in the press, using secret funds to finance publications favouring Mussolini and draw independent newspapers into the orbit of the government. Rossi also funded a secret group of fascist militants charged with eliminating enemies of the regime. One of them was Amerigo Dumini, a young adventurer known as 'the Duce's hitman'. In June 1924, he and several accomplices kidnapped Giacomo Matteotti, a socialist leader and deputy openly critical of Mussolini, stabbing him repeatedly with a carpenter's file before burying his body in a ditch outside Rome.[18]

The murder caused widespread revulsion. Popular opinion turned against Mussolini, who was now more isolated than ever. He made a placatory speech, which in turn alienated his followers, who were under attack by parliament and the press. Fearing that they might turn against him, he finally took the plunge into dictatorship with a violent speech delivered to the Chamber of Deputies on 3 January 1925. Mussolini defiantly announced that efforts to form a parliamentary coalition were futile and that he would now pursue a path of exclusive fascist rule. He alone, he claimed boldly, was responsible for all that had happened. 'If fascism has been a criminal association, then I am the chief of that criminal association.' And he alone would put things right – by force through a personal dictatorship if necessary.[19]

What followed was a campaign of intimidation at every level, as civil liberties were crushed. Within days the police, with the help of the fascist militia, searched hundreds of houses and arrested members of the opposition.

The press was muzzled. Even before Mussolini's speech of 3 January 1925 a decree in July 1924 had given prefects the power to close down any publication without warning. But the liberal press continued to outsell fascist newspapers by a factor of twelve, churning out four million copies a day. Many were now closed down, their most critical journalists persecuted. Police commissioners were attached to the print shops that were still allowed to operate, ensuring that state propaganda was broadcast to all. *Corriere della Sera*, one of the most important opposition papers, was turned into a fascist organ. A draconian law on public security in November 1926 spelled out the reasons for immediate seizure by the police, including writings that were 'damaging to the prestige of the state or its authorities'. A pall of secrecy settled over the country. Telephone lines and the mail were monitored, while blackshirt thugs and undercover police brought the streets under surveillance.[20]

The pace of the revolution was accelerated by several attempts on Mussolini's life. On 7 April 1926 Violet Gibson, an Irish aristocrat, fired a gun at the Duce, grazing his nose. Six months later a fifteen-year-old boy took a shot at him during a parade celebrating the March on Rome. He was lynched on the spot by fascists, fuelling suspicion that the affair had been staged for political ends. From November 1925 to December 1926 all civil associations and political parties came under the purview of the state. Freedom of association was suspended, even for small groups of three or four persons. As Mussolini proclaimed, 'All within the state, nothing outside the state, nothing without the state'.[21]

On Christmas Eve 1925 Mussolini was invested with full executive authority without the intervention of parliament under the new title of Head of Government. In the words of a foreign visitor, he was now 'like a jailer with all the keys hanging at his belt and revolver in hand, pacing unquestioned up and down Italy, as in the quiet and sullen corridors of a vast prison'.[22]

Mussolini was also suspicious of the fascists, however. In February 1925 he named Roberto Farinacci secretary of the National Fascist Party, the only legally permitted political organisation in the country. Farinacci set about curbing the power of the fascists and destroying the party machine, opening the way for a system of personal rule dominated by Mussolini. Thousands of the more radical party members were purged. Much as the Duce had refused to appoint fascist leaders to the coalition government in 1922, he now relied on local prefects named directly by the state to police the nation. Mussolini liked to divide and rule, making sure that party officials and the state bureaucracy oversaw each other, leaving the substance of power to himself.[23]

As some party members were dismissed, others started adulating their leader. Farinacci, for one, assiduously developed the cult of his master. In 1923, during Mussolini's visit back home to Predappio, local leaders had proposed to mark his birthplace with a bronze plaque. Two years later, as Farinacci unveiled the memorial, he announced that every party member should go on a religious pilgrimage to Predappio and take an 'oath of loyalty and devotion' to the Duce.[24]

Realising that their own survival now depended on the myth of the great dictator, other party leaders joined the chorus, portraying Mussolini as a saviour, a miracle worker who was 'almost divine'. Their destinies were tied up with the Duce, the only one capable of holding fascism together. Mussolini was the centre around which leaders as diverse as Grandi and Farinacci could collaborate through common subordination.[25]

Roberto Farinacci, having purged the ranks of the party, was in turn dismissed in 1926, replaced by Augusto Turati, a journalist turned squad leader in the early years of the fascist movement. Turati set about consolidating the cult of the Duce, demanding an oath from party members to ensure their absolute obedience to Mussolini. In 1927 he penned the first catechism, entitled *A Revolution and a Leader*, in which he explained that while there was a Great Council, the Duce was the 'one leader, the only leader, from whom all power flows'. There was, as he put it, 'a spirit, a soul, a light, a reality of conscience in which all brothers can find themselves and recognise themselves: the spirit, the goodness, the passion of Benito Mussolini'. A year later, in a preface to a textbook on the origins and development of fascism, he equated the revolution with Mussolini, and Mussolini with the nation: 'When the entire nation walks on the road of fascism, its face, its spirit, its faith become one with the Duce.'[26]

While Mussolini occasionally professed to dislike the cult around his person, he was actually its main architect. He was a master of the art of projecting his own image, carefully studying certain gestures and poses. He rehearsed in Villa Torlonia, a vast, neoclassical villa on a sprawling estate which became his residence in 1925. In the evenings he would sit in a comfortable chair in a projection room to study every detail of his public performance. Mussolini considered himself to be Italy's greatest actor. Years later, when Greta Garbo visited Rome, his face clouded over: he did not want anyone to overshadow him.[27]

His repertoire changed over time. The famous scowl – imitated by a subservient Farinacci – was abandoned by 1928, while over the years his harsh features softened. His jaw became less rigid. The glaring eyes, so striking in 1922, became more serene. His smile seemed congenial. As George Slocombe noted, 'Except Stalin, no other European leader displays his air of calm, unruffled assurance, the result of uninterrupted years of supreme authority.'[28]

Il Popolo d'Italia ('The People of Italy') had been Mussolini's personal newspaper since 1914, and for many years he had exalted himself as a natural leader in its pages. After he handed the editorship over to his brother Arnaldo in 1922 the paper began describing the Duce as a demi-god.[29]

Cesare Rossi, who had been put in charge of the press in 1922, had to flee the country after Matteotti's murder, but his office flourished. From 1924 onwards the Press Office made sure that all newspapers were filled with what one critic called 'nauseous laudation' of Mussolini. His speeches were widely reproduced. As Italo Balbo, one of the blackshirt leaders, put it, 'Italy is a newspaper in which Mussolini writes the first page every day'.[30]

In 1925 the Press Office took over the Istituto Luce, an institution devoted to producing and distributing cinematographic material. Mussolini ran it directly, previewing and editing news reports from his projection room in Villa Torlonia. Within a few years every cinema, from down-at-heel theatres in working-class neighbourhoods to film palaces with gilded furniture and opulent carpets, was compelled by law to show newsreels produced by Luce with Mussolini as their main subject.[31]

Luce also produced images of the Duce, printed and mounted in albums for his approval. After all the adverse publicity created by the Matteotti affair, photography became crucial in humanising his image. There were photographs of him and his family at Villa Torlonia. The grounds of his villa also served as a backdrop for shots of the Duce in the saddle, riding and jumping his horse over a wooden hurdle in the morning. There were pictures of him racing cars, toying with lion cubs, addressing a crowd, threshing wheat or playing a violin. He appeared as fencer, yachtsman, swimmer and pilot. As the French journalist Henri Béraud observed in 1929: 'Wherever you look, wherever you go, you will find Mussolini, again Mussolini, always Mussolini.' He was on portraits, on medals, in etchings and even on bars of soap. His name adorned newspapers, books, walls and fences. 'Mussolini is omnipresent, he is like a God. He observes you from every angle and you see him in every spot.'[32]

Mussolini was also humanised through a biography first published in English in 1925. Entitled *The Life of Benito Mussolini*, it appeared in Italian as *Dux* the following year. Seventeen editions and eighteen translations would follow. Written by Margherita Sarfatti, his erstwhile mistress, the book mythologised his childhood. The son of a blacksmith, he was born on a Sunday afternoon at two o'clock, as 'The sun had entered the constellation of Leo eight days before'. A 'very naughty, troublesome little boy', he dominated others before he could even walk. He was one of those men 'who are born to compel admiration and devotion from all around him', as people came 'under the sway of his magnetism and the force of his personality'. A description of the wound he sustained in 1917 turned him into an object of almost religious reverence, 'his flesh pierced with arrows, scarred with wounds and bathed in blood', yet smiling gently at those around him.[33]

Although Mussolini edited the text of *Dux* himself, he preferred the official biography by Giorgio Pini, one so blatantly uncritical that it was only translated in 1939. Pini's *Life of Mussolini* was distributed free to schools, where long extracts of Sarfatti were also read in class. Fascist textbooks appeared, specifically tailored to children, all perpetuating the legend of the Duce as a tireless worker devoted to his people. Endorsed by the minister of education in 1927, Vincenzo de Gaetano's *Book for the Young Fascist* equated the movement with the person of Mussolini: 'When one speaks of fascism, one speaks of Him. Fascism is his cause; he has created it, he has infused it with his spirit and given it life.' Some children learned the story of his life by heart. The opening sentence set the tone: 'I believe in the Supreme Duce – the creator of the Black Shirts – and in Jesus

Christ His Only Protector.' On the walls of all schools was the slogan 'From Mussolini to the Children of Italy'; on the cover of their copybooks his portrait.[34]

Mussolini was always fine-tuning his own image. The nation was told that he never slept, working on behalf of his country into the early hours of the morning, so he left the lights on at night in his office at the Palazzo Venezia, an architectural landmark built by the popes in the fifteenth century. The epicentre of the nation was the Sala del Mappamondo, a huge space measuring some eighteen by fifteen metres. It was sparsely furnished, with the Duce's desk standing in a far corner, its back turned to the window. Once they were ushered through the door, visitors had to cross the room, intimidated even before they met his eyes.

A small balcony connected to his office, and he used it to address the crowd below. He prepared his speeches meticulously, sometimes committing them to memory, on occasion writing them down, rehearsing while pacing the Sala del Mappamondo. But he could also be spontaneous, changing the script and adjusting his gestures to the mood of the crowd. He spoke with a metallic voice in short, simple sentences, delivered like the blows of a hammer. His memory was legendary, although he used different strategies to maintain his reputation, for instance by planting questions or rehearsing from an encyclopaedia.[35]

At Villa Torlonia or in the Sala del Mappamondo Mussolini granted audiences to large numbers of admirers. Every day had its quota: 'Schoolteachers from Australia, distant relatives of English peers, American businessmen, boy scouts from Hungary, poets from the Far East, anybody and everybody who desires to stand in the August Presence is warmly received.' As Percy Winner, a correspondent with Associated Press, commented rather astutely, nothing could illustrate better Mussolini's appetite for adulation than the fact that for years he was in contact, seemingly without even a hint of irritation, with a never-ending stream of fawning visitors.[36]

The visits also had a strategic purpose, namely to consolidate his reputation as an international strongman. Respect abroad silenced his critics at home. He took pains to fool foreign journalists and writers with his charm, an effort amply rewarded by a flow of celebratory articles and books, which the fascist press invariably highlighted. Foreign journalists who were critical received no further invitations.

Awed by the immensity of his office, relieved by the cordial reception and calm poise of a man of such fearsome reputation, many walked away thinking they had met a prophet. A mere smile was often enough to disarm an apprehensive visitor. The French writer René Benjamin, recipient of France's most prestigious literary award, the Prix Goncourt, was so daunted by the encounter that he barely managed to cross the vast distance from the door to Mussolini's desk, where he was instantly won over by a broad grin. Maurice Bedel, a compatriot who in 1927 had also won the Prix Goncourt, devoted an entire chapter to the Duce's smile. 'Does he ever stop,' he wondered, 'even for a few brief moments, being a demi-God carried by a violent destiny?' Others were captivated by his eyes. The poet Ada Negri thought they were 'magnetic', but also noticed his hands: 'He has the most beautiful hands, psychic, like wings when they unfold.'[37]

Great leaders also came to pay homage. Mohandas Gandhi, who visited twice, pronounced him 'one of the great statesmen of the time', while Winston Churchill in 1933 described 'the Roman genius' as 'the greatest law-giver among living men'. From the United States alone, he received William Randolph Hearst, New York Governor Al Smith, banker Thomas W. Lamont, future vice-presidential candidate Colonel Frank Knox and Archbishop of Boston William Cardinal O'Connell. Thomas Edison called him the 'greatest genius of modern times' after a short meeting.[38]

Always suspicious of others, Mussolini not only surrounded himself with mediocre followers but also frequently replaced them. The worst, by most accounts, was Achille Starace, a humourless sycophant who took over from Augusto Turati as party secretary in December 1931. 'Starace is a cretin,' one follower objected. 'I know,' Mussolini replied, 'but he is an obedient cretin.'[39]

Starace was a fanatic, and his first task was to subordinate the party even further to Mussolini's will. He did so first by eliminating fascist leaders unwilling to toe the line, then by increasing party membership. It more than doubled from 825,000 in 1931 to over two million in 1936. Many new recruits were opportunists rather than ideologues, more interested in a career than in the tenets of fascism. The result of admitting so many ordinary people into the ranks, as one critic pointed out in 1939, was that the party became depoliticised. 'Fascism has killed anti-fascism and fascism,' he pointed out. 'The strength of fascism,' he continued, 'lies in the lack of fascists.' Loyalty to the leader rather than belief in fascism became paramount, and was expected of everyone, within or outside the Fascist Party. Under Starace, while many party members quite possibly were not fascists, few were not Mussolinists.[40]

This suited Mussolini well. He prided himself that he relied on intuition, instinct and pure willpower rather than on mere intellect, and repeatedly scorned the idea of an ideologically consistent worldview. 'We do not believe in dogmatic programmes, in rigid schemes that should contain and defy the changing, uncertain and complex reality.' In his own career he had not hesitated to change course when circumstances required it. He was unable to develop a political philosophy, and in any event unwilling to be hemmed in by any principle, moral, ideological or otherwise. 'Action, action, action – this summed up his whole creed', noted one of his biographers.[41]

Politics became the mass celebration of an individual. 'Mussolini is Always Right' was the regime's motto. Mussolini was not merely sent by providence, but the very incarnation of providence. Blind obedience was now expected of every Italian. The words 'Believe, Obey, Fight' were painted in long, black letters on buildings, stencilled on walls, emblazoned across the nation.

A so-called fascist style was encouraged by Starace, affecting every aspect of daily life. A 'Hail the Duce' now opened every meeting, while a Roman salute, right arm outstretched, replaced the handshake. The entire population was put into uniform, with even infants posing for photographs in a black shirt. Children wore black uniforms every Saturday – declared 'Fascist Saturday' by the Grand Council in 1935 – and reported to local headquarters to practise marching in step, a toy rifle on their shoulders.[42]

A Ministry of Popular Culture replaced the Press Office, established years earlier by Cesare Rossi. The new organisation was run by the Duce's son-in-law, a talented young man called Galeazzo Ciano who emulated the German Reich's Ministry of Public Enlightenment and Propaganda. Like its German counterpart, it released daily instructions to editors detailing what should be mentioned and what was proscribed. A carrot accompanied the stick, as the secret funds that had fuelled the Press Office ballooned. From 1933 to 1943 more than 410 million lire, the rough equivalent at the time of US$20 million, was spent promoting the regime and its leader in newspapers across the nation. By 1939 even the Duce's mottos appeared on the masthead of subsidised dailies. 'Either Precious Friendship or Brutal Hostility' proclaimed the *Cronaca Prealpina*, invoking a speech Mussolini had held in Florence in May 1930, while *La Voce di Bergamo* announced, 'The Secret of Victory: Obedience'. Some foreign publications accepted subsidies. *Le Petit Journal*, the fourth most popular newspaper in France, benefited from a covert contribution of 20,000 lire.[43]

Secret funds were also used to entice artists, scholars and writers to join the movement. By one estimate, the cost of these subsidies rose from 1.5 million lire in 1934 to 162 million in 1942. One beneficiary was Asvero Gravelli, an early follower and author of a hagiography entitled *Spiritual Interpretations of Mussolini*, published in 1938. 'God and History are two terms that are identified with Mussolini,' Gravelli boldly declared, although he resisted the temptation to compare him to Napoleon: 'Who resembles Mussolini? Nobody. To compare Mussolini to statesmen of other races is to diminish him. Mussolini is the first new Italian.' The author received 79,500 lire for his efforts.[44]

Augusto Turati had started developing radio as a propaganda tool in 1926. His voice could be heard regularly over the ether, together with those of other fascist leaders, including Arnaldo Mussolini. The Duce himself went on air for the first time on 4 November

1925, although the transmission was plagued by technical problems. Radio sets remained beyond the reach of most ordinary people in the 1920s, as Italy was still a poor and largely agrarian country. In 1931 there were a mere 176,000 radio subscribers across the nation, most of them in the cities. When teachers lamented that children could not listen to the voice of Mussolini, Starace ensured some 40,000 free radios were installed in elementary schools between 1933 and 1938. The overall number of subscribers, thanks to state subsidies, soared to 800,000 before the onset of the Second World War. Mere numbers, however, did not reflect the reach of the radio, as loudspeakers were installed in town squares, so that by the middle of the 1930s Mussolini's speeches resounded across the country.[45]

Mussolini himself developed the gift of omnipresence. When in 1929 he had first entered the Royal Hall, an enormous auditorium where large conferences were held in the Palazzo Venezia, he had tried out the stage, looking around the room like a choreographer before deciding that it was too low. 'Those at the back of the room will struggle to see me,' he said, ordering that the platform be elevated, a command delivered on repeated occasions, until his underlings lost count of just how many podiums had been modified to accommodate their master.[46]

In 1932 a four-lane boulevard was cut through the heart of the city from the Colosseum to the Palazzo Venezia, creating a huge open-air space for his balcony speeches, which attracted ever larger crowds. The very idea that any Italian could travel to Rome to see and hear the Duce became part of his legend. Bortolo Pelanda, a seventy-one-year-old farmer, walked some 500 kilometres from Belluno Veronese to Rome to fulfil his dream of listening to Mussolini. Arturo Rizzi built an entire contraption around two bicycles to take his family of eight from Turin to Rome, or so the newspapers reported.[47]

After the March on Rome Mussolini had started touring the country, a ritual that became more frequent over time, especially once he announced his policy of 'Going to the People' in 1932. Every appearance was meticulously stage-managed. Schools and shops were closed for the day, while fascist youth and party activists recruited from the surrounding region poured into the square from chartered buses. They set the tone, cheering, chanting and applauding on command. Ordinary citizens received a pink card delivered by morning mail ordering them to attend the occasion. Failure to comply could bring a fine or a prison sentence. Police mingled in the crowd to ensure that everyone behaved.[48]

Most of all, the crowd was made to wait, sometimes for hours on end, from noon to dusk. Even as Mussolini was still far away, thousands of people closely pressed together craned their necks towards the balcony, eagerly expecting him to appear. Often the Duce only spoke after twilight fell. Giant searchlights were switched on to illuminate the balcony, torches appeared in the crowd, bonfires were lit from nearby buildings. In this theatrical atmosphere, two uniformed guards would step forward, taking positions on each side of the balcony as the crowd began applauding. Trumpets were blasted as the local party secretary moved to the front of the balcony, shouting 'Fascisti! Salute al Duce!'. When the Duce finally stepped into view and smiled, the crowd had been whipped up to fever pitch, releasing the strain of waiting in an eruption of joy.[49]

Every visit was reported by an enthusiastic press, while important speeches were filmed by the Luce Institute and shown in cinemas around the country. The crowd, already carefully selected, knew precisely how to rise to the occasion, having watched the ritual on the silver screen. Cities competed with each other, trying to offer ever more enthusiastic and festive receptions to curry favour with the regime. In Milan, a favourite city of the Duce, enormous temporary balconies were built for his public speeches, bedecked with papier-mâché eagles.[50]

The greatest celebration of the regime was probably the Mostra della Rivoluzione, an exhibition opened on 28 October 1932 to commemorate the tenth anniversary of the March on Rome. Some four million visitors streamed through the grounds of the Palazzo delle Esposizione from 1932 to 1934, with reduced entrance fees for members of party organisations. Mussolini was at the heart of the exhibition, arranged chronologically to mark the most dramatic episodes of the fascist revolution. As Dino Alfieri, its curator, explained, the revolution was 'inextricably linked to the thought and will of Mussolini'. Room T, at the very end of the exhibition, was dedicated to the Duce, with manuscripts and personal belongings carefully displayed under glass, including his handkerchief, still bloodied after Violet Gibson's attempt on his life in April 1926. An exact reconstruction of his office at the *Popolo d'Italia* allowed visitors to get closer to their leader.[51]

Another site of pilgrimage, besides Room T, was the Duce's birthplace. In 1925 party secretary Roberto Farinacci had trekked to Predappio to swear an oath of loyalty to the leader. Seven years later, on the tenth anniversary of the fascist revolution, Achille Starace turned the small medieval village into a site of national celebration, as an entire new town emerged around the cult of Mussolini. 'From the most humble man to his sovereign majesty', people from all backgrounds paid their respects to the leader at Predappio. Day in, day out, thousands of pilgrims arrived by bus in organised tours or alone, sometimes on foot or bicycle, silently shuffling through the family home, bowing their heads in front of the family crypt. His mother Rosa Maltoni was compared to the Virgin Mary and commemorated in the church of Santa Rosa. His father was glorified as a hero of the revolution. Far beyond Predappio, schools, hospitals, bridges and churches were named after Mussolini's parents.[52]

Mussolini received not only thousands of letters and visitors, but also gifts from people from every walk of life. As early as November 1927 Augusto Turati had ordered party members to cease sending donations to their leader, but he could do little to stop admirers from outside the ranks. Henrietta Tower, one of the wealthiest women in the United States and a lifelong resident of Rome, bequeathed a villa with an art collection of 3,000 items including ceramics, tapestries, textiles and paintings when she died in 1933. She was far from exceptional, as three castles and seven large estates were gifted to the Duce between 1925 to 1939 (he accepted on behalf of the state). Writers, photographers, painters and sculptors put their talents to work and sent items celebrating the Duce, including pastel portraits and embroidered busts. Some were displayed in Villa Torlonia. From ordinary people came a daily homage in the form of fresh produce, despite the best efforts of the state to persuade them to desist. On 2 August 1934 alone, dozens of kilos of fruit, sweets, biscuits, pasta and tomatoes were earmarked for destruction.[53]

The large boulevard leading from the Colosseum to the Palazzo Venezia turned Mussolini's balcony into the symbolic centre of fascist power. But by cutting a straight line through the city's most prominent excavations, the Via dei Fori Imperiale, flanked by large bronze statues of Roman generals, also connected the Duce directly to ancient Rome.

The emblem of fascism, a bundle of rods called fasces (*fasci* in Italian) tied around an axe, originated from ancient Rome. It stood not only for strength through unity but also for a resurgence of the lost grandeur of the Roman empire. Like the swastika in Germany, it was carved into buildings, lamps, fountains, doorsteps and even manhole covers. The fascist squads with their ranks and formations were organised on the Roman model. There was the Roman salute, and after 1935 the Roman step. Mussolini even kept a Roman wolf in a cage displayed in the Capitol. Labour Day was no longer celebrated on 1 May but on 21 April, the founding day of Rome. As Mussolini explained, 'The Roman greeting, songs and formulas, anniversary commemorations and the like are all essential to fan the flames of the enthusiasm that keeps a movement in being. It was just the same in ancient Rome.'[54]

Mussolini not only stamped his mark on the capital, he set out to build the 'Rome of Mussolini', a vast metropolis harking back to the days of imperial glory. 'Rome must appear as a marvel to the nations of the world,' he proclaimed in 1926, 'vast, orderly, powerful, as it was in the times of the Augustan Empire.' The centuries that had followed Emperor Augustus he considered 'decadent'. Entire medieval neighbourhoods in the old capital were to be pulled down to make place for modern fascist buildings worthy of a new imperial centre. Mussolini wanted to be remembered as 'the greatest destroyer', the one who rebuilt Rome. His threat was never carried out, although fifteen churches and hundreds of structures were flattened in various parts of the city.[55]

In order to radiate power and prestige Mussolini's Rome was required to double in size. Some 600 square kilometres of marshes south of the capital were drained, the area turned into agricultural land and handed over to the poor. Roads were built. Littoria, named after the lictors who carried the fasces in Roman times, was inaugurated by the Duce in 1931, followed by other model cities, all boasting a town hall, a church, a post office and Fascist Party headquarters built along streets radiating out from a piazza.

As in the time of Augustus, Rome would reach to the sea. A Roma al Mare, 'the new resort of imperial Rome', was planned, linked to the Esposizione Universale Roma, projected to be held in 1942. At the heart of EUR was a neoclassical building standing sixty-eight metres high, clad in white stone, called the Square Colosseum in homage to the older Roman landmark.

But how could the new empire reach beyond the sea? It already, of course, enjoyed the colonial possessions of Libya, Tripoli and Somaliland, but these had been conquered by previous regimes, denounced by Mussolini as weak and corrupt. To be a true emperor, the modern Caesar who founded a new imperial Rome had to expand the empire. There were other reasons. Like Adolf Hitler, who came to power in 1933, Mussolini sought to rival France and Britain, and like his German counterpart he believed that colonial powers alone had access to the necessary raw materials to wage war.

In his search for prestige Mussolini had already presided over a savage war against insurgents in Libya in 1929. In Cyrenaica, the coastal region of their north African colony, the military sowed terror with chemical weapons and mass executions, exterminating close to a quarter of the local population. Some 100,000 Bedouins were expelled, their land given to Italian settlers. The horrors of the war were concealed from the public at home by an obedient press, which hailed Mussolini for bringing Libya into the fold of civilisation after centuries of barbarism.[56]

Mussolini began preparing for war in 1931, telling his generals to be ready by 1935. The following year, he fired Dino Grandi, taking over the reins of the Ministry of Foreign Affairs. After Hitler withdrew from the League of Nations in October 1933, the Duce accelerated efforts to rearm his country. He removed Italo Balbo and assumed control first over the Ministry of War, then over the Ministries of Marine and Air. With the exception of the Ministry of Finance, the levers of government were now entirely in his hands. Mussolini had convinced himself that he was a man of destiny, a Napoleon and Caesar rolled into one, a providential leader whose hand would reshape the modern world. He had come to believe the regime's motto: 'Mussolini is Always Right'. The sycophants around him encouraged his delusions.[57]

In order to be ready for war Mussolini sought a self-sufficient economy. Endless campaigns were launched to whip the population into action. There was a Battle for Grain to reduce imports, with photographs of Mussolini at the threshing machine. There was a Battle for Rice, a Battle for Land, a Battle of Births and a War on Flies, all fronted by the Duce.[58]

Italy already had two colonies in the Horn of Africa. The conquest of Ethiopia would join together the territories of Eritrea and Somalia. Mussolini had visions of a unified Italian East Africa where millions of settlers would extract gold, diamonds, copper, iron, coal and oil, allowing him to build up his empire and dominate the continent. He also wished to wipe out a stain that had left an indelible mark on the country's reputation. In 1896 Emperor Menelik had inflicted a humiliating military defeat on the Italian army at Adwa. The failure still rankled.

Mussolini did not consult anyone except the king before deciding on war. On 2 October 1935, after a year of border skirmishes with Ethiopia, church bells and sirens summoned the population into the town squares, where they listened to their leader declare war over the loudspeakers. The summons had been carefully prepared by Starace. By one estimate some twenty-seven million people took part in the largest staged event in human history.[59]

The financial and military preparations for war, however, were woefully inadequate. The strategy pursued by the Duce, who sidelined his generals to assume overall command, was murderous. Mussolini ordered the use of hundreds of tonnes of mustard gas, sprayed on combatants and civilians alike. In a dark harbinger of the horrors to come under Hitler and Stalin, industrial killing was combined with full-on atrocities, as Ethiopians were decapitated or executed in front of open graves. After a failed attempt on the life of General Rodolfo Graziani, the occupying forces retaliated by killing some 20,000 people in a mere three days in the capital Addis Ababa. Babies were crushed, pregnant women disembowelled and entire families shot, burned, bludgeoned or stabbed to death. When one newspaper compared the conqueror Graziani to Hannibal, Mussolini was furious: he alone could be invoked in the same breath as the giants of ancient Rome. Between late 1935 and 1938 at least a quarter of a million people perished in Ethiopia as a result of the war.[60]

The atrocities were carefully hidden from the public, as the propaganda machine depicted the war as a liberation for Ethiopians, bringing freedom and civilisation to the victims of a feudal caste system. Secret subsidies, once again, helped propagate this vision at home and abroad, with even foreign journalists paid the equivalent of thousands of dollars to visit Addis Ababa and report favourably on their trip.[61]

The kingdom of Italy was now an empire, the diminutive King Victor Emmanuel III promoted to Emperor. Mussolini was granted the title of Founder of the Empire. As in Roman times, spoils of war were brought back from the newly conquered territories. The huge obelisk of Axum, weighing some 160 tonnes and dating from the fourth century, was carted back to Rome and unveiled near the Circus Maximus on 28 October 1937 to commemorate the fifteenth anniversary of the March on Rome. Like an emperor, Mussolini was given his own forum. Called Foro Mussolini, it was built to celebrate the conquest of Ethiopia, with mosaic friezes depicting tanks and warplanes. Other markers appeared across the empire. In order to 'record for future generations the foundation of the empire', a 150-metre profile of the Duce was sculpted into the rocks of a mountain overlooking the Furlo Gorge in central Italy.[62]

When Mussolini proclaimed the annexation of Ethiopia from his balcony on 9 May 1936, the crowds went delirious. As one astute observer pointed out, 'He knew that, possibly for the first time, he was enjoying the unqualified admiration and support of the whole Italian nation.' It was his last day of glory, as his star would begin to wane.[63]

Empire may have been popular at home, but it poisoned relationships with France and Great Britain. The League of Nations condemned Italy, further isolating Mussolini and prompting him to seek a rapprochement with Germany. Mussolini had initially viewed Hitler with suspicion, feeling threatened by a rival. When the German chancellor travelled to Venice in June 1934 for a first meeting, the Duce upstaged him, addressing a cheering crowd on the Piazza San Marco in full military regalia. A pale, insecure Hitler, in a baggy yellow coat and patent-leather shoes, had watched from a balcony in a neighbouring palace, mesmerised by a man so adored by his people. 'He thought that the enthusiasm for Mussolini was genuine,' noted Alfred Rosenberg, the party's ideologue. It was Hitler's first trip abroad, and he realised that he had made a poor impression.[64]

In September 1937, after widespread international condemnation of the war in Ethiopia, the Duce travelled to Berlin. Now he, in turn, was awed by the Führer, who spared no expense to accord his guest the honours due to an esteemed ally. Close to a million people, brought in by special trains from the provinces, dutifully filled the streets of the capital to cheer Mussolini. Large numbers of undercover police moved among the crowd with dogs lurking in the background. The Duce fell under the spell of his host, 'manifestly intoxicated by the spectacle of so much power and fascinated by the man who was plainly resolved to wield it'. Mussolini was no longer the vigorous, sprightly figure who had impressed the Führer in Venice. As the First Secretary of the British Embassy in Berlin observed, his features had coarsened. 'He was fat and bald, and presented the visage of a dissolute Roman emperor of the decadence.'[65]

Mussolini and his blackshirt revolution had been a source of inspiration for Hitler, but now the master began to emulate the pupil. A few months after he returned from Berlin he joined Germany and Japan in a tripartite pact against communism without even consulting the Grand Council. The pact forced Mussolini to betray Austria, invaded by Hitler in March 1938. Having assured everyone, including the Duce, that not a single Czech would be annexed, Hitler then sent his troops into Czechoslovakia, inflicting a blow on the prestige of Mussolini, who had confidently told his ministers there would be no annexation. 'Every time Hitler invades a country, he sends me a message,' he fulminated, fully aware of the hostile reaction of his own people, and bitterly resenting mocking taunts that labelled him the Gauleiter of Italy, a mere subordinate of the Führer.[66]

Mussolini soon regained his poise, deciding to invade Albania in order to keep up with his ally, whose Reich now stretched all the way south to the Italian border. This, too, he managed to botch, even though Albania was a mere enclave already nominally controlled by Italy. Believing that the secret of Hitler's success was that he, not his generals, dictated strategy, Mussolini barely bothered to brief the commander of the expeditionary force. Instead of a lightning strike inspired by the Führer, a confused invasion revealed just how ill prepared and poorly equipped his army was.[67]

As both powers secretly agreed to prepare for a future war in Europe, the alliance with Germany was further expanded into a Pact of Steel, signed in May 1939. Hitler had promised to avoid hostilities for three years to give Mussolini time to prepare for the battles to come. Three months later, Germany invaded Poland. Galeazzo Ciano, now foreign minister, was one of many who realised that Mussolini was dragging his country into the abyss. 'I must fight to the end. Otherwise it will mean the ruin of the country, the ruin of Fascism, and the ruin of the Duce himself.'[68]

Mussolini was now in dire straits. He had failed to prepare his country for an all-out war, but had simultaneously thrown in his

lot with Hitler. He boasted to his counterpart in Berlin that he had
150 divisions backed by reserves of twelve million soldiers, but in
reality only ten divisions with antiquated equipment were ready to
fight. A surprisingly indecisive character hiding behind a façade of
limitless self-belief and willpower, Mussolini agonised, experiencing
bouts of depression, changing his mind, even confessing that
he secretly hoped the Germans would be defeated. But in early
1940 he became convinced that Hitler would win. 'Recently he
has felt more and more the fascination of the Führer. His military
successes – the only successes that Mussolini really values and
desires – are the cause of this,' observed Ciano in his diary. On 10
June 1940 he declared war on the Allied powers.[69]

For almost two decades Mussolini had encouraged the idea that
he alone could be trusted and could do no wrong. He had used
the cult of the leader to debase his competitors, ensuring every
potential rival in the Fascist Party was edged out of the limelight.
Those who remained were united in their devotion to the Duce,
sycophants determined to outdo one another in praising his
genius. They lied to him, much as he lied to them. But most of
all, Mussolini lied to himself. He became enveloped in his own
worldview, a 'slave to his own myth' in the words of his biographer
Renzo de Felice. He knew that those around him were flatterers
who withheld information that could provoke his ire. He trusted
no one, having no true friends, no reliable companion to whom he
could speak frankly. As the years passed Mussolini isolated himself
from others, becoming a virtual prisoner within the walls of the
Palazzo Venezia.[70]

Not content with making all major decisions himself, Mussolini
sought to control everything, apparently with no sense of priority. As
his valet wrote, his was a dictatorship that extended to 'fuel engines,
borax, bicycle rims, translations from Latin, cameras, mirrors, electric
lamps and mineral water'. His hand was everywhere. In the middle
of the war he found time to change the colour of the cover for a
women's magazine from purple to brown. In January 1939, as Europe
was heading towards war, his son-in-law observed units rehearsing
for a parade in front of the Palazzo Venezia. 'The Duce spends many

a half-hour at the window of his office, concealed behind the blue curtains, looking at the movements of the various units. It was his order that the drums and trumpets be used at the same time. It was he who chose the band leader's baton, and in person he teaches the movements to be made, and he changes the proportions and design of the baton. He is a strong believer that in the armed forces it is the form that determines the substance as well.'[71]

As a result, Italy was woefully ill prepared for war. The campaign for economic self-sufficiency Mussolini spearheaded was a success on the propaganda front, but caused a decline in steel production even before war began, as the country had to import millions of tonnes of coal annually. The Battle for Grain likewise increased cereal output, but made the country more dependent on imported fertiliser. While Starace had ordered everyone into military attire, there were too few uniforms for the soldiers, many of whom were equipped with antiquated weapons. Starace himself was dismissed, as were countless other scapegoats, including senior officers in the army, to deflect blame from Mussolini. The Duce, among the many positions he held, was air minister, but he did not know how many of his aircraft were obsolete. There was no military budget and no proper planning staff.[72]

At the height of his glory, in the middle of the 1930s, Mussolini appeared genuinely popular. There were good reasons why foreign travellers – not to mention some historians later on – were impressed by the spell he seemed to have cast on the population. The cult of personality demanded loyalty to the leader rather than faith in a particular political programme. It was deliberately superficial, capable of encompassing the greatest possible number. People were required to appear periodically at the public square and applaud the Duce.[73]

Many also hailed the leader as a way of criticising the abuses of local fascists. 'If only the Duce knew' ('se lo sapesse il Duce!') was a well-worn expression. The greater the sense of frustration and anger people felt towards the Fascist Party, the more they portrayed Mussolini as a blameless leader deliberately kept ignorant of the facts or badly advised by his underlings.[74]

The cult was also tinged with superstition and magic. In a country steeped in religion, people projected onto Mussolini feelings of devotion and worship characteristic of Christian piety. There were holy sites, holy pictures, pilgrimages, even the hope of a healing touch from the leader. His photograph was sometimes used as a talisman, carried around to bring good luck. Most of all, there was faith in a providential figure rather than belief in fascist ideology.[75]

Above all, people had no choice. As Emilio Lussu, a committed anti-fascist, noted in 1936, the regime demanded expressions of popular consent, and the blackshirts pursued these, bludgeon in hand. When the Duce gave speeches, people turned up on orders from the police and cheered on command, 'like extras in a cast of thousands, so that papers could publish photographs of public sites full to the brim with exulting people'.[76]

Little more than the outward appearance of loyalty to the leader was required, and after a few years most people became masters at the game. Mussolini was a superb actor, his subordinates great performers, but the nation at large was a well-rehearsed performance. The penalties for breaking character were harsh. A totalitarian police state had emerged after the Matteotti affair in 1925, and by the mid-1930s it had acquired enormous powers, going to great lengths to put the population under surveillance. The political police, known as PolPol, worked hand in hand with Ovra, or Organisation for Vigilance and Repression of Anti-Fascism, referred to in short as *piovra*, or 'octopus', its tentacles reaching far and wide. There were also the regular state police and the local carabinieri, who were part of the army. There were five special militia for the railways, roads, post, telegraph and telephone services, the ports and the forests. The capital had a metropolitan militia, with some 12,000 agents making the rounds in civilian clothes. Envious neighbours, jealous colleagues or even disaffected members of the same family reported on suspicious conversations. Few people would have dared to speak openly in the presence of more than three others. As one observer put it, Italy was a 'nation of prisoners, condemned to enthusiasm'.[77]

Despite the full weight of the police state, enthusiasm for the leader waned in 1939. Underground newspapers were growing in circulation, some apparently printed on the presses of the *Popolo d'Italia* itself. The credibility of the leader came under attack. One fascist follower opined that the regime represented a mere 30,000 people at most. Nobody believed any longer in the parades, asserted one report from Rome, while people were unhappy with empty shelves in the shops caused by the economic sanctions imposed by the League of Nations. The obligatory newsreels shown in cinemas no longer prompted respectful silence, as viewers used the cover of dark to boo or laugh irreverently. The letter M, seen everywhere in honour of Mussolini, stood for misery, people joked.[78]

Mussolini, fully aware of growing popular disaffection through the secret services, realised that he had to show that his star was still shining brightly with a series of quick successes in war. In June 1940 he was ready to stake his fortune and that of his country by declaring war on France and Great Britain. 'May God help Italy,' wrote his son-in-law.[79]

In the early hours of 28 October 1940, the Italian army crossed the Albanian border to invade Greece. Since Berlin had not informed Mussolini beforehand of their plans to invade Poland, the Netherlands and France, the Duce thought he should surprise Hitler in turn. Mussolini's own staff were kept in the dark. Rodolfo Graziani, now chief of the army staff, only heard of the invasion through the radio. Instead of conducting a lightning war, Italian troops became bogged down in poor weather and were pushed back into Albania within a few weeks. Britain intervened on Greece's side, destroying half of Italy's battle fleet.

'We will break Greece's back,' Mussolini defiantly proclaimed on 18 November, as crowds dutifully cheered outside the Palazzo Venezia. The speech was distributed far and wide by the Ministry of Popular Culture, transmitted over the airwaves in seven languages. But many Italians did not believe their own leader, turning instead to British radio to discover what was happening inside their own country. Over the following three years some 60 million lire were spent on fighting clandestine radio programmes from London, to little avail.[80]

Mussolini was obliged to appeal to Hitler, who came to his rescue in April 1941. Within weeks, the Germans pushed through the Balkans and reached Athens, the Greek capital. There was a price to pay: military experts, economic advisers and secret agents now swarmed all over Italy, interfering in every aspect of the country's affairs. The iron dictator seemed no more than a vassal. 'We were treated, never like partners, but always as slaves,' Ciano bitterly confided to his diary.[81]

Wherever the Duce sent his soldiers, they were defeated. A few months after the Tenth Army moved across the Libyan desert to invade Egypt in September 1940, British troops forced them back. In November 1941 the Italians made their last stand in the ancient imperial capital of Gondar, defeated by the Allied powers with the help of irregular Ethiopian troops. On the Eastern Front, where Mussolini had sent an army corps to help in the war against the Soviet Union, the Italians suffered heavy losses. By July 1942, Mussolini was a broken man, wracked by illness, isolated, disillusioned by the waning of his star. A close collaborator found him 'grey, with sunken cheeks, troubled and tired eyes and his mouth revealing a sense of bitterness'.[82]

The man who had once been in full sight at all times, in the sky, in the sea, on earth, began disappearing from view, eschewing the public. For six months no new images of Mussolini, once described as 'the most photographed man on earth', were published. He also fell silent. On 10 June 1941 he had made a brief appearance to mark the first anniversary of Italy's entry into the war, but for eighteen long months thereafter he was speechless.[83]

On 2 December 1942 Mussolini broke his silence, proving that he was still alive. But it was too little, too late. His voice had changed, people whispered. His speech was superficial. He seemed to have lost his grip on reality, confirming the impression that a leader driven by hubris was steering his country to ruin. Instead of whipping up hatred of the enemy, his speech turned people against him.[84]

From the beginning Mussolini had been forced to compete with the king and the pope for the allegiance of the Italian population.

Mussolini's image may have been everywhere, but it was the king's head that appeared on stamps and coins. Mussolini was only head of government, while the king was head of state. And much as fascism had tried to emulate religion, it was the pope who commanded the loyalty of the country's millions of Roman Catholics.

The Allied powers began bombing Italy ten days after Mussolini's declaration of war in 1940. Almost every city became a target, carried out first by British fliers, then the United States. On 19 July 1943, as Allied planes targeted the capital for the first time, Pope Pius XII was seen visiting the damaged districts in a grubby white cassock, surrounded by devout residents, while Mussolini remained ensconced in his palace.[85]

For months people had accused Mussolini of having brought ruin and misery to their country. The Duce had betrayed Italy. He was a criminal, a murderer, a bloodthirsty tyrant. Some cursed him under their breath, others openly wished for his demise.[86]

The king delivered the final blow. As the acrid smell of smoke still hovered over Rome, the Grand Council of Fascists voted against their leader. One day later, on 25 July 1943, Victor Emmanuel placed Mussolini under arrest. Not a single party member rebelled, despite their solemn oath to protect Mussolini to the death. Achille Starace, like other fascist leaders, immediately tried to ingratiate himself with Pietro Badoglio, the first Duke of Addis Ababa and new head of government.[87]

The historian Emilio Gentile pointed out decades ago that a god who proved to be fallible 'was destined to be dethroned and desecrated by his faithful with the same passion with which he had been adored'. In parts of Italy, angry crowds invaded the local Fascist Party headquarters on the very day of his arrest, flinging effigies, busts and portraits of the overthrown dictator out of the windows.[88]

Mussolini had one friend left, however. The humiliating demise of a close ally was a threat to the image of the untouchable and sacred leader, and Hitler organised a daring rescue operation, sending a group of commandoes to free Mussolini and fly him to freedom. A week earlier, on 3 September 1943, Italy had signed an armistice, prompting German troops to take over the country. Now, as war tore the country apart, they installed Mussolini in Salò to head a new regime, the Italian Social Republic. Mussolini's main achievement was a series of executions of fascist leaders who had voted against him at the last meeting of the Grand Council. His own son-in-law, Galeazzo Ciano, was tied to a chair and shot in the back.

In a January 1945 interview with Madeleine Mollier, wife of the press attaché at the German Embassy, Mussolini seemed resigned to his fate, describing himself as 'little more than a corpse'. 'Yes, madam, I am finished. My star has fallen,' he continued. 'I await the end of the tragedy and – strangely detached from everything – I do not feel any more an actor. I feel I am the last of the spectators.' The end came a few months later, when he was captured by anti-fascist partisans. He and several of his followers, including his mistress Clara Petacci, were summarily shot, their bodies piled into a van and taken to Milan. They were hung upside down from a girder. Achille Starace, arrested shortly afterwards, was taken to see the remains of his leader, then executed and strung up next to the man he had acclaimed as a god.[89]

In the months that followed people sang the fascist hymn with unveiled sarcasm, chiselling away at the symbols of the past dictatorship on buildings and monuments across the country, smashing the statues of their former leader. They blamed only Mussolini, a view made credible, rather paradoxically, by the cult of personality itself. 'One man, and one man alone,' Churchill had famously said in December 1940, absolving all fascists of any responsibility.[90]

2

Hitler

'As I walked with him in the gardens of the Villa Borghese,' Hitler told his guests at a dinner party on 21 July 1941 while the Luftwaffe was bombing Moscow, 'I could easily compare his profile with that of the Roman busts, and I realised he was one of the Ceasars.' The Duce's March on Rome, he explained, was a turning point in history. 'The brownshirts would probably not have existed without the blackshirts.'[1]

Two decades earlier, the Nazi Party, still in its infancy with less than 10,000 members, had been galvanised by the March on Rome, hailing Adolf Hitler as 'Germany's Mussolini' on 3 November 1922. Just as Mussolini presented himself to his people as the Duce, party members now began to refer to Hitler as the Führer, the German word for leader.[2]

Only three years earlier, when Hitler had given his first political speech at a beer hall in Munich, few could have predicted his rise to power. As a young man he had hoped to become an artist in Vienna, but was twice rejected by the Academy of Fine Arts. He enjoyed a bohemian lifestyle, reading widely and pursuing his passion for opera and architecture.

In 1914, having been deemed unfit for service in the Austro-Hungarian army, he managed to enlist in the Bavarian army instead. He took part in some of the bloodiest battles of the First World War and was temporarily blinded by a British gas shell in October 1918. In hospital, he learned of Germany's military collapse and was overcome with despair, which turned into hatred overnight. Like many other nationalists, he believed that the army had been stabbed in the back, betrayed by civilian leaders who had overthrown the Hohenzollern dynasty to establish the Weimar Republic and sign an armistice in the November Revolution.

Hitler returned to Munich, where he had lived before the outbreak of war. He found a city draped in red flags, as the socialist premier Kurt Eisner had established a Free State of Bavaria following the abolition of the Wittelsbach monarchy in November 1918. Eisner's assassination a few months later prompted an uprising among some of the workers, who rushed to proclaim a Bavarian Soviet Republic. It was a short-lived experiment, brutally crushed by government troops and paramilitary volunteers. In the wake of the failed revolution, Hitler was tasked with lecturing soldiers returning from the front against the perils of communism. He thrived, discovering that he had a talent: 'What I had earlier always assumed to be true without knowing it now happened: I could "speak".'[3]

His oratorical skills caught the attention of Anton Drexler, founder of the German Workers' Party (DAP), a loosely organised group of conservatives who mixed nationalism with anti-capitalism in an effort to appeal to larger segments of the population. Hitler joined the party in September 1919, soon becoming their most influential speaker, as people flocked to listen to him. An early follower remembered being unimpressed by a man who looked like 'a waiter in a railway-station restaurant', with heavy boots, a leather waistcoat and an odd little moustache. But once Hitler began speaking, he electrified the audience. 'In his early years he had a command of voice, phrase and effect which has never been equalled, and on this evening he was at his best.' He would begin in a quiet, reserved manner, but gradually build up momentum, using simple language that ordinary people could understand. As he warmed to his subject, he began attacking Jews, chastising the Kaiser, thundering against war profiteers, speaking more and more rapidly with dramatic hand gestures, a finger occasionally stabbing the air. He knew how to tailor his message to his listeners, giving voice to their hatred and hope. 'The audience responded with a final outburst of frenzied cheering and hand-clapping.' By 1921 Hitler could fill as large a venue as the Circus Krone in Munich with more than 6,000 followers.[4]

In February 1920 the party was renamed the National Socialist German Workers' Party (NSDAP, or Nazi Party). Soon it acquired a heavily indebted newspaper called *Völkischer Beobachter*, originally published by the Thule Society, a secretive group of occultists who used the swastika as their symbol and believed in the coming of a German messiah to redeem the nation. Dietrich Eckart, the newspaper's new editor, had pinned his hopes on a journalist called Wolfgang Kapp. In March 1920 Kapp and some 6,000 supporters attempted a putsch against the Weimar Republic in Berlin, but failed after the rank and file of the state administration went on strike. Now Eckhart turned towards Hitler, seeing him as the 'saviour of the fatherland'. Twenty years his senior, Eckhart became his mentor, helping him build up his image, using the *Völkischer Beobachter* to portray Hitler as Germany's next great man.[5]

In the summer of 1921 the party leadership welcomed the arrival of another 'popular and powerful speaker', the leader of a rival organisation called the German Working Association. They proposed a merger. Hitler saw this as a threat to his own position and gambled by tendering his resignation in a fit of anger. Everything hinged on Eckhart, who mediated. Fearful of losing their main attraction, the leadership relented. But Hitler now demanded to be 'chairman with dictatorial powers'. A few months later Eckhart gushed in the pages of the *Völkischer Beobachter* that nobody was more selfless, upright and devoted than Hitler, who had intervened in the fate of the party with an 'iron fist'.[6]

The moment Hitler captured power within the Nazi Party he established a paramilitary organisation called the SA (an abbreviation of *Sturmabteilung*, or Assault Division). Ernst Röhm, a loyal follower, made sure they thrashed dissenters who tried to shout Hitler down in public meetings. The SA also roamed the streets of Munich, beating up their enemies and disrupting events organised by the political opposition.

The Nazi Party was now the Führer's party, and Hitler worked tirelessly at building it up. He designed the garish red flyers used to recruit new members, and he oversaw the parades, flags, pennants, marching bands and music that drew ever larger crowds. Hitler was a meticulous choreographer, attending to every detail. On 17 September 1921 instructions were published to prescribe the exact dimensions and colour scheme of the swastika armband. The brown shirts were introduced after Mussolini marched on Rome.[7]

Like Mussolini, Hitler also gave careful thought as to how best to present himself to the outside world. When an earlier follower suggested that he should either grow a full moustache or clip it, he was unmoved. 'Don't worry,' he said, 'I am setting a fashion. As time goes on people will be pleased to copy it.' The moustache was as much a trademark as the brown shirt. Hitler, again like Mussolini, was short-sighted, but made sure never to be seen in public wearing his spectacles. Wary of facilitating recognition by the police, Hitler – unlike his Italian counterpart – shunned photographers. As his reputation grew, speculation about his appearance added an aura of mystery. Only in the autumn of 1923 did Hitler consent to having his portrait taken by Heinrich Hoffmann, who would soon become the party's official photographer. These first images projected sheer determination and fanatical willpower, showing a grim look, raised eyebrows, lips pressed together, arms resolutely folded. The photographs circulated widely in the press and were sold as postcards and portraits.[8]

As Adolf Hitler turned thirty-four on 20 April 1923 the cult of the leader was launched. A banner on the front page of the party's mouthpiece hailed him as 'Germany's Führer'. Alfred Rosenberg, another earlier ally, celebrated Hitler as the 'Leader of the German Nation', writing about how the man in Munich established a 'mysterious interaction' between himself and his many followers. Hitler, on the other hand, all too aware that his enemies called him a demagogue, a tyrant, a megalomaniac 'Majesty Adolf I', described himself in self-deprecating terms as 'nothing but a drummer and gatherer', a mere apostle waiting for the Christ.[9]

This was all false modesty. As Eckart himself reported, an impatient Hitler could be seen pacing up and down the courtyard shouting, 'I must enter Berlin like Christ in the Temple of Jerusalem and scourge out the moneylenders.' Seeking to emulate Mussolini, on 8 November 1923 he staged a coup by storming a beer hall in Munich with the SA, announcing the formation of a new government with General Erich von Ludendorff, head of the German military during the First World War. The army did not join the rebels. The police easily crushed the coup the following day. Hitler was arrested.[10]

The Beer Hall Putsch had failed. Hitler, behind bars, sank into depression, but soon regained his poise, recognising that martyrdom beckoned. Widespread press coverage established his notoriety at home and abroad. People from all over the country sent presents, and even some of his guards whispered 'Heil Hitler' when they entered the small suite of rooms that served as his cell. The judges at his trial were sympathetic, allowing Hitler to use the courtroom as a propaganda platform, his words reported in every newspaper. He appeared before the court not as defendant but as accuser, portraying the Weimar Republic as the real criminals. He assumed sole responsibility for the putsch. 'I alone bear the responsibility,' he admitted. 'If today I stand here as a revolutionary, it is as a revolutionary against the revolution. There is no such thing as high treason against the traitors of 1918.' Now he scoffed at the idea that he was merely the drummer in a patriotic movement. 'My aim from the first was a thousand times higher ... I wanted to become the destroyer of Marxism.'[11]

The sentence for high treason was surprisingly short, a mere five years, further reduced to thirteen months, but it was still long enough to allow Hitler to write his political biography. By the time he was released, a few days before Christmas 1924, the bulk of the manuscript entitled *Mein Kampf* was finished. The volume appeared in the summer of 1925, although not until 1933 would it become a bestseller.

Mein Kampf summarised much of what Hitler had said in his beer-hall speeches. Behind every one of the country's woes, be it a corrupt parliamentary system or the threat of communism, there lay a Jewish hand. His programme was clear: abrogate the Versailles Treaty, remove the Jews, punish France, build a greater Germany and invade the Soviet Union for 'living space' (*Lebensraum*). But *Mein Kampf* also contained elements of the Hitler legend. A genius child, a voracious reader, a born orator, an unrecognised artist driven by destiny to change the fate of a people. A man overcome by a passion like no other, one that allowed him to recognise the words that would 'open the gates to a people's heart like the blows of a hammer'. A man chosen by heaven as a messenger of its will. As a close follower put it, Hitler was an oracle, a *Traumlaller*, one who speaks prophetically in his dreams.[12]

The oracle was silenced. The state of Bavaria banned Hitler from speaking in public as he emerged from prison a free man. The *Völkischer Beobachter* was proscribed, his party closed down. Most of these restrictions were lifted in February 1925, but as late as 1927 propaganda posters showed the Führer muzzled by bandages with the words 'Forbidden to Speak', as Hitler portrayed himself as a persecuted patriot.[13]

Hitler turned to photography the moment he stepped through the studded iron gate of Landsberg Prison. Heinrich Hoffmann was waiting outside to record the event for posterity, but a prison guard threatened to confiscate his camera. Hitler posed instead in front of the old city gate, standing by the running board of the Daimler-Benz, looking resolutely at the camera, his moustache neatly clipped, hair slicked back. The picture was published around the world.[14]

Hitler could not be heard, but was now seen throughout the ranks and beyond, as Hoffmann published three picture books between 1924 and 1926. The last volume, entitled *Germany's Awakening in Word and Image*, portrayed the leader as a saviour: 'A man stood up from among the people, spreading the gospel of love for the Fatherland.' Posters appeared, some of them showing a crowd of listeners waiting expectantly for the saviour to appear.[15]

On the way back to Munich, Hoffmann asked Hitler what he intended to do next. 'I shall start again, from the beginning.' The party was resurrected and given a new location in the Brienner Strasse, soon referred to as the 'Brown House'. Hitler designed every detail, including the red leather chairs with the crest of the sovereign eagle, copied from ancient Rome, embossed on their backs. On either side of the entrance, two bronze tablets bore the names of those who had lost their lives during the Beer Hall Putsch, now seen as 'martyrs to the movement'.[16]

But membership lagged. Not until 1927 did enrolment reach 57,000, the number attained before the putsch. These were the years of political eclipse, as the economy recovered, assisted by a new currency that tamed inflation and a flood of capital from the United States. Government stabilised. Germany was brought back into the international fold as it entered the League of Nations in 1926. Historians, with hindsight, would call these years the 'Golden Age of Weimar'.

So lukewarm was support for the NSDAP that the ban on speaking was lifted in March 1927. But despite all the theatrics around Hitler's public appearances, with music blaring, flags unfurled and banners waving, and followers with their hands outstretched to greet the leader, many seats remained empty. His rhetorical skills were intact, but his message no longer held the same appeal. The movement was in the doldrums.[17]

Yet even as his popular appeal stalled his image as a god-like figure spread among his followers. Joseph Goebbels, an ambitious, intelligent man with a deformed right foot who had only just joined the party, wondered in October 1925, 'Who is this man? Half commoner, half God! Truly Christ or only John the Baptist?' He was not alone. Even as attendance was below what had been expected at the first party rally in Nuremberg, held in the summer of 1927, the SA in their brown shirts enthusiastically celebrated their leader, who had choreographed the entire event: 'faith in the Führer,' he proclaimed to the assembled masses, 'and not the weakness of the majority is decisive.' Within the ranks of the party, the 'Heil Hitler' greeting became compulsory, symbol of a personal connection with the leader.[18]

Hitler himself was an astute judge of character. As an early believer recalled, he could size up a person at first glance, almost like an animal picking up a scent, sorting those who had 'boundless trust and quasi-religious faith' from those who retained a critical distance. The former were pitted against each other, the latter discarded as soon as they were no longer of use.[19]

Mein Kampf was mocked by enemies, but treated like the Bible by followers. The book repeatedly asserted that geniuses were not found through general elections. 'A camel can pass through the eye of a needle sooner than a great man can be discovered by an election.' His followers saw themselves as apostles who could see even as the minds of unbelievers were blinded. In an open letter to Hitler on the concept of leadership, written in 1928, Goebbels repeated this view, pointing out that 'The great leader *cannot* be elected. He is there when he must be there.' A leader was not chosen by the masses, a leader liberated the masses. The leader was the one, in times of great doubt, to point the way towards belief. 'You are the first servant in the battle for the future,' he continued, suggesting that the leader surround himself with a small group of true men who would roam the country to preach the faith to those who had fallen into despair. A year later, as Hitler turned forty on 20 April 1929, he ascribed to the ideal leader a combination of character, willpower, ability and luck. Hitler already had three of these qualities. His lucky star, Goebbels predicted, would soon shine.[20]

The party's fortunes turned before the end of the year. On 3 October 1929 Gustav Stresemann, a pillar of Weimar democracy, died. A few weeks later Wall Street crashed, sending waves of panic selling around the world. Unemployment soared, passing the three million mark within months to culminate at six million by 1932. Faith in democracy dissolved, inflation took hold, and a sense of despair and hopelessness spread. Hitler was the man of the hour.[21]

A huge propaganda campaign was launched. Whereas other parties were content with a postal appeal or a newspaper advertisement, the Nazis engaged in intense and incessant activities. Hitler had always stressed the importance of the spoken word, and in 1930 one thousand professionally trained speakers fanned out to spread the message, reaching every hamlet. Rallies were organised, meetings held, posters and flyers distributed and swastikas painted on sidewalks.

The party was preaching to the converted, however. Among large parts of the population a wall of resistance existed that their propaganda could not break. The NSDAP referred to itself as 'the Hitler movement', as the figure of the Führer was the one propaganda element that was genuinely effective among a number of disaffected shopkeepers, Protestant farmers and war veterans. While the Nazis' electoral share shot up from 2.6 to 18.3 per cent between May 1928 and September 1930, supporters of rival political parties, in the words of historian Richard Bessel, 'remained remarkably immune to the influence of the cult which was built up around Hitler'.[22]

In September 1931 Hitler's half-niece Geli Raubal shot herself in the chest with his Walther pistol. Two years earlier she had moved into her uncle's apartment in Munich, and her suicide at the age of twenty-three immediately sparked rumours of sexual violence, possibly even murder. It was a publicity disaster, as the press also reminded readers of the homosexuality of SA leader Ernst Röhm. Far from being the party of family values, the NSDAP, enemies of the Nazis alleged, was a collection of sexual deviants.[23]

Six months later Heinrich Hoffmann published a photograph collection entitled *The Hitler Nobody Knows*. It humanised the image of the Führer. Baldur von Shirach, head of the Hitler Youth, provided a foreword. Hitler, he explained, was not only a leader, but also a 'great and good man'. Few people realised that he cultivated simple, spartan habits and worked ceaselessly towards the greater good: 'His capacity for work is extraordinary.' He had no vices. 'It is scarcely known that Hitler is a teetotaller, a non-smoker and a vegetarian.' His hobbies were history and architecture. He read voraciously, boasting a library of 6,000 books, 'all of which he has not just perused, but also read'. Hitler was fond of children and kind to animals. The cover showed a relaxed Führer reclining in an alpine meadow with a shepherd by his side. A hundred candid photographs showed Hitler as a baby, Hitler as artist, Hitler at home, Hitler at work, Hitler at leisure, Hitler reading, chatting, hiking, smiling.[24]

The book appeared in March 1932, in the middle of a presidential campaign. Paul von Hindenburg, a highly respected field marshal aged eighty-four, had been persuaded to run against Hitler. On the first official day of the runoff election, Goebbels published a piece entitled 'Adolf Hitler as a Human Being'. All the themes of the picture book were reinforced. 'Hitler is by nature a good man,' Goebbels testified. A 'human being amongst other human beings, a friend to his comrades, a helpful promoter of every ability and of all talents'. He was kind and modest, which is why all those who knew him 'not only as a politician, but also as a person' were devoted to him. Emil Ludwig, a contemporary biographer, commented: 'All that Hitler lacked, the Germans were persuaded to imagine by his disciple Goebbels.'[25]

The good man showed himself to millions. Goebbels chartered an aeroplane, taking him to dozens of cities in a flying tour that popularised the Hitler cult. 'Hitler over Germany', the headlines screamed. The audience was kept waiting for hours, erupting in applause when Hitler finally descended from the clouds in his plane like a messiah. Young girls gave him flowers, local leaders paid their respects and SA bands played music. The crowds roared.[26]

An election poster pithily titled 'Hitler' made him instantly recognisable, with his face appearing to float free in space, lightened by a dark background. But all the propaganda failed to win Hitler sufficient support to prevail in his presidential bid. Hindenburg won overwhelmingly to become President of the Reich, or head of state, in April. National elections were held a few months later. Hitler kept up the same relentless schedule. His exhausting flying tours finally paid off, as the NSDAP became the most important political party in July 1932, with 37.3 per cent of the electorate.

Hindenburg nonetheless refused to name Hitler Chancellor of Germany, the equivalent of head of government. Rather than compromise, Hitler fumed, declining to join the governing cabinet. He toured the country to denounce the 'reactionary clique' in power in Berlin. Instead of embracing him, in what looked like a decline into oblivion, a more discriminating electorate gave the party less than a third of all votes in new elections held in November 1932. 'The aura is gone ... the magic has failed', one newspaper observed. 'A falling comet in the November fog', another commented. Party members became disillusioned, leaving the ranks in the tens of thousands.[27]

On 30 January 1933 Hitler became Chancellor of Germany. It was the result not so much of an electoral process as of a series of sordid backstage political transactions in which Hindenburg played the leading role. The ageing president did not trust Hitler, but detested his rival even more. When Kurt von Schleicher, last chancellor of the Weimar Republic, proposed to rule as de facto dictator to break parliamentary stalemate, Hindenburg appointed Hitler instead.

Within weeks the Reichstag building where parliament convened was set on fire. Hitler used the incident to claim that a communist plot was in progress. Hindenburg, who did not trust the parliamentary system to contain the threat from the left, was persuaded to pass a decree suspending basic rights.

Terror and propaganda now advanced hand in hand, as hundreds of thousands of brownshirts hunted down their opponents. The mayor of Stassfurt, a social democrat, was shot dead on 5 February 1933. Countless other leaders of the opposition were intimidated, beaten up or paraded through the streets on their way to prison. Still, the NSDAP failed to secure an absolute majority on election day in March 1933, winning only 43.9 per cent of the vote. An Enabling Act was passed the same month, giving Hitler unlimited powers for four years.[28]

An even greater wave of terror followed. In May trade unions were dissolved, while in June all other political parties were disbanded. Violence did not target just political opponents or social outcasts, but was directed at all opponents of the Nazis. An estimated 100,000 people were detained without trial in 1933 alone. Hundreds died in custody. While many were subsequently released, their arrest had the desired effect, making fear a routine part of everyday life.[29]

The moment Hitler became chancellor, some municipal authorities began demonstrating their zeal by renaming streets, squares, avenues, schools, stadiums or bridges after their leader. On 31 March 1933 the centre of Hanover became Adolf Hitler Square. Three days later a central avenue leading from the Charlottenplatz to the Wilhelm Palais in Stuttgart was christened Adolf Hitler Street. For good measure a middle school in the same city was called Adolf Hitler School. In Charlottenburg, Berlin, the local authorities renamed Chancellery Place in honour of the Führer on the occasion of his birthday on 20 April 1933. Within a few years even the smallest village had its obligatory Adolf Hitler Street. Many also had an Adolf Hitler Square.[30]

People also wrote to honour the Führer. On 18 February Herr Weber, owner of a coffee and cake shop in Sondershausen, asked to be allowed to call his establishment the 'Reich's Chancellor A. Hitler'. The Führer declined. Three days later a rose breeder proposed to identity a new variety as 'Adolf Hitler', while an engineer wrote to christen a wind turbine in Berlin the 'Adolf Hitler Tower'. An admirer from Düsseldorf baptised his daughter Hitlerine, while Adolfine, Hitlerike and Hilerine were also popular.[31]

But there were no statues of Adolf Hitler. Unlike most other dictators, the Führer insisted that statues and monuments be reserved for the great historical figures of the past. He was a leader of the future.[32]

Portraits of the Führer adorned every office, but outside the organs of the state demand for his image also rocketed. Some entrepreneurs asked for permission to use his name or profile to sell soap, cigars and sweets. Others bypassed the state altogether and produced bonbons or sausages in the shape of the swastika. To protect the 'sacred nature and value' of state symbols, Goebbels passed a law on 19 May 1933 forbidding any image of the Führer to circulate without the approval of the party.[33]

Hitler was only chancellor, and next to his portrait was that of the president. Hitler made the best of his predicament, using Hindenburg's aura to place himself in a direct line of great German leaders. On 30 January 1933, the two men had appeared side by side on the balcony in the Wilhelmstrasse, greeting some 60,000 brownshirts in a torchlit parade choreographed by Goebbels. Two months later, at the ceremonial opening of the Reichstag in Potsdam, Hitler bowed respectfully to Hindenburg as he received his blessing. The event was shown in every cinema.[34]

By 1934 the brownshirts, who had done the dirty work, became increasingly vocal and demanded to be incorporated into the regular army. But conservative generals viewed them as thugs. Hitler had no wish to antagonise the military establishment. He also feared that Ernst Röhm, chief-of-staff of the SA, had become too powerful. On 30 June, in the Night of the Long Knives, he ordered his elite SS guards to purge the SA. Röhm was arrested and shot, along with dozens of other leaders, while thousands more were thrown into prison. Hindenburg, who retained control over the army as president, congratulated Hitler.

The old field marshal died on 2 August 1934. An hour later the offices of President of the Reich and Chancellor of Germany were united in the person of the Führer, who now commanded the army. The traditional oath of loyalty to the office of the president was altered and given to Adolf Hitler in name by every soldier.[35]

Hitler, having painstakingly built up his image as a charismatic leader, now sought a plebiscite for confirmation. The population was asked to vote on the merger of both offices on 19 August. There was a barrage of propaganda. Posters of Hitler were everywhere, with only one word: 'Yes'. In Bavaria, where BMW had their factories, one observer noted: 'Hitler on every bulletin board, Hitler in every display window, in fact Hitler in every window that one can see. Every tram, every window in every train wagon, every car window: Hitler looks through every window.' In some places the brownshirts, who continued operations on a much-reduced scale after the purge, provided portraits for free, demanding that they be prominently exhibited. They returned within hours if their orders were not followed. Flags were also distributed and hung from windows. Households in central Dresden received instructions on the precise number of swastika flags they should display.[36]

Ninety per cent of the electorate approved. Five million people had the courage to spoil the ballot or vote No. As the Jewish scholar Victor Klemperer confided to his diary, 'One third said Yes out of fear, one third out of intoxication, one third out of fear and intoxication.'[37]

The party's annual rally followed the plebiscite. Since 1927 it had been held in Nuremberg, a small city in Bavaria with fortified buildings dating back to the Holy Roman Empire, considered to be the First Reich. The rallies had grown in size over the years, but none matched the 'Rally of Unity and Strength', as the gathering of 700,000 people was later called. As Hitler's deputy Rudolph Hess announced during the opening ceremony: 'This congress is the first to take place under the unlimited rule of National Socialism. It stands under the banner of Adolf Hitler as the highest and only leader of Germany, under the banner of the "Führer" as a concept embodied in state law.' The rally concentrated on glorifying the Führer. Albert Speer, the party's chief architect, built a huge field with a grandstand surrounded by 152 searchlights casting vertical beams into the night, creating what admirers called a Cathedral of Light around the Führer as he addressed vast formations of uniformed followers enthralled by his every word. As Hess summed up, 'The Party is Hitler and Hitler is Germany just as Germany is Hitler!'[38]

In the years following his release from prison in 1924 Hitler had made his star the guiding principle of the party. Belief in Adolf Hitler became all-important: his intuition, vision and sheer willpower would propel the NSDAP forward. Hitlerism focused entirely on Hitler. As *Mein Kampf* had pointed out, when people adored a genius they released their inner strength. Only Jews denounced reverence for great souls as a 'cult of personality'. Now the people as a whole were asked to unite in their adoration of one man.[39]

The cult of personality abased all others inside the party. Ten days after the 19 August 1934 plebiscite a circular from the NSDAP demanded that portraits of Goering and Goebbels as well as other leaders be taken down from the party premises. When followers assembled for the next rally in Nuremberg a year later the slogan proposed by Hess was shortened to 'Hitler is Germany just as Germany is Hitler'.[40]

Towering above all others had many advantages. Most people detested the thuggish brownshirts and had welcomed the Night of the Long Knives, unaware of the scale of the massacre because Goebbels tightly controlled the newspapers. Many saw in their chancellor a courageous man who put his country above his erstwhile comrades, moving with lightning speed against the powerful men who had become a danger to the state. But the purge had also demonstrated that conflicting forces were at work inside the Nazi movement. Hitler appeared to be the only one who could hold together very diverse and sometimes antagonistic internal party factions. While he exploited their rivalries for his own benefit, all of them had to serve him in common subordination. And when things went wrong, ordinary people blamed his underlings, rarely the Führer, building up his aura of invincibility even further.[41]

Two weeks after the Reichstag fire Goebbels moved into the Ordenspalais, an eighteenth-century palace in the Wilhelmstrasse directly across from the chancellery. As Reich Minister of Propaganda and Enlightenment he worked tirelessly on the cult of the Führer. On 19 April 1933, as Hitler was about to turn forty-four, Goebbels addressed the nation. Many admirers had rushed to join the ranks of the party, he explained, while millions of ordinary believers had only seen him from afar. But even the few who knew him well were overcome by the magic of his personality. 'The longer one knows him,' Goebbels continued, 'the more one admires him, and the more one is ready to give oneself fully to his cause.' Over the next decade Goebbels would glorify the leader in an annual speech on the eve of his birthday, which became a major holiday marked by parades and public celebrations.[42]

Every aspect of daily life fell under the control of the one-party state. In a process called *Gleichschaltung*, or synchronisation, the party took over or replaced completely every organisation from the education system down to a local sports club. All adopted a uniform Nazi outlook. Goebbels oversaw the press, with every newspaper spreading the same message, always dominated by fulsome praise of the Führer.

His word was everywhere. His most important speeches were published in all leading newspapers and distributed by the millions in separate pamphlets produced by the party's printing house. Starting in 1937, every week hundreds of thousands of posters appeared with a quotation for display in party offices and public buildings. Weekly mottos were also printed in the newspapers under a special headline, usually if not always some saying of Hitler's.[43]

Sales of *Mein Kampf* rocketed. At the German Book Week held in Bremen in November 1933 party member and literary critic Will Vesper announced that *Mein Kampf* was 'the holy book of National Socialism and the new Germany that every German must have'. A million copies were sold by the end of the year. Four years later sales passed the four million mark: 'A Book Conquers a Nation!' trumpeted a Berlin newspaper. It became the gift of choice for newly-weds, while free copies were later handed out to soldiers fighting on the front.[44]

Excerpts and abridgements of the sacred text also appeared. In 1934 the chapter entitled 'Nation and Race' appeared as a brochure and was distributed to schools two years later. Collections of quotations from the Führer became popular, for instance, *Words of the Führer* and *Hitler's Words*. But a few years later Hitler intervened, demanding that these publications be banned, as they simplified his thought. He insisted that his words be read in their entirety.[45]

His voice was also everywhere. Hitler first spoke over the radio one day after he became chancellor. It did not go well, with some listeners even complaining that his tone was harsh and 'un-German'. Hitler worked on his broadcasting skills. He was, after all, a practised orator. 'Sound, I think, is much more suggestive than image,' he opined. 'We can get endlessly more out of this.'[46]

Hitler was heard again on the eve of the March 1933 elections. Goebbels was elated: 'This hymn vibrates through the ether over the radio in all of Germany. Forty million Germans stand on the squares and streets of the Reich, or sit in taverns and homes next to the loudspeaker and become aware of the great turning-point in history.'[47]

'Radio is all mine,' Goebbels enthused, soon approving a scheme whereby millions of cheap sets were sold below production cost. 'All of Germany Listens to the Führer with the People's Radio!' became the slogan, and by 1941 some 65 per cent of all households boasted a subscription. But even people without a radio could not escape the voice of their saviour. Loudspeaker pillars were erected in cities, and mobile loudspeakers installed in small towns. In March 1936 Victor Klemperer came across a Hitler speech on a visit to Dresden. 'I could not get away from it for an hour. First from an open shop, then in the bank, then from a shop again.'[48]

Hitler was almost entirely absent from newsreels before he became chancellor. Here, too, Goebbels saw an opportunity to exploit a new technology for propaganda purposes. On 10 February 1933 a team of camera operators and their assistants shot Hitler's thirty-three-minute speech in the Berliner Sportpalast, a huge indoor arena in the Schöneberg district of the capital. But the film failed to capture the bond between the orator and his audience. Goebbels developed doubts, and while Hitler became a regular presence in weekly cinema newsreels his appearances remained fleeting.[49]

Hitler intervened and commissioned Leni Riefenstahl to make *Triumph of the Will*, a lavish documentary of the 1934 party rally in Nuremberg. Riefenstahl used moving cameras, aerial photography and synchronised sound to produce a masterpiece of propaganda, one that presented a murderous regime that had just carried out a bloody purge as a mesmerising, quasi-religious experience in which faithful masses were united with their saviour in a mystical bond. The star was Adolf Hitler, descending like a god from the clouds by plane in the opening scene. *Triumph of the Will* won awards in Germany, the United States, France and other countries. More films followed, including a propaganda piece entitled *Day of*

Freedom: Our Armed Forces and a documentary on the 1936 summer Olympics in Berlin. All of them were screened in special previews for the party elite, shown in theatres around the country and taken to the countryside in mobile cinemas.[50]

Goebbels tried to enlist Hoffmann, but the court photographer was determined to remain 'just a businessman'. His business thrived, with shops in every major city. Since the Führer's image was protected by law, the court photographer had a virtual monopoly over the market. He sold his photos as portraits, postcards, posters and calendars. His book *The Hitler Nobody Knows*, published in 1932, sold some 400,000 copies, and was followed by a series of equally successful picture books, including *Youth around Hitler*, *Hitler in Italy*, *With Hitler in the West* and *The Face of the Führer*. All appeared in a range of formats, from coffee-table books to miniature editions easily tucked into a pocket by soldiers on the front.[51]

Painters, sculptors, photographers, printers and even the Post Office were referred to Hoffmann's studio. His reach extended still farther after Hitler put him in charge of the annual Great German Art Exhibition in 1937. Every year dozens of artworks depicting Hitler, many copied from Hoffmann's photos, filled entire rooms.[52]

Goebbels controlled propaganda, but not schools and universities. To his great disappointment, the Ministry of Culture he had been promised went to Bernhard Rust. Hitler liked to divide and rule, encouraging rivalry among his underlings or giving them overlapping tasks so as to consolidate his own power. It made him the ultimate arbiter, while relegating them to subordinates constantly competing to outdo one another.

Rust, a zealous Nazi, made sure that children were indoctrinated into the cult of the leader from their very first day in school. The Hitler salute was introduced by the end of 1933. His portrait hung in every classroom. Old textbooks were removed, with some burned in giant bonfires, while new ones endlessly hammered home the same message: love the leader and obey the party. Instead of reading Goethe, they recited the poem 'Mein Führer' by Hans

H. Seitz: 'I have seen you now; And will carry your image with me; Whatever may happen; I will stand by you.'[53]

In potted biographies children were told the story of a man who had risen from obscurity to save his people. *The Story of Adolf Hitler Told to German Children* by Annemarie Stiehler concluded: 'As long as Germans walk the earth, they will think of Adolf Hitler with gratitude, the one who fought his way from unknown soldier during the world war to Führer and saved Germany from great need.' In some schools children prayed every day for the Führer: 'Dear God, I beg you; Let me become a pious child; Protect Hitler every day; That no accident may befall him; You sent him in our distress; O God protect him.'[54]

Our Hitler, published in 1933 by Paul Jennrich, enjoined young readers to 'Wake up and follow him!' Youngsters enrolled in the Hitler Youth, an organisation overseen by Baldur von Shirach. Since it was the only youth organisation allowed to exist, membership rocketed after 1934, until three years later it became mandatory for all Germans. They pledged love and loyalty to the Führer. They sang, paraded and prayed in his name: 'Adolf Hitler, you are our great Führer. Thy name makes the enemy tremble.'[55]

Adults or children alike were told 'The Führer is Always Right'. Robert Ley, leader of the German Labour Front and unswerving follower of the Führer, used the slogan at the Nuremberg rally in 1936. It appeared across the nation, proclaimed on banners, posters and in newspapers.[56]

Goebbels, Riefenstahl, Hoffmann, Rust, Shirach, Ley, all worked tirelessly to promote their leader. But the greatest architect of the cult remained Hitler himself, lead actor, stage manager, orator and publicist all rolled into one. He constantly fine-tuned his image. After 1932 he projected himself as a leader in close touch with his people, saluting millions at parades and rallies. But he was also keen to present himself as a great statesman and player on the world stage.

As soon as he moved into the chancellery he hired an interior designer to transform the premises. Hitler detested the old building, seeing its overwrought grandeur as a parable for the political decay of the nation. Rooms were opened to light and air, old partitions removed, floorboards ripped out, crisp, clear and straight lines introduced. As the temple of democracy was torn down, a new Reception Hall was erected, complete with swastika mosaics in the ceiling and bronze lamps along the walls. God was setting his house in order.[57]

Several years later, Hitler's favourite architect, Albert Speer, received a blank cheque to build a new chancellery, a vast building that monopolised the entire northern side of the Vossstrasse. Hitler treasured the polished marble of the main gallery, which was twice the length of the Hall of Mirrors in Versailles: 'On the long walk from the entrance to the reception hall they will get a taste of the power and grandeur of the German Reich!' His office was 400 square metres in size, giving the Führer great joy every time a visitor had to cross the large expanse to reach his desk.[58]

Hitler's apartment in Munich was also refurbished, with every detail carefully designed, down to the door handles. His interior designer Gerdy Troost created an atmosphere of muted, bourgeois luxury, with books and art prominently displayed. 'We might have been in Park Terrace, Glasgow,' one visitor commented. All was designed to convey an air of reassuring familiarity and stability.[59]

The principal stage for Hitler's performance as a cultivated and trustworthy statesman, however, was neither in Berlin nor in Munich. In 1933 Hitler bought a small chalet in the Bavarian mountain retreat of Obersalzberg, which was refurbished and expanded into a sprawling compound named the Berghof (the alpine retreat is sometimes referred to as Berchtesgaden, the name of the local town). Gerdy Troost, who had transformed his home and office, filled the spacious halls and bedrooms with rich fabrics, luxurious tapestries and modern furniture. The centre of the Berghof was the Great Hall, a reception room the size of a small gymnasium, dominated by a giant window that could be lowered to offer a sweeping view of the snow-capped mountains. There Hitler held court, with every detail designed to impress his visitors. They were dazzled by the sheer size of the Great Hall, then overawed by the huge expanse of window, the largest piece of glass ever made at the time. Nothing stood between them and the mountain peak. Furniture was placed along the wall to leave the room's centre uncluttered. But the oversized sofas had deep backs, compelling visitors to lounge, recline or perch on the edge. Hitler sat up straight on a chair, dominating all others.[60]

Outside, Hitler posed for Heinrich Hoffmann's camera, feeding the deer from his terrace, playing with his dog, greeting children. Soon, thousands of well-wishers and tourists arrived, hoping for a glimpse of the Führer. It was 'like a wonderful dream to be so near to the Führer', one woman from Frankfurt recalled. Outsiders were banned in 1936, but leading personalities continued to visit without announcement: they, too, were barred two years later.[61]

Inside, Hitler received a steady flow of dignitaries, from kings and ambassadors to religious leaders and secretaries of state. Many were carefully selected sympathisers, and most were duly impressed. Former British prime minister Lloyd George, who visited in 1936, went back home declaring that Hitler was the 'George Washington of Germany' and a 'born leader of men'. The Duke and Duchess of Windsor came and posed for the camera.[62]

The Berghof, however, also provided the ideal stage for intimidating potential opponents. When Kurt Schuschnigg came to negotiate the fate of his country, Hitler arranged for some of his most brutal looking generals to sit in the background, glaring menacingly at the chancellor of Austria while Hitler ranted for a full two hours.[63]

Still, Hitler was no Mussolini, a dictator who managed to beguile some of the world's greatest leaders. Hitler's best tactic was not so much to charm as to disarm, lulling those who met him into a false sense of security. Hitler was a master of disguise, hiding his personality behind a carefully constructed image of a modest, kind and simple man. He knew how to absorb and give expression to the emotions of a crowd, and equally he knew how to read his visitors, adapting his tone and demeanour to hide his intentions and downplay the threat he represented. When the

American journalist Dorothy Thompson published *I Saw Hitler* in 1932, describing him as 'formless and faceless' after a lengthy interview, 'the very prototype of the Little Man' who would only smite 'the weakest of his enemies', Hitler was amused. She was just one in a long line of people who underestimated what the little man could – and would – do.[64]

From the chancellery and the Berghof, the two power centres of the Third Reich, Hitler set out to pursue the vision he had expressed in *Mein Kampf*, although he did so more by following his intuition, seizing opportunities when they presented themselves, than by adhering to any definite programme. Germany withdrew from the League of Nations in October 1933. Conscription was reintroduced in violation of the Treaty of Versailles in March 1935, the armed forces expanding to six times the permitted number. Even as Hitler made promises of peace, he prepared his country for war. In March 1936 he took his first international gamble, as his army marched into the demilitarised zone in the Rhineland. His own military advisers had warned him of the risks, and his troops were under strict instructions to retreat if they encountered any opposition from France. But nothing happened, except for a vote of weak condemnation by the League of Nations. 'With the certainty of a sleepwalker, I walk along the path laid out for me by providence,' Hitler quipped. He himself now began to believe in his own infallibility.[65]

The Rhineland coup crushed Hitler's opponents. They were further isolated by a carefully orchestrated show of unity between the leader and his people, held in the guise of a referendum two weeks later. A wave of terror had already thinned the ranks of critics of the party, as people were sent to prison for the slightest infraction. Robert Sauter, an ordinary citizen who queried the reliability of newspapers, was confined for five months. Paul Glowania, a resident in Ludwigshaven, expressed doubts about the regime in the privacy of his own home, was overheard, denounced and sentenced to a year. 'Germany is silent, nervous, suppressed; it speaks in whispers; there is no public opinion, no opposition, no discussion of anything,' noted W. E. B. Du Bois, the African-American civil rights activist who spent months travelling through the country in 1936.[66]

Propaganda, combined with terror, convinced the others to vote Yes. Even in a small town of 1,500 people, there were posters everywhere, on fences and houses, including giant portraits of Hitler. In Breslau every display window was mandated to feature a dedicated Hitler corner. Shopowners who refused were threatened with a day in a concentration camp. Elsewhere brownshirts appeared on the doorstep of each household, telling their occupants how many posters must be displayed. Cases of resistance still occurred, with portraits of Hitler covered in paint or torn down overnight. The result of the referendum was that 99 per cent voted Yes. 'It is the miracle of our age that you have found me among so many millions,' he told ecstatic supporters at the party rally in September 1936, 'and that I have found you is Germany's great fortune.'[67]

Hitler now had the popular backing he needed to expand the Third Reich. But in order to wage war he believed that the economy must become self-sufficient. As early as 1933 exports had been curbed, price controls introduced, grain stores built and consumption rationed. In 1936 Hermann Goering was put in charge of the Four-Year Plan, cranking up the effort to reach economic independence by 1940. It brought widespread shortages. The American journalist William Shirer reported from Berlin that long queues of sullen people waited before the food shops, as there were shortages of meat, butter, fruit and fats. Import substitutes meant that clothes were increasingly made from wood pulp, gasoline from coal and rubber from coal and lime. Cost-conscious people wondered how much money was wasted on propaganda, not to mention the millions lavished on the mountain retreat for the 'simple worker of his people'.[68]

Panem et circenses, bread and circuses, was an old principle well understood by modern dictators, but the entertainment was also faltering: the parades and rallies all looked the same, the speeches sounded alike. 'Gone is the belief in the magical powers of Hitler,' one commentator ventured. Still, many credited Hitler for having freed the country from the shackles of Versailles. Hitler had elevated their country to its rightful position in the world and restored their army to its former glory.[69]

Most of all, the cult provided protection against disillusionment with the system. People blamed the party, not their leader. The more disenchanted they became, the more they characterised Hitler as a man kept in deliberate ignorance by his underlings. He only wanted the best for his people. 'If only Hitler knew' became a popular expression.[70]

Hitler, having portrayed himself as a sleepwalker guided by the hand of destiny, knew that he had to show that his star was still in the ascendant. In March 1938 he gambled again. Even before the collapse of the Austro-Hungarian empire in 1918 there had been calls for the unification of Austria and Germany into a Greater Germany. The Treaty of Versailles forbade the union and stripped Austria of the Sudetenland, giving the German-dominated area to Czechoslovakia. In February 1938 Hitler had browbeaten the chancellor of Austria into appointing Nazi sympathisers to key positions in Vienna. On returning home, Schuschnigg scheduled instead a plebiscite on the issue of unification. Hitler was furious, sent an ultimatum and invaded on 12 March. He himself crossed the border the very same day in a motorcade, to be welcomed by cheering crowds. Austria became the province of Ostmark.

The international response was subdued and encouraged Hitler to eye the Sudetenland. Still, like many gamblers, he vacillated, torn between confidence and self-doubt. In September 1938 he loudly threatened war at the annual party rally. Within days Neville Chamberlain travelled to the Obersalzberg, where his host received him on the Berghof's front steps. Halfway through a three-hour conversation, Hitler suddenly switched roles, transforming himself from an unpredictable megalomaniac who threatened war into a perfectly reasonable negotiating partner. Hitler pledged not to use force against Czechoslovakia. Chamberlain agreed to the cessation of the Sudetenland, signing the Munich Agreement two weeks later. 'He looks entirely undistinguished,' the prime minister admitted to his sister, but Hitler was 'a man of his word'. Hitler clapped his hands in sheer delight the moment Chamberlain left the Berghof. The Sudetenland was occupied without a shot being fired.[71]

On 20 April 1939 Adolf Hitler was fifty. 'The fiftieth birthday of the creator of Greater Germany. Two days of flags, pomp and special editions of the newspapers, boundless deification,' noted Victor Klemperer. The celebrations had been under preparation for weeks by Goebbels, who addressed the nation over the radio on 19 April, asking Germans to join him in fervent prayer to almighty God: 'May he grant the German people's deepest wish and keep the Führer in health and strength for many more years and decades.' Shortly afterwards party leaders appeared at the chancellery to offer their congratulations. At nine in the evening the Führer showed himself to the crowds. Hundreds of thousands formed a guard of honour along the road from the Wilhelmstrasse all the way to Adolf Hitler Place in Charlottenburg, where Hitler inaugurated a new section of the new east–west axis, also called the Via Triumphalis. The ten-lane avenue was ablaze, with powerful lights throwing gilded swastikas and imperial eagles, mounted on columns every twenty metres, into sharp relief against a dark sky.[72]

Birthday presents, piled high in several rooms at the chancellery, were opened around midnight. There were gifts from his entourage. Albert Speer, the Führer's architect who had built the Via Triumphalis, used one of the salons to erect a four-metre-high model of a gigantic Arch of Triumph to be built in Berlin. Small bronze casts, white marble nudes and old paintings were heaped on long tables. There were also tributes from the people. Farmers sent their produce. A group of women from Westphalia had knitted 6,000 pairs of socks for the Führer's soldiers. Others had baked a two-metre-long birthday cake.[73]

The real festivities came the following day, as the former corporal acted as an emperor, reviewing his mighty war machine before an astonished world. He wore his usual brown uniform, but sat on a throne-like chair placed on a raised dais, covered with red plush, protected by a giant canopy decorated with eagles and iron crosses. Tanks, artillery, armoured cars, and tens of thousands of soldiers in full fighting regalia greeted their Führer along the Via Triumphalis, with 162 warplanes flying overhead in close formation.[74]

The Via Triumphalis cut through the heart of the capital, but it also linked Hitler to the country's imperial past. Albert Speer had designed the avenue as an extension of the Unter den Linden, developed by Prussia as a Via Triumphalis after its victory in the Napoleonic Wars. The axis was part of a grandiose plan to transform Berlin into the capital of a thousand-year Reich, a gleaming city called Germania that would rival Egypt, Babylon and ancient Rome. The plan, based on original sketches provided by the Führer himself, included a gigantic Grand Hall designed to host 180,000 people. The Arch of Triumph, meanwhile, would reach an enormous 117 metres. As Speer later put it, Hitler demanded 'the biggest of everything to glorify his works and magnify his pride'.[75]

'The Führer is celebrated by the nation like no other mortal has ever been,' Goebbels effused. Hitler seemed to have miraculously united a nation still deeply divided only six years earlier. In an important reflection on the Nazi regime, the German journalist and historian Sebastian Haffner calculated that more than 90 per cent of the population were followers of the Führer.[76]

Victor Klemperer was more prudent: 'Who can judge the mood of eighty million people, with the press bound and everyone afraid of opening their mouth?' When Hitler spoke in the Theresienwiese, an open space in his old stamping ground of Munich, half a million people had been expected, but at most 200,000 turned up. 'They stood there as if the speech had nothing to do with them,' one observer noticed. Most had been frogmarched to the event from neighbouring enterprises and factories. Speer himself remembered that in 1939 the cheering crowds were entirely stage-managed, even if some were genuinely enthusiastic.[77]

'The fiftieth birthday of Hitler was celebrated with such extravagance that one might really believe that his popularity is soaring. But those who really know the common people realise that much, but by no means all, is mere appearance,' wrote an anonymous critic of the regime. For two weeks before the event, people were bombarded with exhortations to decorate their homes, and woe betide any who failed to comply. Even churches were given specific instructions by the Ministry of Propaganda on how to ring their bells on the great day.[78]

Whether or not they adored the Führer, as Goebbels proclaimed, they lived in fear of war. Even fanatical followers heaved a sigh of relief after Austria was peacefully incorporated into the Reich, but they did not trust the Munich Agreement. Chamberlain, upon his return to London, had received a boisterous welcome, holding a flimsy piece of paper flapping in the wind: 'Peace for our time,' he had confidently declared. Wild crowds had also cheered in other parts of Europe, but not in Germany. People thought it a bluff. 'They don't understand Hitler,' they whispered.[79]

Chamberlain was convinced that Hitler had merely hoped to absorb the Sudetenland, when in fact the Führer wished to eliminate all of Czechoslovakia. This he did on 15 March 1939, as the country was invaded and divided up among Germany, Hungary and Poland. A week later American president Franklin Roosevelt sent a message asking Hitler to pledge that he would not attack other nations in Europe. Chamberlain himself announced that Britain would intervene if Polish independence was threatened. Despite the appearance of strength and unity, a thick cloud of fear hung over the birthday celebrations.[80]

A few months later, as apprehensions of war mounted, Hitler stunned the world by signing an alliance with Stalin. The arch-enemies were now allies, meaning that there would not be a war on two fronts. But Hitler made a fatal miscalculation. With the Soviet Union on his side, he thought that France and Britain would not dare to intervene in Poland. It was a huge gamble, but Hitler trusted his intuition, which had proved him right so far. He had built an image of himself as the man of destiny and had come to believe in it. He dismissed dissenting opinions, including those of his own generals. When Hermann Goering suggested that it was not necessary to wager everything, Hitler replied: 'In my life I have always put my whole stake on the table.' Germany invaded western

Poland on 1 September, the Soviet Union eastern Poland on 17 September.[81]

On 3 September Britain and France declared war. People were in a state of shock. Instead of the wild enthusiasm of 1914, the declaration of war aroused, in Heinrich Hoffmann's words, 'abysmal despondency'. 'Today, no excitement, no hurrahs, no cheering, no throwing of flowers, no war fever, no war hysteria,' observed William Shirer from Berlin. 'There is not even any hate for the French and British.'[82]

Hitler, too, was taken aback. Hoffmann found him 'slumped in his chair, deep in thought, a look of incredulity and baffled chagrin on his face'. But he recovered soon enough, as reports of swift military advances in Poland began to flow in.[83]

The invading troops reached Warsaw within a week, but the streets of Berlin saw no wild rejoicing. 'In the subway going out to the radio studio I noted the strange indifference of the people to the big news,' Shirer confided to his diary. Resignation took over, as rationing increased, with French and English ships enforcing an economic blockade that affected almost every commodity, halving imports of cotton, tin, oil and rubber. In many shops – confectioner's, fishmonger's, grocer's – the Führer's picture, with flag cloth and victory green, replaced the rationed goods in window displays. Income tax increased by a hefty 50 per cent to finance the war effort.[84]

By October even rubber overshoes were restricted to 5 per cent of the population. Over the winter temperatures plummeted to below zero centigrade. Half the population was freezing and without coal. Robert Ley read a Christmas proclamation over the radio: 'The Führer is always right. Obey the Führer!'[85]

When Hitler celebrated his birthday on 20 April 1940 no church bells rang, because many of them had been melted down to make bullets. Despite his victories in Denmark and Norway, invaded a few weeks earlier, a mere seventy-five well-wishers stood outside the chancellery waiting for a glimpse of the leader.[86]

Hitler realised that he could not break the economic blockade. Again he risked everything, making a bid for victory now that his troops still had sufficient supplies. On 10 May 1940 the German army marched into the Netherlands, Belgium and France. It was a resounding success, with tanks easily outflanking French fortifications to reach Paris on 14 June. Four days later an armistice was signed in the very same carriage of the Compagnie des Wagons-Lits where Marshal Ferdinand Foch had dictated his terms to the German delegation on 11 November 1918.

When the invasion of France had been announced six weeks earlier, many people had responded with apathy. 'Most Germans I have seen,' commented William Shirer, 'are sunk deep into depression.' Now they cheered Hitler, who was welcomed back home as the 'Creator of a New Europe'. Hitler had overseen the choreography of the Victory Parade himself, insisting that it 'reflect the historical victory' achieved by his troops. As his train pulled slowly into the railway station, a crowd that had waited for hours cheered jubilantly. The Führer shed a tear, visibly overcome with emotion. People thronged the route back to the chancellery. 'The streets are covered in flowers and look like a colourful carpet,' wrote Goebbels, as 'excitement fills the entire city.'[87]

Spontaneous scenes of joy erupted across the country, as people celebrated the armistice. There was relief after the dread of war, but also genuine euphoria at the ease with which Hitler had achieved his objectives. Again, it seemed, the hand of providence had guided the Führer to victory.[88]

In an eloquent speech at the Reichstag, Hitler offered peace to Britain. It was one of his best performances, calculated to rally a population that longed for peace behind the inevitable fight against Britain. The sway of his body, the inflections of his voice, the very choice of words, the cocking of his eyes, the turning of his head for irony, the gestures with his hands, the clever combination of the confidence of a conqueror with the humbleness of a true son of the people, everything created the impression of a sincere man of peace. 'He can tell a lie with as straight a face as any man,' noticed William Shirer. Part of the show was for his generals, massed together on the first balcony: with one imperious flick of the hand, he promoted twelve generals to the rank of field marshal. Hermann Goering became Reich Marshal.[89]

Britain refused to sue for peace. To their intense consternation, many ordinary people now realised that the war would not end speedily. The Battle of Britain followed, but Reich Marshal Goering failed to bomb the island into submission. Hitler adopted another plan, one close to his heart ever since he had written *Mein Kampf*, namely, the conquest of Russia. Germany depended heavily on deliveries of oil and grain from Stalin. The Soviet Union appeared weak, their troops having suffered great losses after a botched invasion of Finland in the winter of 1939–40. Hitler was convinced he could win a quick victory. He gambled again and betrayed his ally, as some three million soldiers crossed the Russian border in June 1941.

German troops soon became bogged down in a costly war of attrition. After Japan attacked the American fleet at Pearl Harbor on 7 December 1941, Hitler declared war on the United States, a country that had never loomed very large in his thinking. He apparently underestimated its ability to produce wheat, coal, steel and men. The war on two fronts that everyone had dreaded now became a reality. One defeat succeeded another, as the Führer, sure of his own genius, brushed aside the army's high command, interfering in every aspect of the war. He repeatedly refused to withdraw his troops from Stalingrad, the city named after his nemesis. After hundreds of thousands of German soldiers died in one of the bloodiest battles in the history of warfare, the remaining Wehrmacht troops surrendered in February 1943.[90]

For years Germans had been told that Hitler was the master of the short, lightning war, a blitzkrieg conducted far away from home. In a speech at the Berliner Sportpalast on 18 February 1943, broadcast over the radio and reproduced in every newspaper, Goebbels told the population that total war was now inevitable.[91]

Hitler disappeared from view. To quell rumours of his declining health, he spoke briefly on 21 March 1943. It was a dull performance, delivered so hastily that some listeners suspected it was the work of an impersonator. His hand suffered from a tremor which worsened over time, which no doubt contributed to his reluctance to appear in public. As his secretary noted, he believed that an iron will could prevail over everything, yet was unable to master his own hand.[92]

On the eve of the Führer's birthday on 20 April 1943 Goebbels explained in his annual peroration that men of great calibre did not need to show themselves before the full footlights of the world stage. In endless days of work and wakeful nights Hitler was toiling hard on the nation's behalf, carrying the heaviest burden, and facing the greatest grief.[93]

Some derided Goebbels. Others were in a state of deep shock. Many realised that Stalingrad was a turning point, that Germany was losing the war. There were harsh words for the regime, although people knew how to express themselves without becoming liable to criminal prosecution. It was clear to all that if major strategic blunders had been made, only one man could possibly be responsible, a man who might not rest until all was destroyed.[94]

By summer 1943, as Mussolini fell from power, criticism of the regime became more open. People listened to foreign radio, keen to learn more about the advancing enemy troops. The Hitler salute was in striking decline. 'Many party members no longer wear the party badge,' observed one report from the Security Service of the SS. 'Let us hope the English will be in Berlin before the Russians' became a wish that was heard ever more frequently, noted the estranged diplomat Ulrich von Hassell.[95]

With total war came even more drastic rationing, as ordinary people were placed on a starvation diet. Still, they fared better than others. The moment Poland was invaded, the systematic killing of Jews and other undesirables began. Extermination camps were set up in occupied Poland in 1941, and soon millions of Jews from all over Europe were transported in sealed freight trains, for destruction in gas chambers. Their belongings were confiscated, catalogued, tagged and sent to Germany to assist the war effort.

Paper and cardboard, too, were rationed, but not for Heinrich Hoffmann's photography business, since pictures of the Führer were considered 'strategically vital'. Every month, some four tonnes of paper were earmarked for his company.[96]

On 6 June 1944 the Allied powers landed in Normandy. The nightmare of encirclement now became real, as two powerful armies moved towards Germany in a giant pincer movement. Hitler, still convinced of his own genius, badgered his generals and pored obsessively over maps, but since no victory was forthcoming he became increasingly suspicious of those around him. On 20 July 1944 several military leaders made an attempt on his life by placing a bomb inside a briefcase at the Wolf's Lair, a command post in Prussia. Hitler escaped with a few bruises. It reinforced his belief that fate had chosen him, as he pressed on with the war effort, thinking that a miracle weapon or a sudden change of fortune would rescue him and his people at the eleventh hour.

By then he had become a different person. Heinrich Hoffmann described him as 'a shivering shadow of his former self, a charred hulk from which all life, fire and flame had long since departed'. His hair was grey, his back stooped, and he walked with a shuffle. Among his own entourage, Albert Speer noted, discipline began to slacken. Even his most devoted followers at the Berghof remained seated when he entered a room, as conversations continued, some falling asleep in their chairs, others talking loudly with no apparent inhibition.[97]

On 24 February 1945, with the Russians at the gates, a proclamation by the Führer was read over the radio. Hitler predicted a turnabout in the fortunes of war. He was widely mocked, even by party members: 'another prophecy by the leader,' one of them exclaimed ironically. Soldiers talked openly of his 'megalomania'. With the rumble of the front in the distance, ordinary people began taking down the swastikas from public buildings, angry at the failure of the leadership to surrender. Others removed his picture from their living room. 'I cremated him,' said one old lady.[98]

During the last months of the war, Hitler withdrew into his bunker, built underneath the new chancellery. It was 'the last station in his flight from reality,' wrote Speer. Still he ordered the

fight to continue, determined to bring death and destruction to a
nation that did not deserve him.[99]

On 20 April 1945, Hitler's fifty-sixth birthday, the first enemy shell
hit Berlin. Bombardment was relentless. Two days later nothing
but a white façade standing amidst smoking rubble was left of the
Ministry of Propaganda. Old and trusted associates began deserting
the sinking ship, Heinrich Himmler and Hermann Goering among
them. Hitler shot himself on 30 April. He had heard of Mussolini's
undignified end and had ordered that his remains be incinerated
to prevent any desecration. His body, together with that of Eva
Braun, his long-term mistress whom he had married a day earlier,
was dragged out of the bunker, doused in petrol and set alight.

A wave of suicides followed among the most committed
Nazis, including the entire Goebbels family, Heinrich Himmler,
Bernhard Rust and Robert Ley. Thousands of ordinary people also
killed themselves. As soon as the Red Army arrived, a Protestant
clergyman reported, 'whole good, churchgoing families took their
lives, drowned themselves, slit their wrists or allowed themselves
to be burned up along with their homes'. But the Führer's death
prompted no spontaneous displays of public grief, no outpouring of
sorrow by distraught believers. 'Strange,' one woman reported from
Hamburg after the radio announced Hitler's death, 'nobody wept
or even looked sad.' A young man who had long wondered how his
countrymen would react to the death of their leader was astonished
by the 'monumental, yawning indifference' that followed the radio
announcement. The Third Reich, Victor Klemperer observed, was
gone overnight, almost as good as forgotten.[100]

All resistance collapsed the moment Hitler died. Expecting
the same ferocious partisan war they had fought at home, Red
Army officers were taken aback by the docility of the population.
They were also surprised by the number of people who produced
communist flags out of scarlet Nazi banners with the swastika cut
from the centre. In Berlin this turnabout was referred to as 'Heil
Stalin!'.[101]

3

Stalin

'Everywhere in Moscow one sees nothing but Lenin,' the French journalist Henri Béraud observed in 1924, a few months after the death of the communist revolutionary and head of state. 'Lenin posters, Lenin drawings, Lenin mosaics, Lenin scorched in pokerwork, Lenin in linoleum, Lenin inkwells, Lenin desk blotters. Entire shops devoted to selling his bust, in every size, every material and every price, from bronze, marble, stone, porcelain and alabaster to plaster. And that does not include pictures of Lenin, from formal portraits to lively snapshots and newsreels.' Lenin, Béraud ventured, was probably the most photographed head of state – after Mussolini.[1]

Even before Lenin died his comrades had begun glorifying him. In August 1918 a disillusioned revolutionary called Fanny Kaplan approached Lenin as he was leaving the Hammer and Sickle Factory in Moscow. She fired several shots. One bullet lodged in his neck; another went through his left shoulder. Against all odds, he survived. 'Only those marked by destiny can escape death from such a wound,' his physician remarked. Eulogies to the great leader followed, printed and distributed in hundreds of thousands of copies. Leon Trotsky, founder and commander of the Red Army, praised him as a 'masterpiece created by nature' for a 'new era in human history', the 'embodiment of revolutionary thinking'. Nikolai Bukharin, editor of the party newspaper *Pravda*, wrote about 'the genius leader of the world revolution', the man with an 'almost prophetic ability to predict'.[2]

Lenin recovered and put a halt to the outpouring, but when poor health finally forced him to withdraw from public appearances in 1922 the cult took on new life. The Bolsheviks, like the fascists and the Nazis, were a party held together not so much by a programme or platform but by a chosen leader. It was Lenin's will, vision and, most of all, intuition that had guided the revolution, rather than the communist principles proposed by Marx half a century earlier. Lenin was the embodiment of the revolution. If he could no longer lead in person, then his followers had to invoke his name or claim direct inspiration from his revolutionary spirit.[3]

The deification of Lenin also served as a substitute for a popular mandate. Even at the height of their popularity in November 1917 the Bolsheviks won less than a quarter of the vote. They used violence to seize power, and the more power they acquired the fiercer the violence became. Fanny Kaplan's assassination attempt was followed by a Red Terror, as the regime systematically targeted whole groups of people, from striking factory workers to peasants who deserted the Red Army. Thousands of priests and nuns, declared class enemies after the revolution, were killed, some crucified, castrated, buried alive or thrown into cauldrons of boiling tar. The entire imperial family was shot or stabbed to death, their bodies mutilated, burned and dumped in a pit. If violence alienated many ordinary people, neither the abstract language of 'class struggle' nor the 'dictatorship of the proletariat', foreign words that villagers in a largely illiterate countryside could barely pronounce, won them over. Appeals to the leader as a holy figure, on the other hand, were far more successful in creating at least the illusion of some sort of bond between the state and its seventy million subjects.[4]

Lenin did not name a successor, but in 1922 he hand-picked Stalin for the new post of General Secretary as a means of reining in Trotsky, who opposed the New Economic Policy spearheaded by Lenin. The policy effectively reversed the forced collectivisation introduced after the revolution, when factory workers had been ordered to produce by decree, their goods confiscated by the state.

Christened war communism, this system had left the economy in ruins. The New Economic Policy moved back towards the market, allowing individuals to operate small enterprises. Forced grain requisitions ceased, replaced by a tax on agricultural produce. Trotsky came to view the New Economic Policy as a surrender to capitalists and rich peasants, and demanded instead an even greater role for the state in the economy.

Stalin acquired great powers as General Secretary, despite possessing obvious defects. He was no great orator, speaking with a thick Georgian accent in a voice that carried poorly. He lacked any sense of timing. He performed with an almost complete absence of gesture. And, unlike many of his colleagues, he lacked the aura of a revolutionary who had spent years abroad in exile. He could write fluently, but was not an outstanding theoretician who could expound on communist doctrine. Stalin made the best of his shortcomings, presenting himself as a modest servant devoted to promoting the greater good while others were constantly seeking the limelight.

He described himself as a *praktik*, a practical man of action rather than an exponent of the revolution. By all accounts he had exceptional organisational abilities, a huge capacity for work and great strength of will. His rivals often dismissed him as a mere administrator, 'the outstanding mediocrity of our party', as Trotsky phrased it. But Stalin was a cunning, unscrupulous operator who exploited other people's weaknesses to turn them into willing accomplices. He was also a gifted strategic thinker with a genuine political touch. Like Hitler, he showed concern for the people around him, regardless of their position in the hierarchy, remembering their names and past conversations. He also knew how to bide his time.[5]

As Lenin convalesced, Stalin became his intermediary, using his new powers to draw closer to the leader. But the relationship was tempestuous, and in 1923 the two fell out. The ailing leader dictated a series of notes that became known as Lenin's Testament, a document suggesting that Stalin had a crude temperament and should be removed from the post of General Secretary.

Alive Lenin was a threat, dead an asset. The moment Lenin passed away on 21 January 1924 Stalin became determined to pose as his most faithful pupil. He was the first among the inner circle to enter his master's bedroom, theatrically taking the dead man's head in both hands to bring it close to his chest, kissing him firmly on the cheeks and on the lips.[6]

For several weeks Lenin's embalmed corpse was displayed in a glass catafalque on Red Square, where the winter cold kept his body intact. The party was divided over what to do next. Russia had a long tradition of mummifying its holy men. In the Monastery of Caves in Kiev, where reclusive monks used to worship before the revolution, the catacombs were lined with dozens of saints, their faces blackened, their emaciated hands resting on ragged, dusty clothes. Comparable treatment for the revolutionary leader carried religious overtones that clashed with the atheist outlook of several leaders, including Lenin's wife. Felix Dzerzhinsky, as chair of the funeral commission, prevailed, with the backing of the General Secretary. Lenin, in death as in life, was to serve the cause of the working class, as millions would come to pay their respects before his coffin.[7]

Once spring arrived a few months later a team of scientists took Lenin's body away and set about experimenting with chemicals to prevent its decomposition. In August 1924 Lenin reappeared, his whitened, marble-like body displayed in a more permanent mausoleum. It attracted long queues of worshippers, patient, poor, mystical, the same crowd, noted Henri Béraud, that could be seen 'muttering its prayers in front of gilded icons and candles burning with a yellow flame'.[8]

Having captured Lenin's corpse, Stalin set about asserting ownership over his words. He took the Lenin Institute under his wing, overseeing the publication of all significant Lenin documents. But Lenin's collected writings did not define a doctrine. By delivering a series of lectures on Leninism, serialised in *Pravda* under the title 'Foundations of Leninism', Stalin staked his claim as guardian of his master's legacy. Leninism, he wrote, was the Marxism of the imperial age, and Lenin the sole great heir of Marx and Engels.[9]

However, when party delegates convened in Moscow in May 1924 to examine Lenin's Testament, Stalin encountered a setback. After Grigory Zinoviev and Lev Kamenev, two party elders disturbed by Trotsky's ambition, spoke out in favour of Stalin, the Central Committee decided to read the document only to select delegates as opposed to the entire assembled congress. Trotsky, reluctant to appear divisive in his coming bid for power, did not intervene. Stalin, pale as death, humbly asked for release from his duties, hoping that his show of contrition would prompt the Central Committee to refuse his request. His gamble paid off, but left him seething with resentment. He was the disciple of a man who seemed to have demanded his removal.[10]

After regaining his composure, Stalin began surrounding himself with reliable, loyal supporters, including Vyacheslav Molotov, Lazar Kaganovich and Sergo Ordzhonikidze. He used his position as General Secretary to replace supporters of all his rivals with his own henchmen. He acquired personal assistants to gather information and undertake his shadier tasks. Lev Mekhlis, Stalin's personal secretary, began overseeing every aspect of Stalin's public image, vetting photographs that appeared in the press.[11]

In November 1924 Stalin cornered Trotsky. Whereas Stalin presented himself as Lenin's pupil, Trotsky had made the tactical error of posing as Lenin's equal by publishing his own collected writings. Not only did Trotsky appear vain, but he provided textual evidence of many differences over issues on which he had opposed Lenin. Stalin published a vicious piece entitled 'Trotskyism or Leninism?', denouncing his rival as the proponent of a permanent revolution that put him at loggerheads with the very principles of Leninism. Careful readers understood that the title meant Trotsky or Stalin.

Stalin also targeted Trotsky's criticism of the New Economic Policy. Other Bolsheviks, including Zinoviev and Kamenev, the two powerful Central Committee leaders who had helped Stalin survive Lenin's testament, disliked the turn towards the market. Stalin whittled away at them, portraying them as doctrinaire leftists whose ideas would lead the Soviet Union to perdition. Nikolai

Bukharin, a tireless defender of the mixed economy, assisted him. In 1925 Stalin himself addressed peasant representatives who refused to sow crops unless they were granted land leases. With a flick of the hand Stalin promised leases for twenty years, forty years, possibly even in perpetuity. When asked if this did not seem like a return to private land ownership, he responded 'We wrote the constitution. We can change it too.' Reports of the meeting circulated around the world. Stalin came across as the level-headed, pragmatic boss of the party, a leader attuned to his people.[12]

By 1926 Trotsky, Zinoviev and Kamenev were forced into a United Opposition against Stalin, who promptly turned on them and denounced them for bringing instability to the party by forming a faction. Since factions had been outlawed years earlier, Trotsky was expelled from the Politburo. His followers dwindled to a mere handful. In October 1927, at a full Central Committee meeting, Trotsky once more tried to bring up Lenin's Testament. By then, however, many party delegates had come to view Stalin as the self-effacing, efficient, hard-working defender of Lenin. The marginalised Trotsky, by contrast, seemed condescending, noisy and self-absorbed. Stalin crushed him, retorting that three years earlier the party had examined the document and refused his resignation. Delegates erupted in applause. Within a month the party expelled Trotsky and dozens of his followers. In January 1928 Trotsky was sent into exile to Kazakhstan. One year later he was deported from the Soviet Union.[13]

Just as soon as his main rival was dispatched Stalin began implementing Trotsky's policies. Trotsky had warned against a 'new capitalist class' in the countryside. After grain supplies tumbled by a third in late 1927, threatening Moscow and Leningrad with starvation, Stalin sent procurement squads into the villages, ordering them to grab what they could at gunpoint. Those who resisted were persecuted as kulaks, a derogatory term meant to designate 'rich' farmers but used for anyone who opposed collectivisation. This was the opening battle in a war against the countryside that would culminate a few years later in famine.

Those within the party, including Bukharin, who still adhered to Stalin's earlier views were lambasted as rightists. Crushing fear now pervaded the party, with its members denounced and summarily arrested as 'left oppositionists' or 'right deviators'. Homes were searched and relatives taken away. People disappeared overnight. Stalin also cracked down on managers, engineers and planners, including foreigners accused of deliberate sabotage.[14]

In the midst of a purge of the party ranks, a huge parade was organised for May Day 1928. Ever since 1886, when the Chicago police had fired on strikers demanding an eight-hour workday, socialists around the world had celebrated 1 May. Marches by workers with unfurled banners and red flags were regular events in many cities around the world, sometimes degenerating into street fights with the police. Lenin, early in his career, had seen the potential of these celebrations, writing that they could be developed into 'great political demonstrations'. In 1901 Stalin himself had been involved in bloody clashes around May Day in Tiflis (Tbilisi), the capital of his native Georgia.[15]

In 1918 Lenin made May Day an official holiday. A decade later, in 1928, Stalin had the Labour Code amended, adding 2 May to the festivities. Preparations for these showpiece events began weeks in advance, with gigantic wood and cardboard structures erected at the main intersections of Moscow, depicting workers, peasants and soldiers marching towards the future. On 1 May Stalin and his principal lieutenants appeared on the wooden ramparts of the Lenin Mausoleum, saluting a flood of humanity cheering and singing under banners and floats. Then came a giant parade of rumbling tanks, armoured cars, machine guns and searchlights, with aeroplanes buzzing overhead. It was an enormous display of organisational strength, meticulously planned from above, with every word scripted and every slogan approved by decree. Hundreds of thousands waited meekly for hours for their turn to cross the square and glimpse the leader.[16]

By 1929 Stalin was ready to impose his mark on the Soviet Union. Lenin had already transformed Russia into the world's first one-party state, accomplishing what Hitler would try to achieve in the name of *Gleichschaltung* after 1933: the systematic elimination of all organisations outside the party. Alternative political parties, trade unions, the media, churches, guilds and associations all came under the thumb of the state. Free elections had been banned immediately after November 1917, and the rule of law was abolished, replaced by revolutionary justice and a sprawling gulag system.

Stalin sought to go further and permanently alter the country's economy by turning an agricultural backwater into an industrial powerhouse within a mere five years. Huge industrial cities were built from scratch, turnkey factories imported from abroad, engineering plants expanded and new mines opened to meet the need for coal, iron and steel, all at breakneck speed. No eight-hour workday existed in the Soviet Union, as factory workers toiled seven days a week. The key to industrial expansion lay in the countryside, with grain taken from the villagers sold on the international market to earn foreign currency. In order to extract more grain, the countryside was collectivised. Villagers were herded into state farms, from which the kulaks were excluded. Stalin viewed collectivisation as a unique opportunity to liquidate the entire kulak class, as some 320,000 households were broken up, their members sent to concentration camps, forced to work in mines or transported to distant regions of the empire.[17]

The party, under Stalin's leadership, was now sacrosanct, the party line presented as a mystical will that was beyond debate. Stalin became the personification of that sanctity, the *vozhd*, or great leader, a term previously reserved for Lenin. On 1 May 1929 Marx receded into the background, while Stalin ascended to equal status with Lenin. As one American journalist noted, 'On Red Square, on the buildings opposite the Kremlin walls, huge faces of Lenin and Stalin were displayed. Their gigantic full-length portraits were mounted on scaffolding on Theatre Square, looming high above the Metropole Hotel on one side and the Grand Hotel on the other.'[18]

The great leader was fifty on 21 December 1929, an occasion celebrated by 'numberless telegrams', the party's mouthpiece *Pravda* explained, as workers the world over greeted Stalin. Congratulatory slips of paper were even smuggled out of prisons in Poland, Hungary and Italy. This was not hero-worship, the propaganda machine clarified, but an expression of devotion from millions of workers everywhere to the idea of the proletarian revolution. Stalin was the party, the embodiment of all that was best in the working class: 'flamboyant enthusiasm kept in bounds by an iron will, unshakable faith in victory based on sober revolutionary Marxian analysis, a proletarian contempt of death on the civil war fronts', the circumspection of a leader whose mind 'illuminated the future like a searchlight'.[19]

Other demonstrations of flattery abounded, as Stalin's underlings composed paeans to their leader, enthusiastically abasing themselves. Lazar Kaganovich, the stocky, thick-moustached secretary of the party, praised him as 'the closest, most active, most faithful assistant of Lenin'. Sergo Ordzhonikidze described his master as a true and unfaltering disciple of Lenin armed with the iron will to lead the party to the final victory of the world proletarian revolution.[20]

Few people, however, had ever seen Stalin except from a distance, as he stood on the rostrum in Red Square twice a year to celebrate May Day and the October Revolution. Even then he appeared almost like a sculpture, a robust figure adopting a stolid, calm pose in a military overcoat with a peaked cap. He rarely appeared in newsreels and never spoke in public. Not once had his voice been heard over the radio. His photographs, strictly controlled by his personal secretary, were all standardised. Even in posters Stalin seemed cold and distant, the embodiment of an unflinching will to push through the revolution.[21]

Over the course of a decade Stalin had moved from inconspicuous commissar to undisputed leader of the party. But he had repeatedly been forced to do battle with powerful forces arrayed against him. In a testament that would haunt Stalin for the rest of his life, Lenin, after handing him supreme power, had had second thoughts and called for his removal. Time and again, Trotsky, a formidable orator, gifted polemicist and respected leader of the Red Army, had confronted him. Sheer vindictiveness and cold calculation had kept Stalin moving forward, but over the years he also developed a sense of grievance, viewing himself as a victim. A victor with a grudge, he became permanently distrustful of those around him.[22]

The image of a stern, aloof leader towering above his potential critics suited him well, but Stalin soon began to cultivate a more human aspect. Trotsky in inner exile cut a dramatic figure, making Stalin resemble the keeper of a caged lion. As soon as he was abroad, he tried to appear more Leninist than Stalin. He began publishing a *Bulletin of the Opposition*, using his detailed knowledge of corridor politics to report on controversies within the party leadership. His autobiography *My Life*, published in Russian and English in 1930, portrayed Stalin as a mediocre, jealous and devious character whose covert machinations had led to a betrayal of the revolution. Trotsky reproduced Lenin's Testament: 'Stalin is rude, disloyal, and capable of abuse of the power that he derives from the party apparatus. Stalin should be removed to avoid a split.' Stalin had coined the term Trotskyism, and now Trotsky in turn popularised the notion of Stalinism.[23]

A year earlier, on the occasion of his fiftieth birthday, the leader's Georgian colleague Avel Enukidze had introduced a few human touches, bringing together some elements of the Stalin myth. Stalin was the son of a cobbler, a precocious and gifted student, but also a young rebel, thrown out of a theological seminary. He lacked all vanity. He was a man of the people with a knack for explaining complicated matters very simply to workers, who affectionately nicknamed him 'Soso'. He never wavered in his defence of Bolshevism and gave himself entirely to revolutionary work. 'Stalin will remain the same to the end of his life,' Enukidze proclaimed.[24]

Stalin was not merely the leader of the party. He was also de facto head of the Communist International, or Comintern, making him the figure pointing the way forward towards the worldwide proletarian revolution. Yet at home and abroad he still remained, unlike Trotsky, a mysterious, distant figure. In November 1930 Stalin invited the United Press correspondent Eugene Lyons to meet him personally in his office. Lyons, a fellow-traveller who had worked in the New York office of TASS, the official Soviet news agency, had been carefully selected from dozens of reporters in Moscow. Stalin met him at the door. He smiled, but there was a shyness that instantly disarmed the correspondent. His shaggy moustache, Lyons reported, gave his swarthy face a friendly and almost benign look. Everything spoke of simplicity, from his relaxed manner, the austerity of his attire and the spartan nature of his office to the quiet, orderly corridors of the headquarters of the Central Committee. Stalin listened. He was thoughtful. 'Are you a dictator,' Lyons finally asked. 'No, I am not,' Stalin replied gently, explaining that in the party all decisions were collective and no one person could dictate. 'I like that man,' exulted Lyons on the way out. 'Stalin Laughs!', a sycophantic piece of work edited by Stalin himself, appeared on the front page of major newspapers around the world, 'ripping the cloak of secrecy' surrounding the recluse of the Kremlin.[25]

Stalin had inserted an intimate domestic note into the interview, talking about his wife and three children. A week later Hubert Knickerbocker interviewed Stalin's mother, a simple woman wearing a common dress of grey wool. 'Soso was always a good boy!' she exulted, happy to talk about her favourite subject.[26]

More prestigious intellectual figures followed, popularising and diffusing the image of a kindly, simple, modest man who was no dictator despite wielding huge power. A year later the socialist author George Bernard Shaw received a military guard of honour in Moscow and a banquet to celebrate his seventy-fifth birthday. He toured the country, visiting model schools, prisons and farms, with villagers and workers carefully drilled to praise the party and their leader. After a two-hour private audience, masterfully staged by Stalin, the Irish playwright found the dictator a 'charmingly good-humoured fellow' and proclaimed: 'There was no malice in him, but also no credulity.' Shaw never tired of promoting the despot, and died in 1950 in his bed with a portrait of his idol on the mantelpiece.[27]

Emil Ludwig, a popular biographer of Napoleon and Bismarck, likewise met Stalin in December 1931, and was struck by the simplicity of a man who had so much power but 'took no pride in its possession'. But the individual whose biography did most to propagate the image of a simple man who grudgingly accepted the adoration of millions was probably Henri Barbusse, a French writer who moved to Moscow in 1918 and joined the Bolshevik Party. When they first met in 1927 Stalin completely captivated Barbusse, whose laudatory articles were translated in *Pravda*. Following another encounter in 1932 the Culture and Propaganda Department of the Central Committee carefully vetted Barbusse, who also organised the Paris-based World Committee Against War and Fascism. In October 1933 Barbusse collected 385,000 francs Stalin had sent to Paris, the rough equivalent of US$330,000 in today's money. In the words of André Gide, another French literary figure whom Stalin had approached, substantial financial advantages awaited those who wrote 'in the right direction'.[28]

Stalin provided all the documentation for his biographer, with every detail supervised by his underlings within the propaganda machine. In *Stalin: A New World Seen through One Man*, published in March 1935, Barbusse portrayed Stalin as a new messiah, a superhuman whose name millions chanted at every parade on Red Square. Yet even as those around him adored him, he remained modest, crediting his master Lenin for every victory. His salary was a meagre five hundred roubles, his home had only three windows. His eldest son slept on a couch in the dining room, the younger one in an alcove. He had one secretary, in contrast to former British prime minister Lloyd George who had employed thirty-two. Even in his personal life this 'frank and brilliant man' remained 'a simple man'.[29]

From Henri Barbusse to George Bernard Shaw foreign celebrities helped Stalin get around a paradox at the very heart of his cult: the Soviet Union was supposedly a dictatorship of the proletariat, not the dictatorship of one individual. In communist polemics, only fascist dictators like Mussolini and Hitler proclaimed that their word was above the law, their people obedient subjects who must bend to their will. Therefore, even as his cult pervaded all aspects of everyday life, the very idea that Stalin was a dictator became taboo.

Ostensibly the people glorified him, against his own wishes, and it was they who demanded to see him, as he reluctantly displayed himself to millions during the Red Square parades.[30]

Every aspect of his image stood in contrast to those of his nemeses. Hitler and Mussolini would rant and rave in front of their followers, while at party gatherings the self-effacing secretary would sit in watchful silence in the back row of a crowded platform. They spoke at people, he listened to them. They were dominated by emotion, he stood for reason, carefully weighing his every word. His words were few, and therefore treasured and studied by all. As Emil Ludwig put it, even his quietness conveyed power, as there was something slightly menacing in 'the dangerous weight of the silent'.[31]

Stalin may, as Henri Barbusse claimed, have had only one secretary, but after his fiftieth birthday in 1929 he used the party machine to shore up his cult, as posters, portraits, books and busts began to proliferate. In the summer of 1930 the Sixteenth Congress of the Communist Party became a demonstration of fealty to Stalin, who spoke for seven hours. Praise, now obligatory, circulated inside the congress, in the newspapers and on the radio.[32]

In the countryside, where a merciless campaign of collectivisation was being enforced, statues of Lenin and Stalin could be seen at the peak of the 1932 famine. An estimated six million people died of hunger in Ukraine, the Urals, the Volga, Kazakhstan and parts of Siberia, as huge stocks of grain as well as milk, eggs and meat were sold on the international market to finance the Five-Year Plan. Even as they were reduced to eating grass and tree bark, villagers were forced to acclaim their leader.[33]

In 1930 the Sixteenth Congress had been greeted by 'stormy, prolonged applause extending into a lengthy ovation'. Four years later, at the Seventeenth Congress, this was no longer deemed adequate, and the stenograms recorded a 'tremendous ovation' as well as shouts of 'Long Live our Stalin!' The gathering was hailed as a Congress of Victors, as the delegates celebrated the successes of agricultural collectivisation and rapid industrialisation. But behind the scenes members grumbled about Stalin's methods. Some feared his ambition even as they publicly acclaimed him. Rumour had it that he had received so many negative votes that some paper ballots had to be destroyed.[34]

Stalin did nothing. He knew the virtue of patience, displaying a nerveless, calculated restraint in the face of adversity. But when in late 1934 an assassin shot Sergey Kirov, the boss of Leningrad, Stalin took drastic measures. This marked the start of the Great Terror, as party members who had at some point or another defied Stalin were arrested. In August 1936 Zinoviev and Kamenev, the first to undergo a show trial, were found guilty and executed. Others followed, including Bukharin and twenty other defendants allegedly part of a 'Bloc of Rightists and Trotskyites'. More than 1.5 million ordinary people were ensnared by the secret police, interrogated, tortured and in many cases summarily executed. At the campaign's height in 1937 and 1938 the execution rate was roughly a thousand per day, with people accused of being class enemies, saboteurs, oppositionists or speculators, some denounced by their own neighbours or relatives.[35]

The cult flourished as the terror unfolded. In 1934, Stalin was not the only one glorified by his underlings. By the end of the 1920s virtually every leader, down to directors of local enterprises, had their workers carry their portraits in triumph on public holidays. Some leaders became little Stalins, copying their master in their own fiefdoms, immortalising themselves in portraits and statues, surrounded by sycophants who sang their praises. One such was Ivan Rumiantsev, himself a flatterer who acclaimed Stalin as a 'genius' in 1934. He viewed himself as the Stalin of the Western Region, compelling 134 collective farms to be named after him. In the spring of 1937 Rumiantsev was denounced as a spy and shot.[36]

Sometimes Politburo members had entire cities renamed in their honour. Stalingrad existed, but so did Molotov and Ordzhonikidze. When a leader fell from favour, names were summarily revised, as happened to the ill-fated cities of Trotsk and Zinovevsk. But by 1938 only one other name was allowed equal standing with Stalin's, that of Mikhail Kalinin, nominal President of the Union of Socialist Soviet Republics, or head of state from 1919 to 1946. His role was purely symbolic, but he served admirably, dutifully signing each and every one of Stalin's decrees. When his wife was arrested for calling Stalin a 'tyrant and a sadist', Kalinin did not lift a finger.[37]

In June 1934, three months after the Congress of Victors, Stalin began overseeing every aspect of the state propaganda machine. His image became still more ubiquitous, with one American visitor observing large portraits 'on the hoardings surrounding the new metro excavations in Moscow, on the façades of public buildings in Kazan, in the Red Corners of shops, on the walls of guardrooms and prisons, in shops, in the Kremlin, the cathedrals, the cinemas, everywhere'.[38]

In the intervals between signing death warrants and directing show trials Stalin met with writers, painters, sculptors and playwrights. The individual, in every aspect of art, vanished, as Stalin imposed a style known as 'socialist realism'. Art had to glorify the revolution. Fairy tales were prohibited as unproletarian: children were to be enthralled with books about tractors and coal mines. In what one historian has called a 'hall of mirrors', the same motifs were endlessly repeated as committees vetted texts and images. Since Stalin was the embodiment of the revolution, he was the most prominent of them all: 'it was not a rare incident for workers to compose a letter to Stalin during a meeting in the Stalin House of Culture of the Stalin Factory on Stalin Square in the city of Stalinsk.'[39]

Stalinsk was but one of five cities named after the great leader. There were also Stalingrad, Stalinabad, Stalino and Stalinagorsk. Great parks, factories, railways and canals were all named after him. The Stalin Canal, dug all the way from the White Sea to Leningrad on the Baltic Sea by convict labour during the first Five-Year Plan, was opened in 1933. The best steels were christened stalinite. 'His name is shouted at you through every printed column, every billboard, every radio,' noted Eugene Lyons: 'His image is ubiquitous, picked out in flowers on public lawns, in electric lights, on postage stamps; it is for sale in plaster-of-Paris and bronze busts in nearly every shop, in crude colours on teacups, in lithographs and picture postcards.'[40]

The number of propaganda posters fell from 240 in 1934 to 70 in 1937, but their print runs increased as the focus shifted towards the leader himself. When ordinary people made a fleeting appearance, it was always in relation to him: gazing up at him, carrying his portrait in parades, studying his texts, saluting him, singing songs about him and following him into a utopian future.[41]

Stalin, now all-pervasive, acquired a benign smile. The Congress of Victors had, after all, announced in 1934 that socialism had been achieved, and Stalin himself proclaimed one year later that 'life has become more joyous'. There was a smiling Stalin surrounded by adoring crowds, and a smiling Stalin with joyous children presenting flowers. One image, circulated in its millions, showed him at a Kremlin reception in 1936 taking flowers from a small girl in a sailor suit named Gelia Markizova (her father was later shot as an enemy of the people). Stalin was Grandfather Frost, the Russian Santa Claus, beaming benevolently as children celebrated New Year's Day. Everything, it seemed, was a gift from Stalin. Buses, tractors, schools, housing, collective farms, all were bestowed by Him, the ultimate dispenser of goods. Even adults, it seemed, were children, Stalin their father, or, rather, the 'little father', or *batiushka*, a term of endearment used for tsars who expressed concern over the welfare of their subjects. The constitution, passed at the height of the show trials in December 1936, was Stalin's Constitution.[42]

Every new expression was engineered from above. After the young writer Aleksandr Avdeenko concluded a speech in 1935 with a vote of thanks to the Soviet Union he was approached by Lev Mekhlis, Stalin's personal secretary, who suggested that he should have thanked Stalin instead. A few months later Avdeenko's words at the World Congress of Writers in Paris were broadcast to the Soviet Union, ending every sentence with a ritualistic 'Thank you Stalin!' and 'For I am joyous, thank you Stalin!' His career thrived, and on three subsequent occasions he received the Stalin Prize.[43]

Less joyous writers were consigned to the gulag, the country's sprawling system of concentration camps. Osip Mandelstam, one of Russia's greatest poets, was arrested for reciting a sarcastic poem critical of the leader to close friends in 1934 and died in a transit camp a few years later. Others, from poets and philosophers to playwrights, were simply shot.

Since the cult was supposed to reflect popular adoration, poems and songs composed by the labouring masses were widely propagated. From a Soviet Daghestan woman came the adulatory lines: 'Above the valley, the mountain peak; Above the peak the sky. But Stalin, skies have no height to equal you, only your thoughts rise higher. The stars, the moon, pale before the sun that pales in turn before your shining mind'. Seidik Kvarchia, a collectivised farmer, composed a *Song of Stalin*: 'The man who fought in front of all fighters, Who succoured orphans, widows and the aged; Before whom all enemies do tremble'.[44]

Despite the carefully cultivated impression of spontaneity, by 1939 a rigid canon was imposed. Official newspapers, orators and poets all sang the same hymn, praising the 'unmatched genius', 'the great and beloved Stalin', 'the leader and inspirer of the working classes of the whole world', 'the great and glorious Stalin, head and brilliant theoretician of the world revolution'. People knew when to applaud at public gatherings, and when to invoke his name on public occasions. Repetition was key, not innovation, meaning that excessive flattery could be dangerous, too. Stalin, noted Nadezhda Mandelstam, wife of the murdered poet, had no need of zealots of any kind: he wanted people to be obedient instruments of his will, with no convictions of their own. The party machine, more often than not through the chief of Stalin's personal chancellery, Alexander Poskrebyshev, prescribed every word and picture. But Stalin himself was also a compulsive editor, poring over editorials, editing speeches and reviewing articles. In 1937 he neatly excised the expression 'Greatest Man of our Time' from a TASS agency report on the May Day parade. Stalin was a gardener, constantly pruning his own cult, cutting back here and there to allow it to flourish in good season.[45]

Stalinism entered the vocabulary when Stalin judged the time to be ripe. Lazar Kaganovich, the first true Stalinist, allegedly proposed

'Let's replace Long Live Leninism with Long Live Stalinism!' at a dinner with Stalin in the early 1930s. Stalin modestly declined, but the term occurred with increasing frequency from the very moment the constitution was passed on 5 December 1936: 'Our constitution is Marxism-Leninism-Stalinism'. Several weeks later, on New Year's Eve, Sergo Ordzhonikidze used the expression to great applause in a speech entitled 'Our Country is Invincible', proclaiming how Stalin motivated an army of 170 million people armed with 'Marxism-Leninism-Stalinism'.[46]

Stalin's 1924 lectures, published as *Foundations of Leninism*, sold swiftly after 1929, and by 1934 more than sixteen million copies of the leader's various works were in circulation. But Leninism was not Stalinism. A founding text similar to *Mein Kampf* was required. This was all the more urgent since no official biography of Stalin existed. Potential hagiographers found the task daunting, as the past was continually changing. It was one thing to airbrush a dead commissar out of a photograph, quite another to keep on amending a biography. Even Henri Barbusse's book fell from favour soon after its publication in 1935, since it mentioned leaders who had been arrested.[47]

The *Short Course on the History of the All-Union Communist Party* was the answer. It presented a direct line of succession from Marx and Engels to Lenin and Stalin. Every episode of the party's history was covered, presenting the reader with a clear narrative in which the correct party line, represented by Lenin and his follower Stalin, had been opposed by a string of devious anti-party cliques that had been successfully eliminated along the path to socialism. The *Short Course* was commissioned in 1935 by Stalin, who demanded several revisions and edited the full text on five occasions before allowing its publication, to great fanfare, in September 1938. The book became a canonical text that deified Stalin as the living fount of wisdom, selling more than forty-two million copies in Russian alone, with translations into sixty-seven languages.[48]

On 21 December 1939 Stalin turned sixty. Six months earlier in Berlin leaders had queued up at the chancellery to offer their best wishes to Hitler. In Moscow the congratulations were a public exercise in self-abasement, as party leaders published lengthy paeans in a twelve-page edition of *Pravda*. 'The Greatest Man of our Time,' gushed Lavrentiy Beria, the new head of the NKVD. 'Stalin, the Great Driver of the Locomotive of History,' declared Lazar Kaganovich. 'Stalin is Today's Lenin,' proclaimed Politburo member Anastas Mikoyan. Stalin, the entire Presidium of the USSR Supreme Soviet wrote, was 'The most beloved and dearest man of our country and of the working people of all the world'. Upon the 'Great Continuer of Lenin's Task – Comrade Stalin', they bestowed the order of Hero of Socialist Labour.[49]

Stalin required abasement from his entourage, boundless enthusiasm from the masses, whose gifts arrived from every corner of the Soviet Union. It was their long-awaited chance to repay Stalin, the ultimate carer and provider, with a token of their undying gratitude. There were drawings from children, photographs from factories, paintings and busts by amateurs, telegrams from admirers, a tidal wave of offerings that required a month of acknowledgements in the pages of *Pravda*. Selected items were displayed in the Museum of the Revolution as a testament to the people's devotion.[50]

Among the many foreign well-wishers was Adolf Hitler. 'Please accept my most sincere congratulations on your sixtieth birthday. I take this occasion to tender my best wishes. I wish you personally good health and a happy future for the peoples of the friendly Soviet Union.'[51]

For the best part of a decade Stalin and Hitler had observed each other with a mixture of growing wariness and grudging admiration. 'Hitler, what a great fellow!' Stalin exclaimed after the Night of the Long Knives. Hitler, for his part, found the Great Terror deeply impressive. But Stalin had read *Mein Kampf* carefully, including those passages where its author promised to erase Russia from the map. 'Never forget,' Hitler had written, 'that the rulers of present-day Russia are bloodstained common criminals. We are dealing with the scum of humanity.'[52]

After the Munich Agreement in September 1938 Stalin called a halt to the Great Terror. Its main executioner, Nikolai Yezhov, was purged in November and replaced by Beria. By this time Stalin was surrounded by sycophants. Every potential opponent within the leadership had fallen victim to the purges. Since insufficient zeal in supporting the party line could be construed as disloyalty, the secret service had even turned against those who remained silent. Stalin had no friends, only underlings; no allies, only flatterers. As a result, he alone took all major decisions.

On 23 August 1939 Stalin stunned the world by signing a non-aggression pact with Hitler, in what seemed a brilliant if highly risky move in an unprincipled power game. By freeing Germany from the need to wage war on two fronts, the Soviet Union could sit back and watch the capitalist countries fight each other to exhaustion. Within weeks it became clear that there were secret clauses to the pact, as the Soviet Union invaded half of Poland.

Hitler also gave Stalin a free hand in Finland, and in November 1939 the Soviet Union attacked its tiny neighbour. What should have been an easy victory turned into a bloody stalemate, with more than 120,000 Soviet casualties. The Great Terror had clearly crippled the Red Army, since some 30,000 officers had fallen victim to Stalin's purges. Three of the army's five marshals had been executed. A peace treaty was signed in March 1940, but the experience left the Kremlin in shock. Finland exposed the military weakness of the Soviet Union.[53]

The country's carefully fostered reputation as a peace-loving nation was also shattered. The League of Nations expelled the Soviet Union. Abroad, some who identified with the ideals of socialism now viewed Joseph Stalin as the equivalent of Adolf Hitler.

Stalin had badly miscalculated. In order to prepare a defensive line against Germany, he invaded the Baltic States of Estonia, Latvia and Lithuania and made them into Soviet protectorates. This plan, too, was short-sighted, based on his belief that Hitler would become bogged down in France. But German troops reached Paris within less than five weeks. It now seemed as if Hitler would be able to secure one of Germany's flanks far sooner than expected and turn his tanks against the Soviet Union. By May 1941 a mounting tide of evidence from Stalin's own intelligence services pointed to a massive German military build-up along the frontier. Stalin, relying on experience and intuition, dismissed it as mere provocation. In the words of historian Robert Service, in his supreme confidence Stalin had unwittingly prepared 'the conditions for the greatest military disaster of the twentieth century'.[54]

Stalin was in bed in his dacha some two hundred kilometres outside Moscow when more than three million German soldiers poured across the border. Chief of General Staff Georgy Zhukov, who had warned him repeatedly of an impending invasion, phoned his master, who hurried back to the Kremlin. He still believed it was a conspiracy, until hours later the German ambassador clarified the situation: Germany was at war with the Soviet Union. Stalin was distraught, but recovered quickly, establishing a Supreme Command packed with his political commissars. Then he abandoned the Kremlin, returning to his dacha, where he skulked for several days.

German tanks rolled across the vast plains of western Russia, with separate formations smashing their way to Leningrad in the north and Kiev in the south. Along the way many Soviets welcomed the troops as liberators, especially in Ukraine where millions had starved during the famine. But Hitler viewed all as racial degenerates, to be reduced to serfdom.

On 3 July 1941 Stalin spoke over the radio, preparing the Soviet people for war by appealing to patriotism rather than communism. Crowds gathered to listen to the broadcast in city squares, 'holding their breath in such profound silence that one could hear every inflection of Stalin's voice', according to one foreign observer. For several minutes after he had finished the silence continued. Overnight, at home and abroad, he became the defender of freedom. Alexander Werth, a journalist based in Moscow, remembered that 'the Soviet people now felt that they had a leader to look to'.[55]

Stalin, back in control, ordered that every town be defended to the last, very much against the advice of his generals. Instead of ordering a strategic withdrawal from Kiev, he allowed the

Ukrainian capital to be encircled, with half a million troops trapped inside. But the arrival of winter a month later, combined with fierce resistance from Russian troops, halted the German advance on Moscow. In December 1941 the United States entered the war, tilting the balance back in favour of the Soviet Union. By then over two million Red Army soldiers had been killed, and 3.5 million taken prisoner.

Stalin did not quite vanish from view after his radio address, but appeared only fleetingly during the war's first years. He did not write for the newspapers, and he rarely spoke in public, passing up every opportunity to inspire and motivate his people. *Pravda* published occasional photographs, showing him as army commander with a military cap and a single red star, his uniform decorated with imposing epaulettes. But he seemed more a disembodied symbol of the war effort than a Supreme Commander leading his people in the Great Patriotic War. No information was divulged on his activities or his family life. His seclusion had the advantage, one foreign journalist noted, that there was no clash between image and reality since the public knew so little about their leader.[56]

Only after the Battle of Stalingrad turned the tide of war in February 1943, ending the threat to the oil fields of the Caucasus, did Stalin return to centre stage. He promoted many of his officers, awarding himself the title of Marshal of the Soviet Union. Newspapers were peppered with new expressions, from 'Stalinist strategy' and 'the Stalinist military school of thought' to the 'military genius of Stalin'. His proclamations following each victory were solemnly read over the radio and marked by a salute of guns, with 1944 celebrated as the year of the 'ten Stalinist blows'.[57]

Stalin also presented himself as a key player on the world stage, a great and dignified statesman with a grey moustache and silver hair. He was shown in the company of foreign dignitaries in a wood-panelled room in the Kremlin, standing back as his underlings signed treaties. He appeared next to British prime minister Winston Churchill and US president Franklin D. Roosevelt in summit meetings in Tehran, Yalta and Potsdam, planning the post-war world. His smile returned, as he sat majestically in his marshal's greatcoat, one of the world's great statesmen.[58]

The world's great figures who shuffled through Stalin's office said good words about him. 'I like him the more I see him,' pronounced Churchill, unaware of just how much Stalin despised and belittled him. The Americans agreed. A credulous Roosevelt perceived something beyond a revolutionary in Stalin's nature, namely a 'Christian gentleman'. Truman, who succeeded to the presidency after Roosevelt passed away, confided to his diary: 'I can deal with Stalin. He is honest – but smart as hell.' His secretary of state James Byrnes held that 'The truth is he is a very likeable person.' Stalin enthralled foreign journalists, who routinely referred to him as Uncle Joe.[59]

Even some of Stalin's own people liked him. Terror and propaganda had advanced hand in hand throughout the 1930s, with millions starved, imprisoned or executed. Only the most foolhardy foreign admirer could believe that his own victims genuinely adored the perpetrator of so much human misery. When Nadezhda Mandelstam was forced to seek work in a textile factory in Strunino, a small town just outside Moscow, she discovered that during the Great Terror local people were so embittered that they routinely referred to Stalin as 'the pockmarked fellow'. But almost everyone was traumatised by a war waged with unparalleled savagery, as the invaders went far beyond the battlefield to torture, murder and enslave, determined to crush people they considered racially inferior.[60]

Entire cities were starved into submission, with a million lives claimed just in the twenty-eight-month siege of Leningrad. More than seven million civilians were killed in occupied areas, not counting a further four million who died of hunger or disease. Some twenty-five million people were made homeless, with 70,000 villages erased from the map. Perhaps understandably, some people looked up to Stalin, needing someone to believe in. The propaganda machine conflated Stalin and the motherland as one and the same. He was the leader of a just war, the Supreme Commander of a Red

Army that would not only liberate the motherland but also exact revenge.[61]

Yet even as war worked wonders in enhancing his reputation, large swathes of the population apparently remained indifferent. Propaganda relentlessly projected an image of a potent and sage leader rallying the masses against the common enemy, but when a British journalist spent a week travelling by train from Murmansk to Moscow, speaking to dozens of soldiers, railway workers and civilians from all walks of life, Stalin's name was not mentioned once.[62]

Distrust of the one-party state ran deep in the countryside, where young men were drafted into the army. Many new recruits were religious villagers who wrote letters back home ending with the words 'Long Live Jesus Christ'. In 1939 some of them defaced busts of Lenin and Stalin, driving political instructors to sheer despair. It was the propagandists in the army who cared most about Stalin. These attitudes changed after the imposition of ruthless discipline in 1941. In July 1942 Stalin issued Order Number 227, 'Not a Step Backward!', treating disobedience or retreat as treason. Special units were placed behind the front line to shoot laggards, leaving the troops in no doubt as to whom they should fear most, Stalin or Hitler. More generally, the regime showed little regard for the lives of its soldiers. Those injured or mutilated while fighting received heartless treatment, with many rounded up and deported to the gulag.[63]

The Red Army was destroyed and renewed at least twice, but Stalin could afford to lose more tanks and more people than Hitler. On their way to Berlin, the German capital, the troops engaged in widespread looting, pillaging and rape, more often than not with the approval of their commanders, including Stalin.[64]

Stalin ran the war as he ran everything else, singlehandedly. In the words of Isaac Deutscher, one of his earliest biographers, 'He was in effect his own commander-in-chief, his own minister of defence, his own quartermaster, his own minister of supply, his own foreign minister, and even his own chef de protocol.' As the red flag went up over Berlin, he was the great victor. Yet Stalin, more paranoid than ever, distrusted the army. The real hero was Chief of General Staff and Deputy Chief Supreme Commander Georgy Zhukov, who had led the westward march towards Hitler's bunker. In Moscow the population called him 'our St George', from the patron saint of the capital. Zhukov led the victory parade in Red Square on 24 June 1945, although he understood his master well enough to refer to him as 'the captain of genius' in his tribute. The party line relentlessly glorified 'Our great genius and leader of troops, comrade Stalin, to whom we owe our historic victory'. That same month, Stalin gave himself the ultimate accolade, bestowing upon himself the title of Generalissimo.[65]

A year later, after his colleagues had been tortured into providing incriminating evidence, Zhukov was consigned to inner exile in the provinces. His name was no longer mentioned. Victory Day celebrations were suspended after 1946, memoirs by soldiers, officers and generals forbidden. In the official memory of the war, everyone receded into the background, allowing Stalin alone to shine. In 1947 a *Short Biography* of Stalin, designed for ordinary readers, was published to great fanfare. Strikingly similar to Henri Barbusse's hagiography published in 1935, it sold as many as eighteen million copies by 1953. The chapter on the Great Patriotic War mentioned none of his generals, least of all Zhukov, portraying Stalin as the architect of victory.[66]

During the war Stalin had encouraged rumours of more freedom to come, but these were crushed as soon as the fighting ended. Millions of Russians who had become involuntary prisoners of the Germans were considered besmirched and potentially treacherous. Treated as traitors, many were sent to camps, others shot. Stalin also feared that foreign ideas had contaminated the rest of the population.

As tensions between the three allies developed into a Cold War in 1947 the screws tightened further. Andrei Zhdanov, in a campaign closely scripted by Stalin, imposed ideological orthodoxy. Everything foreign was attacked, everything local extolled, from literature, linguistics, economics and biology to medicine. Stalin

personally intervened in several scientific debates, posing as an
arbiter acting in the interests of Marxism. In a 10,000-word essay
in *Pravda* he hinted that Russian was the language of the future,
dismissing a leading linguist as anti-Marxist. In 1948 he lambasted
genetics as a foreign and bourgeois science, bringing research in
biology to a halt. For over a decade Stalin had ruled over a fearful
and obsequious court. Now he battered entire fields of science
into submission, promoting flatterers who fawned over his genius
while sending dissenting professors to the gulag. Only one branch
was exempt, namely research into the atomic bomb, for which
unlimited resources were made available.[67]

Stalin's cult began to assume industrial proportions. Stalin
had not only liberated the Soviet Union, but also occupied half
of Europe. From Poland in the north to Bulgaria in the south
the Red Army took over huge territories that were progressively
converted into satellite states. Future leaders known as 'little Stalins'
were flown in from Moscow to oversee the colonisation of their
respective countries – Walter Ulbricht in East Germany, Bolesław
Bierut in Poland, Mátyás Rákosi in Hungary. Initially progress
was slow, since Stalin had ordered them to proceed cautiously, but
everywhere by 1947 the secret services were incarcerating real and
imagined enemies or sending them to camps. The communists also
began to nationalise schools, dismantle independent organisations
and undermine the Church. Demand for posters, portraits, busts
and statues of Stalin skyrocketed, as new subjects were required to
worship their distant master in the Kremlin, celebrated in Warsaw
as 'Poland's unbending friend', in East Berlin as 'the best friend of
the German people'.[68]

At home, too, statues and monuments to Stalin's glory multiplied,
even though he himself, increasingly frail and exhausted, withdrew
from public life. The peak of his cult came when he turned seventy
in 1949. As he celebrated his birthday at the Bolshoi Theatre in
Moscow, searchlights picked out a giant figure of Stalin in full
military uniform, suspended from balloons high above the Red
Square. Millions of small red flags fluttered over Moscow the
following day, with banners proclaiming the same message: 'Glory

to the Great Stalin'. The authorities distributed some two million posters, plus thousands of portraits, many illuminated at night. Monumental busts, *Pravda* proudly announced, had by then been placed on thirty-eight Central Asian mountain peaks. The first had appeared in 1937, as mountaineers had carried a statue to the highest summit in the Soviet Union, named Stalin Peak.[69]

Gifts were borne to Moscow on special trains decorated with red flags. But by contrast with previous occasions, Stalin's birthday was now a global event. People across the socialist camp vied to demonstrate their love for the leader in the Kremlin, the head of the international communist movement. More than a million letters and telegrams arrived from all corners of the world. Not until the summer of 1951 did the chorus of greetings abate, with *Pravda* publishing several hundred every day. Signatures from ordinary people were also required. In Czechoslovakia some nine million affixed their names, collected in 356 volumes, to a congratulatory message. North Korea easily outdid them, sending along precisely 16,767,680 signatures filling 400 hefty tomes.[70]

Gifts poured in, with workers from Eastern Europe sending an aircraft, several motorcars, a railway engine and a motorcycle. From China came a magnificent statue of Hua Mulan, a legendary woman warrior from the sixth century, and also Stalin's portrait engraved on a grain of rice. Many of the presents, meticulously inventoried, were exhibited in the Pushkin Museum of Fine Arts, including some 250 statues and 500 busts. There were many spectacular pieces, perhaps none quite so impressive as a seventy-square-metre carpet representing Stalin in his office.[71]

Stalin appeared on his birthday flanked by the leaders of Eastern Europe and by Mao Zedong, who in October had triumphantly proclaimed the People's Republic of China. A few months earlier the first Soviet atomic bomb had been successfully tested, making Stalin the leader of a global superpower. It was a show of force as the socialist camp retreated behind an iron curtain, marking a turning point in the Cold War.

Stalin continued to purge to the very end. Paranoia is hard to measure, but age seemed to make him even more pitiless. Family was no exception, since Stalin wished to hover above all others like a distant deity, mysterious and detached from his own personal history, which relatives knew only too well. In 1948 his sister-in-law Anna Allilueva was deported for ten years after publishing a memoir that offered seemingly innocuous glimpses into his earlier life. Except for his own children none of his relatives were safe. His court was terrified, reduced to fawning on his wisdom and competing for his favours even as he baited and humiliated them, playing on their fear or pitting them against each other. Constantly and inexorably, new purges unfolded, as the population in the gulag more than doubled to 2.5 million between 1944 and 1950. In between purges Stalin approved ever more extravagant monuments to his own glory. On 2 July 1951 he commissioned a statue of himself on the Volga–Don Canal using thirty-three tonnes of bronze. Stalin began self-deification as he sensed the coming of the end.[72]

On 1 March 1953 Stalin was found lying on the floor, soaked in his own urine. A blood vessel had burst in his brain, but no one had dared to disturb him in his bedroom. Medical help, too, was delayed, as the leader's entourage was petrified of making the wrong call. Stalin died three days later. His body was embalmed and displayed, but crowds of mourners determined to catch a last glimpse of their leader ran out of control. Hundreds were trampled to death in the ensuing panic. After an elaborate state funeral on 9 March he was laid to rest next to Lenin. Tower bells were rung and salute guns fired. Every train, bus, tram, lorry and car in the country came to a halt. Complete silence descended over Red Square. 'A single sparrow swooped over the mausoleum,' observed one foreign correspondent. An official announcement was made, then the flag slowly raised back to full mast. Eulogies came in from the beneficiaries of the regime, none more eloquent than those penned by Boris Polevoi and Nicolai Tikhonov, winners of the Stalin Prize. Millions grieved. One month after his funeral Stalin's name vanished from the newspapers.[73]

4

Mao

When Stalin appeared at the Bolshoi Theatre to show himself to the cameras for his seventieth birthday gala, he stood between Mao Zedong and Nikita Khrushchev. Mao looked dour, awed by his counterpart in the Kremlin but resentful at the way he was being treated. He had expected to be welcomed as the leader of a great revolution that had brought a quarter of humanity into the communist orbit, but had been met at Yaroslavsky Station by two of Stalin's underlings who did not even accompany him to his residence. Stalin had granted Mao a brief interview, praising him for his success in Asia, but for several months a shroud of silence had been placed in the Soviet Union over the victory of the Chinese Communist Party.

After the birthday celebrations Mao was whisked off to a dacha outside the capital and made to wait several weeks for a formal audience. Meetings were cancelled, phone calls never returned. Mao lost patience, ranting about how he was in Moscow to do more than 'eat and shit'. With every passing day he was made to learn his humble place in a communist brotherhood which revolved entirely around Stalin.[1]

For the previous twenty-eight years the Chinese Communist Party had depended on Moscow for financial support. Mao, a tall, lean and handsome young man aged twenty-seven, had been handed his first cash payment of 200 yuan by a Comintern agent in 1921 to cover the cost of travelling to the founding meeting of the party in Shanghai. But the money came with strings attached. Lenin realised that the principles of Bolshevism had little popular appeal beyond the shores of Europe, and demanded that communist parties join their nationalist counterparts in a united front that would overthrow foreign powers. He had a point. After several years membership of the party lingered in the low hundreds in a country of more than 480 million people.

In 1924 the Chinese Communist Party joined the Nationalist Party, which also received military aid from Moscow. It was an uneasy alliance, but two years later the nationalists under Chiang Kai-shek launched a military campaign from their base in the south, attempting to seize power from local warlords and unify the country. In Mao's home province of Hunan they followed instructions from Russian advisers and funded peasant associations in the hope of fomenting a revolution. Social order unravelled in the countryside, as poor villagers used the opportunity to turn the world upside down. They became the masters, assaulting the wealthy and powerful, creating a reign of terror. Some victims were stabbed with knives, a few even decapitated. Local pastors were paraded through the streets as 'running dogs of imperialism', their hands bound behind their backs with a rope around their necks. Churches were looted.[2]

It was a revelation for Mao, who was enthralled by the violence. 'They strike the gentry to the ground,' he wrote admiringly in his report on the peasant movement. He made a bold prediction, foreseeing how 'Several hundred million peasants will rise like a mighty storm ... They will smash all the trammels that bind them and rush forward along the road to liberation. They will sweep all the imperialists, warlords, corrupt officials, local tyrants and evil gentry into their graves.'[3]

For years Mao had tried to find his way. As a young man he had read voraciously, viewing himself as an intellectual who penned nationalist essays. He had worked as a librarian, a teacher, a publisher and a labour activist. In the countryside he finally discovered his calling: although he was still a lesser figure in the party, he would be the one to lead the peasants towards liberation.

The violence in the countryside repelled the nationalists, who soon turned away from the Soviet model. A year later, after his troops entered Shanghai in April 1927, Chiang Kai-shek launched a bloody purge in which hundreds of communists were executed. The Chinese Communist Party went underground. Mao led a motley army of 1,300 men into the mountains, in search of the peasants who would propel him to power.

Mao turned ideology on its head, abandoning the urban workers to espouse the very peasants despised by orthodox Marxism. Relegated to remote mountainous areas, he and his followers spent years learning how to mobilise the raw power of poor peasants to overthrow government posts, plunder local resources and control increasingly large tracts of land. They became experts at guerrilla warfare, using ambushes and raids to harass the less mobile troops of the nationalists, their arch-enemy.

All along there were ideological clashes with the Central Committee, which stayed underground in Shanghai, close to the factory workers. Some took a dim view of his unorthodox tactics. Zhou Enlai, a suave, educated young man in charge of the party's military affairs, described Mao's troops as 'just bandits who roam here and there'. But by 1930 Mao began to attract the attention of Stalin. Mao knew how to deal with the 'kulak scum' in the countryside, and he knew how to fight off his competitors. He was single-minded in the pursuit of power, driven by a ferocious ambition that was served well by a manipulative personality and great political skills. It was also ruthless. In one incident that took place in a town called Futian, a hundred officers of a battalion that had mutinied against his leadership were confined to bamboo cages, stripped naked and tortured, many of them being finished off with bayonets.[4]

On 7 November 1931, the anniversary of the October Revolution, Mao proclaimed a Soviet Republic in a mountainous area of Jiangxi province, financed by Moscow. It was a state within the state, issuing its own coins, paper money and stamps. Mao was its head, lording over some three million subjects. But members of the Central Committee joined him from Shanghai, and they were critical of guerrilla warfare. They stripped Mao of his positions, handing command over the battlefront to Zhou Enlai instead. The result was a disaster, as Chiang Kai-shek mauled the Red Army, forcing the communists to flee in October 1934. What later became known as the Long March was an arduous trek of 9,000 kilometres through some of the country's most forbidding terrain.

Mao used the Long March to claw his way back to power. On the way to Yan'an, a remote and isolated mountain area on a loess plateau in Shaanxi province, he exploited the defeat of the Jiangxi Soviet to isolate his rivals, dislodging Zhou Enlai to take back control of the Red Army.

The troops arrived in October 1935, reduced from some 86,000 to a mere 8,000, but they were loyal, dedicated followers. Always the demagogue, Mao turned the Long March into a manifesto: 'The Long March has announced to some 200 million people in eleven provinces,' he wrote, 'that the road of the Red Army is their only road to liberation.'[5]

It was not all bravura. Mao was counting on a world war, hoping that it would ignite a global revolution. And he knew he had Stalin's attention. Months earlier Moscow had shifted its foreign policy, increasingly apprehensive of an attack from either Germany or Japan. In 1931 Japan had invaded Manchuria, a vast region rich in natural resources that stretched from the Great Wall north of Beijing all the way to Siberia. There were endless border disputes with the Soviet Union, including air intrusions. By July 1935 the Comintern openly referred to Tokyo as a 'fascist enemy'.[6]

Stalin, like his master Lenin more than a decade earlier, now encouraged communists abroad to seek a united front with those in power instead of trying to overthrow them. But this strategy demanded that the authority of communist party leaders be elevated. A full-blown campaign to exalt Mao began. The Comintern acclaimed him as one of the 'standard-bearers' of the world communist movement. Later that year *Pravda* published a long tribute entitled 'Mao Zedong: Leader of the Chinese Working People', followed by a pamphlet entitled 'Leaders and Heroes of the

Chinese People'. Mao was the *vozhd*, great leader, a title reserved for Lenin and Stalin alone.[7]

Mao took the cue. A few months later, after careful vetting, he invited Edgar Snow, a young, idealistic reporter from Missouri, to come to Yan'an. Every detail about how the journalist should be handled was dictated: 'Security, secrecy, warmth and red carpet.' Snow spent several months at the communist base, as Mao offered a mythical version of his own life, speaking about his childhood, youth and career as a revolutionary. Mao checked and amended every detail of what Snow wrote.[8]

Red Star over China, published in 1937, was an instant success. It introduced the mysterious leader of the Chinese Communist Party to the rest of the world, describing him as 'an accomplished scholar of classical Chinese, an omnivorous reader, a deep student of philosophy and history, a good speaker, a man with an unusual memory and extraordinary powers of concentration, an able writer, careless in his personal habits and appearance but astonishingly meticulous about details of duty, a man of tireless energy and a military and political strategist of considerable genius'.[9]

Mao was the poor child of the soil who had pulled himself up through sheer willpower and pride, determined to fight for his humiliated compatriots. He was a man of simple habits, living in a loess cave, growing his own tobacco leaves. He was down to earth, a rebel with a lively, rustic sense of humour. He worked tirelessly. He was a poet. He was a philosopher. He was a great strategist. But most of all, he was a man of destiny, called upon by deep historical forces to regenerate his country. 'He might very well,' Edgar Snow announced, 'become a very great man.'[10]

Red Star over China was a sensation, selling 12,000 copies in the United States within a month of publication. It was immediately translated into Chinese, turning Mao into a household name. The photograph on the cover of the book, showing Mao wearing a military cap with a single red star, became an iconic image.[11]

Stalin had asked for an alliance between the communists and the nationalists. Mao knew full well that Chiang Kai-shek had no intention of collaborating with him, and promptly declared his willingness to form a 'broad revolutionary national united front' against Japan. He also asked Stalin for an extra two million roubles in military aid.[12]

Mao's offer made him look like the leader most concerned about the fate of the nation, as the threat of war with Japan loomed ever larger. On 12 December 1936 Chiang was kidnapped by members of his own alliance and forced to cease all hostilities against the communists. The truce was a blessing, giving Mao the time to build up his strength under a new united front.

More good fortune came in July 1937, when Japan crossed the border from Manchuria, capturing Beijing within weeks. Over the next few years the Japanese army would do what the communists would never have been able to achieve, namely attack, destroy or displace the nationalist troops from all major cities along the coast. One gruesome battle followed another, with the best of Chiang's divisions in Shanghai sustaining a three-month assault by enemy tanks, naval gunfire and aircraft. Hundreds of thousands of people died in the Battle of Shanghai. The fate of Nanjing was even worse, as the Japanese systematically murdered and raped civilians in the nationalist capital during the winter of 1937–8.

All along, the communists remained safely ensconced in the hinterland. By January 1940, according to a report from Zhou Enlai himself, more than a million soldiers had been killed or wounded, although this figure included no more than 31,000 casualties from the Red Army. Chiang Kai-shek and his government were forced to retreat to the provisional capital of Chongqing in Sichuan. Some 3,000 tonnes of bombs were dropped on the city in hundreds of air raids until the United States entered the war after Pearl Harbor.[13]

Not a single bullet was ever fired at Yan'an. Mao's strategy of guerrilla warfare far behind enemy lines had some outspoken critics, but Stalin stood by Mao. In the summer of 1938 Moscow demanded that party members unite behind their leader, crushing those who had hoped to prevail against him. A few months later the Kremlin described Mao as a 'wise tactician' and 'brilliant theorist'. An abridged version of *Red Star over China* was rushed into print.[14]

For the very first time Mao was without a serious rival. He used the opportunity to rewrite the past. At a plenum held in the autumn of 1938 the first item on the agenda was his report on the history of the party since its foundation seventeen years earlier. At 150 pages, it lasted three days. Mao ticked off everyone who had crossed him in the past, describing them as 'right opportunists' or 'left opportunists'. A few were accused of being Trotskyists. It was the first canonical version of the party's history, one in which a long series of errors against the correct party line had been committed until Mao Zedong had finally triumphed, leading the Red Army to Yan'an with the Long March.[15]

Mao's next step was to establish himself as a theoretician. In this task he was helped by Chen Boda, a bookish but ambitious young man trained in Moscow who would become his ghost writer. Together they penned *On New Democracy*, a pamphlet published in January 1940 that portrayed the communist party as a broad front striving to unite all 'revolutionary classes', including the national bourgeoisie. Mao promised a multi-party system, democratic freedoms and protection of private property. It was an entirely fictitious programme, but one that held broad popular appeal.[16]

Many thousands of students, teachers, artists, writers and journalists poured into Yan'an in the following years, attracted by the promise of a more democratic future. But Mao was suspicious of these free-thinkers and demanded absolute loyalty instead. In 1942 he launched a Rectification Campaign. In the words of historian Gao Hua, the aim was 'to intimidate the whole party with violence and terror, to uproot any individual independent thought, to make the whole party subject to the single utmost authority of Mao'.[17]

Mao orchestrated the entire campaign, supervising everything down to the last detail, but he allowed his henchman Kang Sheng to take centre stage. A sinister man with a pencil moustache and thick spectacles, always dressed in black, Kang had been trained in Moscow, where he had helped the secret police eliminate hundreds of students from China during the Great Terror. Under his supervision endless witch-hunts were carried out in Yan'an, as people were forced to denounce each other. Thousands of suspects were locked up, investigated, tortured, purged and occasionally executed. The spine-chilling howls of people imprisoned in caves could be heard at night.[18]

When the campaign came to an end, more than 15,000 alleged enemy agents and spies had been unmasked. Mao had allowed the terror to run amok, assuming the role of a self-effacing, distant yet benevolent leader. Then he stepped in to curb the violence, letting Kang Sheng take the fall. Those who had managed to survive the horror turned to Mao as a saviour.[19]

Mao also set up a Central General Study Committee, which he packed with close allies, among them Liu Shaoqi, a dour, puritanical party member who would emerge as Number Two. The Study Committee ran everything in Yan'an, in effect converting the Communist Party into Mao's personal dictatorship. Leading members who had crossed Mao in the past were humiliated, forced to write confessions and apologise publicly for their mistakes. Zhou Enlai was one of them, and he tried hard to redeem himself by proclaiming his undying support for Mao. This was deemed insufficient, as he was tested in a series of denunciation meetings in which he had to call himself a 'political swindler' who lacked principles. It was a gruelling exercise in self-abasement, but Zhou managed to emerge from the ordeal as Mao's faithful assistant, determined never to oppose him again. Unlike Stalin, Mao rarely had his rivals shot, turning them instead into accomplices who were on permanent probation, having to work tirelessly to prove themselves.[20]

On 1 July 1943, the twenty-second anniversary of the founding of the party, Mao announced that the Rectification Campaign had 'guaranteed ideological and political unanimity in the party'. This was the green light for an unlimited cult of personality. All had to acclaim Mao Zedong, and all had to study Mao Zedong Thought, a term coined four days later by Wang Jiaxiang, a Soviet-trained ideologist. Foremost among his hagiographers was Liu Shaoqi, who hailed Mao as a 'great revolutionary leader' and 'master of Marxism Leninism'. Liu's praise was the signal for others to rally around their leader, referring to him as the 'great revolutionary helmsman', a 'saving star', a 'genius strategist' and a 'genius politician'. The panegyrics were 'nauseatingly slavish', observed Theodore White and Annalee Jacoby, two American journalists. When Mao spoke, hardened men tempered by years of guerrilla warfare would studiously take notes 'as if drinking from the fountain of knowledge'.[21]

The party's mouthpiece, *Liberation Daily*, overseen by Mao, used giant headlines proclaiming 'Comrade Mao Zedong is the Saviour of the Chinese People!' By the end of 1943 portraits of Mao were everywhere, prominently displayed next to those of Marx, Engels, Lenin and Stalin. Badges bearing his head circulated among the party elite, while his profile appeared in gold relief on the façade of a huge auditorium. People sang to his glory: 'The East is Red, the Sun is Rising; China has Brought Forth a Mao Zedong; He Seeks the People's Happiness'.[22]

In April 1945, after a seventeen-year interval, a party congress was finally convened. Hundreds of the delegates had been persecuted during the Rectification Campaign, some of them replaced by men loyal to Mao. All of them hailed their leader, who was elected Chairman of the top organs of the party. Mao Zedong Thought was enshrined in the party constitution. In his opening report, Liu Shaoqi mentioned the Chairman's name more than a hundred times, referring to him as 'the greatest revolutionary and statesman in all of Chinese history' as well as 'the greatest theoretician and scientist in all of Chinese history'. Mao, at long last, had turned the party into an instrument of his own will.[23]

When Japan surrendered on 15 August 1945 Mao controlled 900,000 troops in rural pockets across the north of China. A few days earlier Stalin had declared war on Japan, sending close to a million troops across the Siberian border to occupy Manchuria and the north of Korea, where they waited for their Allied counterparts to join them on the 38th parallel. Mao had grandiose plans to incite a rebellion in faraway Shanghai, but Stalin's immediate concern was to ensure the departure of the American troops from China and Korea. In order to achieve this goal, he recognised Chiang Kai-shek as the leader of a united China in a Sino-Soviet treaty.

Soviet troops in Manchuria, however, quietly handed over the countryside to the communists, who began pouring into the region from Yan'an. The Soviets helped Mao transform his ragtag army of guerrilla fighters into a formidable fighting machine, opening sixteen military institutions, including air force, artillery and engineering schools. Some Chinese officers went to the Soviet Union for advanced training. Logistical support also arrived by air and by rail. In North Korea alone a full 2,000 wagonloads were allocated to the task.[24]

The Americans, on the other hand, in September 1946 imposed an arms embargo on their wartime ally Chiang Kai-shek. Chiang, convinced that China would never be able to defend itself without control over Manchuria, the industrial powerhouse and strategic gateway of the country, kept on pouring his best troops into the region. Mao never let up, determined to wear down his enemy in a pitiless war of attrition, whatever the cost.

In 1948 the communists began laying siege to cities in Manchuria, starving them into surrender. Changchun fell after 160,000 civilians died of hunger. Unwilling to undergo the same fate, Beijing capitulated soon afterwards. Like dominoes, other cities fell one after the other, unable to resist the war machine built up by the communists. Chiang Kai-shek and his troops fled to Taiwan. By the end of 1949, after a long and bloody military conquest, the People's Republic of China was proclaimed.[25]

The moment the red flag fluttered over Beijing, a hastily sketched portrait of Mao Zedong went up over the main gate of the Forbidden City. Over the following months portraits of the Chairman appeared in schools, factories and offices, often with precise instructions on how they should be displayed. His distinctive wart soon became a trademark and was affectionately touched in, like a Buddha figure. The study of Mao Zedong Thought became compulsory, as adults from all walks of life had to go back to class, poring over official textbooks to learn the new orthodoxy. Revolutionary songs, including 'Mao Zedong is our Sun' or 'Hymn to Chairman Mao' were belted out daily by schoolchildren, soldiers, prisoners and office workers. These tunes were also blasted from loudspeakers, installed on street corners, railway stations, dormitories, canteens and all major institutions. Carefully choreographed parades were held twice a year, as clockwork soldiers, mounted cavalry, tanks and armoured cars were reviewed by the Chairman on top of a rostrum in Tiananmen Square.[26]

With the cult of personality came a harsh regime modelled on the Soviet Union. 'The Soviet Union's Today is our Tomorrow' was the slogan of the day. Mao emulated Stalin, seeing the key to wealth and power in the collectivisation of agriculture, the elimination of private property, all-pervasive control of the lives of ordinary people and huge expenditures on national defence.[27]

The promises made in *On New Democracy* were broken one by one. The regime's first act was to overthrow the old order in the countryside. This was done in the guise of land reform, as villagers were forced to beat and dispossess their own leaders in collective denunciation meetings, accusing them of being 'landlords', 'tyrants' and 'traitors'. Some did so with relish, but many had no choice as they risked being targeted themselves. Close to two million people were physically liquidated, many more stigmatised as 'exploiters' and 'class enemies'. Their assets were distributed to the perpetrators, creating a pact sealed in blood between the poor and the party.[28]

In the cities every individual was given a class label (*chengfen*) based on their loyalty to the revolution: there were 'good', 'wavering' and 'hostile' people. A class label determined a person's access to food, education, health care and employment. Those marked as 'hostile' were stigmatised for life and beyond, since the label was passed on to children.[29]

A Great Terror followed from October 1950 to October 1951, as the regime turned against 'counter-revolutionaries', 'spies', 'bandits' and others standing in the way of revolution. Mao fixed the killing quota at one per thousand, but in some regions two or three times as many were killed, often at random. The following year former government servants were subjected to a massive purge, while the business community was brought to heel. All organisations operating outside the party – religious communities, philanthropic societies, independent chambers of commerce, civil associations – were eliminated by 1953.[30]

A literary inquisition ensured artists and writers conformed to the dictates of the party. Books considered undesirable were burned in giant bonfires or pulped by the tonne. The Commercial Press, one of the largest in the country, had roughly 8,000 titles in print in the summer of 1950. A year later a mere 1,234 of these were considered acceptable for 'the masses'. In every domain of the visual and literary arts the socialist realism devised by Stalin was imposed. The most prominent theme was Mao, not Stalin. His works, essays, poems, lectures, musings and mottos were churned out by the million, from cheap paperbacks to expensive gilded editions. A huge amount of propaganda work was published, telling the story of oppression and the road to liberation, sometimes in Mao's own words and handwriting. Newspapers and magazines, too, spread his wisdom far and wide. Photographs of the Chairman dominated the front pages.[31]

In 1949 the Chairman handpicked a photographer named Hou Bo. She had joined the party at the age of fourteen, and her pictures were soon printed in the millions. 'The Founding of the PRC' (1949), 'Mao Zedong Swimming Across the Yangzi' (1955) and 'Chairman Mao at Ease with the Masses' (1959), some of them heavily touched up, were among the most widely distributed images of the twentieth century.[32]

No parks, streets or cities were named after Mao. The Chairman instead fashioned a more intangible monument to himself, as philosopher king of the East. At its heart was the idea that he had combined the theory of Marxism-Leninism with the concrete practice of the Chinese revolution. Instead of applying Marxism dogmatically to conditions very different from those in Russia, Mao had overseen the Sinification of Marxism. In December 1950 the Chairman published an article entitled 'On Practice', followed in April 1952 by 'On Contradiction'. Both were hailed as philosophical developments of the dialectical materialism of Marx, Engels, Lenin and Stalin. Although these essays contained little that was original, the idea of the Sinification of Marxism captured the imagination of admirers at home and abroad.[33]

Mao also posed as a renaissance man, a philosopher, sage and poet wrapped in one, a calligrapher immersed in the literary traditions of his country. Even as traditional poetry vanished from the shelves, the Chairman's own verses were widely distributed. A highpoint was the publication of *Chairman Mao's Nineteen Poems*. The compendium actually contained twenty-one pieces, but Mao was keen to imitate a well-known classical anthology entitled *Nineteen Ancient Poems*. It immediately prompted a movement to study his work, as learned professors and party secretaries vied with each other to praise this 'historic breakthrough in literary history'.[34]

While Mao's poetry was only marginally better than that of Stalin, who also liked to dabble in rhyme, he did have a genuine gift for words. His pithy slogans found their way into every household, whether it was 'Women Hold up Half the Sky', 'Revolution is Not a Dinner Party', 'Power Comes from the Barrel of a Gun' or 'Imperialism is a Paper Tiger'. His motto was 'Serve the People', proclaimed from posters and placards everywhere, the white characters written in a flamboyant hand against a red background. His mighty brush was used to name government buildings, grace public monuments and adorn mugs, vases and calendars. To this day his calligraphy dominates the masthead of the *People's Daily*.[35]

Mao, like Stalin, was a remote, god-like figure, rarely seen, rarely heard, ensconced deep within the Forbidden City that was once occupied by emperors. But he excelled at corridor politics, constantly meeting members at all levels of the party hierarchy. His personal appearance was deceptive. He came across as gentle, humble and almost grandfatherly in his concern for others. He was a poor public speaker, hampered by a thick Hunanese accent, but a good conversationalist who knew how to put his audience at ease. He walked and spoke slowly, always with great gravitas. He smiled often and benevolently. 'He seems so gentle that few people notice the cold, appraising eyes or are aware of the ceaselessly calculating mind within.' When he entered a room for a meeting, those present were required to stand up and applaud.[36]

Mao emulated Stalin, but his mentor feared the emergence of a powerful neighbour that might threaten his dominance over the socialist camp. Stalin had made him wait for weeks on end before signing a Treaty of Friendship, Alliance and Mutual Assistance in 1950. He also whittled down funding for China's first Five-Year Plan, warning Mao that he was moving too fast in collectivising the economy.

Stalin's death in 1953 came as a liberation for Mao. The Chairman could finally crank up the pace of collectivisation, as he imposed a monopoly on grain by the end of the year that obliged farmers to sell their crops at prices fixed by the state. Two years later collectives resembling state farms in the Soviet Union were introduced. They took back the land from the farmers, transforming the villagers into bonded servants at the beck and call of the state. In the cities all commerce and industry became functions of the state, as the government expropriated small shops, private enterprises and large industries alike. But the Socialist High Tide, as the campaign of accelerated collectivisation was known, had devastating effects on the economy and caused widespread popular discontent.[37]

In 1956 Mao encountered a setback. On 25 February, the final day of the Twentieth Congress of the Soviet Communist Party, Nikita Khrushchev held an unscheduled secret session in the Great Kremlin Palace. In a four-hour speech delivered without interruption, he denounced the suspicion, fear and terror created by Stalin. In a devastating attack on his former master, Khrushchev accused him of being personally responsible for brutal purges, mass deportations, executions without trial and the torture of innocent party loyalists. Khrushchev further assailed Stalin for his 'mania for greatness' and the cult of personality he had fostered during his reign. Members in the audience listened in stunned silence. There was no applause at the end, as many of the delegates were dazed, leaving in a state of shock.[38]

Copies of the speech were sent to foreign communist parties, where it set off a chain reaction. In Beijing the Chairman was forced on the defensive. Mao was China's Stalin, the great leader of the People's Republic. The secret speech could only raise questions about his own leadership, in particular the adulation surrounding him. De-Stalinisation was nothing short of a challenge to Mao's own authority. Just as Khrushchev pledged to return his country to the Politburo, Liu Shaoqi, Deng Xiaoping, Zhou Enlai and others in Beijing spoke out in favour of the principles of collective leadership. They also used Khrushchev's critique of state farms to slow down the pace of collectivisation. It looked as if the Chairman was being sidelined.[39]

At the Eighth Party Congress in September 1956, Mao Zedong Thought was removed from the party charter, while the cult of personality was decried. Hemmed in by Khrushchev, Mao had little choice but to put a brave face on these measures, even contributing to them in the months prior to the meeting. But in private the Chairman was seething, accusing Liu Shaoqi and Deng Xiaoping of taking control of the agenda and relegating him to the background.[40]

The Hungarian revolt gave Mao an opportunity to regain the upper hand. As Soviet troops crushed the rebels in Budapest in November 1956 the Chairman blamed the Hungarian Communist Party for having brought misfortune on itself by failing to listen to popular grievances and allowing them to fester and spiral out of control. Mao posed as a democrat, championing the ordinary man, demanding that non-party members be allowed to voice their discontent. In February 1957 he asked the party to 'let a hundred flowers bloom, let a hundred schools contend', urging ordinary people to overcome their hesitations and speak out.

Mao badly miscalculated. He had hoped for an outpouring of adulation in which his admirers would punish a party that had written Mao Zedong Thought out of the constitution. Instead, people wrote pithy slogans in favour of democracy and human rights, some even demanding that the communist party relinquish power. Students and workers took to the streets in the tens of thousands, clamouring for democracy and freedom of speech. Mao was stung by the extent of popular discontent. He put Deng

Xiaoping in charge of a campaign that denounced half a million students and intellectuals as 'rightists' bent on destroying the party, shipping many off to labour camps established along the outer reaches of the empire.[41]

Mao's gamble had backfired, but at least he and his comrades-in-arms were united again, determined to suppress the people. Back at the helm of the party, Mao was keen to push through the radical collectivisation of the countryside. In Moscow, where he and other communist party leaders from all over the world had been invited to celebrate the fortieth anniversary of the October Revolution in November 1957, he gave his showpiece pledge of allegiance to Khrushchev by recognising him as the leader of the socialist camp.

Deep down Mao believed that it was he who should assume the mantle of leadership over all socialist countries. Even when Stalin was still alive, Mao viewed himself as a more determined revolutionary. It was Mao, after all, who had led a quarter of humanity to liberation. He was both the Lenin and the Stalin vof China. When Khrushchev announced that the Soviet Union would catch up with the United States in per capita production of meat, milk and butter, Mao took up the challenge and proclaimed that China would outstrip Britain – then still considered a major industrial power – in steel production within fifteen years. Mao was determined to outclass Khrushchev, pushing for a Great Leap Forward into communism that would upstage the Soviet Union.

The Great Leap Forward was the Chairman's first attempt to steal the Soviet Union's thunder, as people in the countryside were herded into giant collectives called people's communes. By turning every man and woman in the countryside into a foot soldier in one giant army, to be deployed day and night to transform the economy, he thought that he could catapult his country past the Soviet Union. Mao was convinced that he had found the golden bridge to communism, making him the messiah leading humanity to a world of plenty for all.

Mao used the campaign to relaunch the cult of personality, battering his rivals into submission in a series of party meetings in the early months of 1958. 'What is wrong with worship?' he asked rhetorically. 'The truth is in our hands, why should we not worship it?' 'Each group must worship its leader, it cannot but worship its leader,' Mao observed, explaining that this was the 'correct cult of personality'.[42]

His message was immediately picked up by loyal followers. Ke Qingshi, the mayor of Shanghai, quivered enthusiastically: 'We must have blind faith in the Chairman! We must obey the Chairman with total abandon!'[43] All ranking leaders, at one point or another, had to offer a self-criticism. Zhou Enlai was repeatedly demeaned and humiliated, forced to confess to his errors on three occasions before all the assembled party leaders. In the end he told the audience that Mao was the 'personification of truth' and that errors occurred only when the party became divorced from his great leadership.[44]

Zhou Enlai was allowed to stay on, but many inside the party ranks were less fortunate. The leadership of entire provinces was overthrown, as 'anti-party' cliques were removed almost everywhere. In Yunnan province alone, an inquisition purged thousands of members, including one in fifteen within the upper echelons of the party.[45]

Mao insisted on absolute loyalty, turning everyone into a flatterer. As a result, decisions were made on the basis of the Chairman's whims, often without any concern for their impact. Already in the summer of 1959 it was clear that the Great Leap Forward was a disaster. But even a mild letter of criticism by Minister of Defence Peng Dehuai at a party gathering in Lushan was interpreted by the Chairman as a stab in the back. Peng was described as the leader of an 'anti-party clique' and removed from all influential positions. Liu Shaoqi stepped in, covering the Chairman with praise. 'The leadership of Comrade Mao Zedong,' Liu observed, 'is in no way inferior to the leadership of Marx and Lenin. I am convinced that if Marx and Lenin lived in China, they would have guided the Chinese revolution in just the same way.' As Mao's doctor put it, the Chairman 'craved affection and acclaim. As his disgrace within the party grew, so did his hunger for approval.'[46]

Most of all, Lin Biao rallied to the Chairman's defence, accusing Peng Dehuai in his frail, squeaky voice of being 'ambitious, conspiratorial and hypocritical'. Lin was widely considered one of the most brilliant strategists of the civil war and had personally ordered the siege of Changchun in 1948. A gaunt man with a chalky complexion, he suffered from a wide array of phobias about water, wind and cold. The mere sound of running water gave him diarrhoea. 'Only Mao is a great hero, a role to which no one else should dare to aspire,' he crowed, adding, 'We are all very far behind him, so don't even go there!'[47]

In private Lin was far more critical than Peng, confiding in his private diary that the Great Leap Forward was 'based on fantasy and a total mess'. But he knew that the best way to maintain power was to shower the Chairman with flattery. Lin had realised long ago how crucial it was to exalt Mao: 'He worships himself, he has blind faith in himself, adores himself, he will take credit for every achievement but blame others for his failures.'[48]

Anyone who had expressed reservations about the Great Leap Forward was hunted down, as some 3.6 million party members were purged as 'rightists' or 'little Peng Dehuais'. They were replaced by hard, unscrupulous elements who trimmed their sails to benefit from the radical winds blowing from Beijing, using every means at their disposal to extract grain from the countryside.[49]

Instead of steering the economy past that of the Soviet Union, the Great Leap Forward turned into one of the greatest catastrophes of the twentieth century, as tens of millions of people were worked, beaten or starved to death. By October 1960 Mao was forced to retreat from his grandiose plan, although it took more than a year for the economy to begin recovering.[50]

In January 1962, as some 7,000 leading cadres from all over the country gathered to talk about the failure of the Great Leap Forward, Mao's star was at its lowest. Rumours were circulating, accusing the Chairman of being deluded, innumerate and dangerous. Some of the delegates held him responsible for the mass starvation of ordinary people. Liu Shaoqi himself had been genuinely shocked by the disastrous state of the countryside. During the proceedings he even used the term 'man-made disaster', drawing gasps from the audience. Lin Biao, again, came to the rescue, hailing the Great Leap Forward as an unprecedented accomplishment in Chinese history: 'The thoughts of Chairman Mao are always correct. He is never out of touch with reality.' Zhou Enlai stepped forward, taking the blame for everything that had gone wrong.[51]

The Chairman was pleased with Lin, but suspicious of everyone else. His entire legacy was in jeopardy. Mao feared that he would meet the same fate as Stalin, denounced after his death by Khrushchev.

He went on the counter-attack as early as August 1962, laying the groundwork for the Cultural Revolution. Counter-revolutionary forces, he explained, were everywhere, and they were trying to lead the country back onto the road towards capitalism. He launched a Socialist Education Campaign with the motto 'Never Forget Class Struggle'. A year later Mao exhorted the nation to learn from Lei Feng, a young soldier who had dedicated his life to serving the people. His posthumous diary, a record of his ideological progress, was published and studied across the country. Lei Feng explained how 'the blood given by the party and Chairman Mao has penetrated every single cell of my body'. Mao even appeared to him in a vision: 'Yesterday I had a dream. I dreamt of seeing Chairman Mao. Like a compassionate father, he stroked my head. With a smile, he spoke to me: "Do a good job in study; be forever loyal to the party, loyal to the people!" My joy was overwhelming; I tried to speak but could not.'[52]

Glowing testimonials from workers and villagers were published in letters to newspapers all over China. Tens of thousands of meetings were held, extolling Lei Feng as a model communist. Plays and movies were produced. Songs were composed, some of them running into dozens of verses. Storytellers roamed the villages to enthral illiterate villagers with Lei Feng's love of the Chairman. A Lei Feng exhibition opened at the Beijing Army Museum, where a huge screen at the entrance inscribed with Mao Zedong's calligraphy exhorted visitors to 'Learn from Comrade Lei Feng!' Lei Feng was the poor man's Mao, a simplified Mao for the masses.

He was meant to rouse people from the apathy caused by Mao's Great Famine and heighten their hatred for class enemies.[53]

Lin Biao, who had been rewarded for his performance at Lushan with Peng Dehuai's job as minister of defence, promoted the study of Mao Zedong Thought within the armed forces. Soldiers were asked to commit short passages from Mao's collected writings to memory. In January 1964, a mimeographed compendium of these quotations was published, with a fuller version distributed to the People's Liberation Army later that year. It came covered in gaudy red plastic, and was no bigger than the palm of a hand, easily fitting inside the pocket of a standard military uniform. Lin Biao provided an inscription, taken from Lei Feng's diary: 'Read Chairman Mao's book, listen to Chairman Mao's words, act according to Chairman Mao's instructions and be a good fighter for Chairman Mao.' By the time a new edition appeared in August 1965, millions of copies of the *Quotations of Chairman Mao*, also known as the Little Red Book, were being distributed far beyond the ranks of the army.[54]

Mao basked in the adulation and ordered the country to emulate Lin Biao and the People's Liberation Army. 'The merit of the Liberation Army,' he said, 'is that its political ideology is correct.' In response, the army began to assume a more prominent role in civil life, setting up political departments in government units to promote Mao Zedong Thought. The army also fostered a more martial atmosphere, in tune with the Socialist Education Campaign. Military 'summer camps' for students and workers were organised in the countryside. In primary schools children were taught how to use airguns by shooting at portraits of Chiang Kai-shek and American imperialists. Military training camps were set up for older students from reliable backgrounds, where they learned how to throw grenades and shoot with live bullets. In the summer of 1965 more than 10,000 university and 50,000 middle-school students in Shanghai spent a week in camp.[55]

On 1 October 1964, to celebrate National Day, the army organised a monumental show on Tiananmen Square with several choirs and ballet dancers in military uniform. A colossal figure of Chairman Mao opened the procession, which edged forward to the

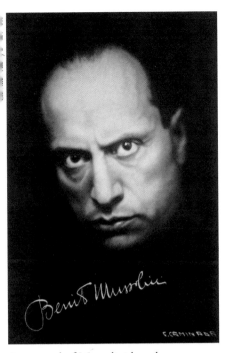

A postcard of Mussolini based on a photograph by Gianni Caminada, 1921.

Mussolini on horseback at his Villa Torlonia, September 1930.

Mussolini on the balcony of the Palazzo Venezia in Rome after his declaration of war on Ethiopia on 2 October 1935. The photo was widely reproduced, but is a montage of a picture of a crowd with a photograph of Mussolini taken between 1931 and 1933.

A huge portrait of the Duce at the Duomo in Milan, November 1933.

Mussolini declares war on Ethiopia over the radio, 2 October 1935.

Effigy of Mussolini carved by soldiers in Adwa Valley, Ethiopia, February 1936.

Hitler rehearsing in 1925 while listening to a recording of his own speeches. After seeing the photographs, Hitler ordered Heinrich Hoffmann to destroy the negatives, but he disobeyed.

Hitler election poster, 1932.

Hitler surrounded by admiring young militants in Berlin, photograph by Heinrich Hoffmann, 1933.

Hitler welcomed by supporters at Nuremberg in 1933.

Heinrich Hoffmann Photography shop,
Düsseldorf, July 1939.

Hitler and Uschi Schneider, the daughter
of Herta Schneider, a close childhood
friend of Eva Braun, at the Berghof,
Berchtesgaden, 1942.

Joseph Stalin at his desk in the Kremlin, 1935.

Stalin with Gelia Markizova, June 1936.

A tractor in a field with Stalin's portrait, circa 1940.

Germans cheer Stalin, 14 August 1951, East Berlin.

Soviet sailors swimming with portraits of Stalin in celebration of Navy Day, Sevastopol, July 1950.

A group of pioneers at a monument to Stalin, Uzbekistan, circa 1940.

Mao on the cover of *Red Star Over China*, 1937.   Mao surrounded by students, Shaoshan, 1959.

A People's Commune outside Shanghai, 1964.

The employees of a bookstore send the *Selected Works of Mao Zedong* to peasants in a suburban district of Beijing, circa 1966.

A parade in Beijing, circa 1970.

A group of children in uniform read the Little Red Book during the Cultural Revolution, circa 1968.

Kim Il-sung offering 'on-the-spot guidance' at a machine factory, circa 1967.

A choir sings in front of a huge portrait of Kim Il-sung in the Palace of Culture, Pyongyang, circa 1981.

Father and son, 1992.

Workers sweeping the ground in front of a giant bronze statue of Kim Il-sung, Pyongyang, 1994.

Fiftieth anniversary of the Workers' Party of Korea, a year after the death of Kim Il-sung, 1995.

An unassuming Duvalier, circa 1963.

Duvalier with gun as he rides through Port-au-Prince, circa 1963.

A parade in Port-au-Prince celebrating Duvalier, 1968.

Homeless man lying beneath portrait of Papa Doc, 1974.

Ceauşescu is presented with a presidential sceptre, March 1974.

The Ceauşescus surrounded by children in traditional costumes, December 1979.

Huge crowds celebrate Ceauşescu in Bucharest, January 1988.

The Palace of the People, photographed a few days after Ceaușescu was shot on Christmas Day 1989.

Children welcoming the Ceaușescus, November 1989.

Gate at the entrance of Harar with portraits of Brezhnev, Castro and Mengistu in the centre, circa 1981.

Mengistu leading a mass meeting, June 1977.

Mengistu and Castro celebrate the fourth anniversary of the revolution in Addis Ababa, September 1978.

Mengistu shaking hands with Kim Il-sung, February 1986.

tune of 'Chairman Mao, the Sun in our Hearts'. 'Armed with Mao Zedong Thought', the nation was told, the people would be able to overcome 'capitalist and feudal attempts at restoration as well as attacks by our enemies at home and abroad'. Two weeks later China exploded its first atom bomb, joining the world's superpowers.[56]

By the spring of 1966 Mao was ready to launch the Cultural Revolution. It was his second attempt to become the historical pivot around which the socialist universe revolved. Instead of trying to transform the economy, which had resulted in the disaster of the Great Leap Forward, the Chairman focused on culture. Mao must have wondered how one man, Nikita Khrushchev, could have single-handedly engineered a complete reversal of policy in the mighty Soviet Union, attacking Stalin in 1956 and proposing 'peaceful co-existence' with the imperialist camp. The answer was that culture had been neglected. The capitalists were gone, their property confiscated, but capitalist culture still held sway, making it possible for a few people at the top to erode and finally subvert the entire system.

Lenin had carried out the Great October Socialist Revolution, setting a precedent for the proletariat of the whole world. But modern revisionists like Khrushchev had usurped the leadership of the party, leading the Soviet Union back onto the road to capitalist restoration. The Great Proletarian Cultural Revolution would be the second stage in the history of the international communist movement, safeguarding the dictatorship of the proletariat against revisionism. The foundation piles of the communist future were being driven in China, as the Chairman guided the oppressed and downtrodden people of the world towards freedom. Mao was the one who inherited, defended and developed Marxism-Leninism into a new stage, that of Marxism-Leninism-Mao Zedong Thought. There was no mention of Stalin.[57]

These were grandiose ideas, but Mao also used the Cultural Revolution to get rid of his real and imaginary enemies, in particular delegates who had discussed the Great Leap Forward in January 1962.

Ten years earlier Mao had miscalculated by allowing intellectuals to speak their minds during the Hundred Flowers. This time he was better prepared. First, he placed the country on alert by having four party leaders arrested in May 1966, accusing them of being part of an 'anti-party clique' that had been plotting a return to capitalism. Then, on 1 June, classes across the country were suspended as students were unleashed against their teachers.

Students at every level had undergone years of indoctrination during the Socialist Education Campaign. Encouraged by the party machine, they harassed, denounced, humiliated and even tortured suspected class enemies. But a few went too far, taking to task leading party members. They were punished for their activities by work teams sent by Deng Xiaoping and Liu Shaoqi, put in charge of the Cultural Revolution in the Chairman's absence from Beijing. In mid-July Mao returned to the capital. Instead of supporting his two colleagues he accused them of suppressing the students and 'running a dictatorship'. Both were sidelined, while Lin Biao took over from Liu Shaoqi as Number Two.

'To Rebel is Justified' became Mao's battle cry, and rebel students did. Red Guards appeared in August 1966 donning improvised military uniforms, carrying the Little Red Book. They vowed to defend the Chairman and carry out the Cultural Revolution. In the early hours of 18 August, close to a million of them spilled out on Tiananmen Square, waiting to see the Chairman. As the sun began to rise over the eastern end of the square, Mao came down from the rostrum, wearing a baggy army uniform. The crowd erupted in cheers, brandishing the Little Red Book.[58]

Between August and November 1966 Mao reviewed some twelve million Red Guards at eight mass rallies. In the end, when even the giant square in front of the Forbidden City could no longer contain them, he rode through the city in an open jeep, reaching two million students in one fell swoop. Each rally was meticulously prepared, with Red Guards marched in groups or ferried by a fleet of 6,000 lorries to the square in the middle of the night, always unannounced for security reasons. They were ordered to sit in rows, waiting for hours on end. When the Chairman finally showed himself, they jumped up, craning their necks, surging forward, cheering 'Long Live Chairman Mao!'[59]

Many were ecstatic at catching a glimpse of the Chairman; others were disappointed. A few were frightened. But all of them knew precisely what to do and what to say, as the key sentence had been publicised endlessly by press, radio and television after every mass rally in Beijing: 'I am the happiest person in the world today. I have seen our Great Leader Chairman Mao!'[60]

At the end of the first rally on 18 September, Lin Biao made a lengthy speech, appealing to the excited youngsters to destroy 'all the old ideas, old culture, old customs and old habits of the exploiting classes'.

This they did with gusto, as they burned books, overturned tombstones in cemeteries, tore down temples, vandalised churches, and more generally attacked all signs of the past, including street names and shop signs. They also carried out house raids. In Shanghai alone, a quarter of a million homes were visited, as all remnants of the past were seized, whether ordinary books, family photographs, antique bronzes or rare scrolls.[61]

As the old world came under attack, a new proletarian culture, Mao proclaimed, would be forged. All understood that the only acceptable alternative was the cult of Chairman Mao. The most visible aspect of this cult was a rash of slogans. They went up everywhere. As one close observer noted: 'There have always been plenty of them in the past but all previous records have now been broken. Every stretch of clean wall must have its carefully inscribed quotation or tribute to Mao.' Some of the favourite slogans were 'Our Great Teacher, Great Leader, Great Commander, Great Helmsman' or 'Long Live Chairman Mao!' Shops, factories and schools were plastered with them, a few stretching across the top of entire buildings. Quotations were painted on the outside of buses, lorries, cars and vans.[62]

In this new world drenched in red, all the senses were bombarded. Red Guards on temporary platforms called upon the people in shrill voices to join the revolution. Bystanders were harangued in fiery rhetoric peppered with quotations from the

Chairman. High up in the skies, air hostesses on internal flights treated passengers to regular readings from the Little Red Book. But the most fearful weapon was the loudspeaker. Loudspeakers had long been used in propaganda campaigns, but now they were switched on permanently, spewing out the same quotations – always at full volume. Red Guards read from the Little Red Book in police boxes, connected to loudspeakers on the streets. Gangs of revolutionary youths paraded through the cities, belting out revolutionary songs praising the Chairman and his thought. The same songs were broadcast on radio, which in turn was connected to loudspeakers in courtyards, schools, factories and government offices. One favourite was 'When Sailing the Seas, We Depend on the Helmsman', another 'The Thought of Mao Zedong Glitters with Golden Light'.[63]

Nobody wanted to fall behind in the cult of the leader. As the range of objects condemned as 'feudal' or 'bourgeois' expanded, ordinary people increasingly turned to the only politically safe commodities available. Mao photos, badges, posters and books became all the rage, as entire branches of industry were converted to produce cult objects.

In Shanghai alone seven new factories were built with a total surface of 16,400 square metres, the size of about three football fields, to keep up with demand for photos, portraits, posters and books. In Jiangsu province industrial plants were refitted to print the Little Red Book. Factories producing red ink worked around the clock but still ran dry.[64]

The books needed covers – shiny, bright and red. The quantity of plastic needed for the Little Red Book alone reached 4,000 tonnes by 1968. As early as August 1966 the Ministry of Trade curbed the production of plastic shoes, plastic slippers and plastic toys as factories around the country geared up to contribute to Mao Zedong Thought.[65]

The planned economy struggled to keep up with popular demand. When it came to Mao badges, for instance, the national output stood at more than fifty million badges per month in 1968, but it was not enough. A thriving black market emerged to compete with the state. Some government organisations produced badges for their own members, but also expanded their operations into a legal twilight zone, lured by the profit motive. Underground factories appeared, entirely devoted to feeding the black market. They competed with state enterprises for rare resources, stealing aluminium buckets, kettles, pots and pans. Such was the demand that in some factories even the protective layer of aluminium on expensive machinery was ripped away to feed the badge frenzy.[66]

There were thousands of different badges, a few fashioned crudely from acrylic glass, plastic or even bamboo, some carefully crafted with hand-coloured porcelain, the majority with an aluminium base and a profile image of Mao in gold or silver, invariably looking to the left. Like the Little Red Book, the badge became a symbol of loyalty to the Chairman, and was worn just above the heart. Badges were the most hotly traded pieces of private property during the first years of the Cultural Revolution, open to every form of capitalist speculation. The amount of aluminium diverted away from other industrial activities was so enormous that, in 1969, Mao ordered a halt: 'Give me back my aeroplanes.' The fad declined rapidly, and largely ceased after the death of Lin Biao in 1971.[67]

The first phase of the Cultural Revolution was marked by vicious factional fighting, as ordinary people, party cadres and military leaders were divided over the true aims of the Cultural Revolution. As different factions opposed each other, all of them equally certain that they represented the true voice of Mao Zedong, the country slid into civil war. Soon people were fighting each other in the streets with machine guns and anti-aircraft artillery. Still the Chairman prevailed. He improvised, destroying millions of lives along the way. Periodically he stepped in to rescue a loyal follower or throw a close colleague to the wolves. A mere utterance of his decided the fates of countless people, as he declared one or another faction to be 'counter-revolutionary'. His verdict could change overnight, feeding a seemingly endless cycle of violence in which people scrambled to prove their loyalty to the Chairman.

As the violence spiralled out of control over the summer of 1967 the Chairman intervened. He toured the country, calling for a Great Alliance. On 1 October, in a great show of coordinated unity, half a million soldiers marched across Tiananmen Square, led by an enormous silver-coloured, plastic figure of Mao pointing the way forward. They were followed by hundreds of thousands of ordinary people, forced to march together, many in contingents with members from opposed factions.[68]

Everywhere study classes in Mao Zedong Thought were convened. The People's Liberation Army had stood behind Mao Zedong Thought years earlier, and now it used the cult of their leader to impose order and discipline. The cult of personality, as Lin Biao phrased it, would unite 'the entire party, the entire army, and the entire people'. A new campaign called the Three Loyalties and Four Boundless Loves was launched in March 1968. It brought the worship of Mao to new heights, requiring absolute loyalty to the Chairman, his thought and the 'proletarian revolutionary line'. In schools, offices and factories, altars were set up to Chairman Mao. Large characters reading 'The Red Sun in Our Hearts' were cut out in bright, shiny red paper, forming an arc over a picture of the Great Helmsman. Sunrays emanated from his head. Everywhere people met the gaze of the Chairman the moment they woke up and reported back to him in the evening, bowing in front of his portrait.[69]

There was even a loyalty dance, consisting of a few simple moves with outstretched arms from the heart to the Chairman's portrait. The dance was accompanied by the song 'Beloved Chairman Mao'. On state television, entire evenings were devoted to ritual song and dance. A giant bust usually occupied the centre of the stage, producing rays that throbbed and flickered with electricity, as if light and energy poured forth from the godhead.[70]

Busts and statues of Mao sprouted like mushrooms after rain. More than 600,000 of them appeared in Shanghai alone, most made of death-white plaster, others using reinforced concrete, aluminium and tinplate. Some towered above pedestrians at a majestic fifteen metres, others stood at a more modest three metres. Scarce resources were expended in the informal competition, and in 1968 the city used 900 tonnes of tinplate alone. The Steel Institute turned to stainless steel to erect its monument at a cost of 100,000 yuan.[71]

The first phase of the Cultural Revolution came to an end in the summer of 1968 as new, so-called 'revolutionary party committees' took over the party and the state. They were heavily dominated by military officers, concentrating real power in the hands of the army. Over the next three years they turned the country into a garrison state, with soldiers overseeing schools, factories and government units. They also organised a series of purges, as all those who had spoken out at the height of the Cultural Revolution in 1966–7 were punished. At first millions of undesirable elements, including students and others who had taken the Chairman at his word, were banished to the countryside to be 're-educated by the peasants'. This was followed by a nationwide witch-hunt for 'spies', 'traitors' and 'renegades', as special committees were set up to examine the alleged enemy links of ordinary people and party members alike. A campaign against corruption further cowed the population into submission, as almost every act and every utterance – inadvertently tearing a poster of the Chairman, questioning the planned economy – became a potentially criminal act.[72]

Across the country people were forced to prove their devotion to the Chairman, denouncing colleagues, friends, neighbours and family members. In one senseless and unpredictable purge after another entire communities were ripped apart, producing docile, atomised individuals loyal to no one but the Chairman. And everywhere recalcitrant elements were forced to undergo re-education, whether study classes in Mao Zedong Thought for ordinary people or May Seventh Cadre Schools for party members.

In April 1969 the Ninth Party Congress passed a new constitution, establishing that 'Marxism-Leninism Mao Zedong Thought' was to be the theoretical basis of the party. Mao Zedong Thought was reaffirmed as the country's guiding ideology. At long last the Chairman was able to reverse the decisions made by the Eighth Party Congress in September 1956. By now Liu Shaoqi had been expelled from the party and denounced, along with dozens of other elderly party leaders, as a 'renegade, traitor and scab hiding in the party and a running dog of imperialism, modern revisionism and the nationalist reactionaries who has committed innumerable crimes'. He died in solitary detention six months later, covered in bedsores, his hair long and unkempt. A new Central Committee was elected in which less than one in five members were carryovers from 1956.[73]

Mao, however, was wary of the military, in particular Lin Biao, who had pioneered the study of Mao Zedong Thought in the army. Mao had used Lin Biao to launch and sustain the Cultural Revolution, but the marshal in turn exploited the turmoil to expand his own power base, placing his followers in key positions throughout the army. He died in a mysterious plane crash in September 1971, bringing to an end the grip of the military on civilian life, as the army was in turn purged, falling victim to the Cultural Revolution.

Mao's cult, closely associated with Lin Biao and the People's Liberation Army, was scaled back almost overnight. China moved even further away from the Soviet Union, turning instead towards the United States in 1972. Cities were spruced up for Nixon's visit, with posters removed and anti-imperialist slogans toned down. Shanghai underwent a facelift. It took a small army of women to scrub out a huge slogan opposite the Peace Hotel proclaiming 'Long Live the Invincible Thoughts of Chairman Mao'. New slogans appeared, welcoming the 'Great Unity of the Peoples of the World'. All signs of the Chairman were removed from window displays. Thousands of statues were dismantled, discreetly sent off for recycling.[74]

The Chairman, too, was primped and preened. His meeting with Nixon was a huge propaganda coup. The news sent shock waves around the world, as the balance of the Cold War shifted away from the Soviet Union. In Beijing, Mao gloated that the United States was 'changing from monkey to man, not quite a man yet, the tail is still there'. He had reduced Nixon, the leader of the most powerful nation on earth, to a mere emissary seeking an imperial audience. Leaders of countries from Europe, Latin

America, Africa and Asia soon flocked to Beijing, all seeking recognition.[75]

During his final years in court the Chairman continued to play one faction against the other. When Zhou Enlai was diagnosed with cancer Mao refused to approve his treatment, allowing him to die in early 1976. His own death came a few minutes past midnight on 9 September 1976. In schools, factories and offices people were assembled to listen to the official announcement. Those who felt relief had to hide their feelings. This was the case with Chang Jung, a student from Sichuan who for a moment was numbed with sheer euphoria. All around her people wept. She had to display the correct emotion or risk being singled out, and buried her head in the shoulder of the woman in front of her, heaving and snivelling.[76]

She was hardly alone in putting on a performance. Traditionally, in China, weeping for dead relatives and even throwing oneself on the ground in front of the coffin was a required demonstration of filial piety. Absence of tears was a disgrace to the family. Sometimes actors were hired to wail loudly at the funerals of important dignitaries, thus encouraging other mourners to join in without feeling embarrassed. And much as people had mastered the art of effortlessly producing proletarian anger at denunciation meetings, many knew how to cry on demand.

People showed less contrition in private. In Kunming, the provincial capital of Yunnan, liquor sold out overnight. One young woman remembers how her father invited his best friend to their home, locked the door and opened the only bottle of wine they had. The following day they went to a public memorial service where people cried as if they were heartbroken. 'As a little girl, I was confused by the adults' expressions – everybody looked so sad in public, while my father was so happy the night before.'[77]

Some people felt genuine grief, especially those who had benefited from the Cultural Revolution. And plenty of true believers remained, especially among young people. Ai Xiaoming, a twenty-two-year-old girl eager to enter the party and contribute to socialism, was so heartbroken that she wept almost to the point of fainting.[78]

In the countryside, however, apparently few people sobbed. As one poor villager in Anhui recalled, 'not a single person wept at the time'.[79]

Mao entered a mausoleum, like Stalin. Unlike Stalin, he remained there. His portrait still hangs high in Beijing, while his face beams from every banknote in the People's Republic. Mao used the cult to turn others into adulators who enforced his every whim. He made party leaders accomplices to his crimes. And by becoming complicit they and their successors turned themselves into the custodians of his image, determined not to repeat the mistake Khrushchev had made in his secret speech.

5

Kim Il-sung

On 14 October 1945 a mass rally was held in a sports field in Pyongyang to welcome the Red Army. Half a year earlier, when Stalin had met Roosevelt at Yalta, the Allied powers had negotiated the fate of Korea, a Japanese colony since 1910. They had agreed to jointly occupy the peninsula, deciding at the last minute to divide the country along the 38th parallel. Pyongyang became the provisional capital of north Korea under Soviet control.

Flanked by Soviet officers, Kim Il-sung made his first public speech on that day. There was a stir in the audience when he was introduced by General Lebedev, as people associated his name with a legendary guerrilla fighter, a great patriot who had roamed at will over Manchuria ten years earlier, harassing the Japanese enemy. But Kim did not look the part. He was only thirty-three years old and seemed inexperienced, nervously clutching his script. In the words of one witness he looked 'like a delivery boy from a Chinese eatery', with a close-cropped haircut and a blue suit that was too small for his pudgy frame. He stumbled through a speech peppered with Marxist jargon in a monotonous voice, heaping extravagant praise on Stalin. A rumour swept through the crowd, accusing him of being a fake, a stooge imposed by the Soviet Union. It was an inauspicious beginning for the man who would rise to dominate North Korea.[1]

Kim was born a Christian, his father educated by missionaries. In 1919, when Kim was just seven years old, the family followed hundreds of thousands of other Koreans across the border into Manchuria to escape colonial oppression. In 1931 Japan caught up with them, turning Manchuria into a puppet state. Kim, by now nineteen, joined the Chinese Communist Party. But Korean partisans were suspected of spying on behalf of the Japanese, and more than a thousand of them were interrogated and tortured in a series of brutal purges. Hundreds were killed. Kim, too, was arrested, although he was exonerated in 1934.[2]

By then Kim was one of the few communist Koreans left. He soon commanded several hundred guerrilla fighters, carrying out raids in Manchuria and across the border in Korea. In June 1937 he and his men attacked a police garrison in a small village called Pochonbo, a mere forty kilometres from Mount Paektu, a sacred mountain believed to be the birthplace of the founder of the first kingdom. It was a strategically insignificant operation, but one which attracted widespread press coverage since it was the first time the communists were able to mount an attack inside Korea. The Japanese placed Kim on a list of most-wanted bandits, turning him into a household name among the many millions who hated their colonial masters.[3]

By 1940 Kim was the most wanted rebel in Manchuria, forced to cross into the Soviet Union. There he and his followers were sheltered, trained and indoctrinated by the Red Army. In 1942 he was promoted to captain, but three years later he was denied the chance to enhance his reputation further by marching victoriously into Pyongyang. A suspicious Stalin gave this role to the more trustworthy 'Soviet Koreans', a group with longstanding ties to Moscow. Kim and sixty of his partisan fighters instead found their own way into north Korea, disembarking in the port city of Wonsan a month after Japan had surrendered. It was an ignominious return for Kim, not as liberator of his country, but as a lowly captain in a foreign uniform. He insisted that his journey back home be kept secret.[4]

In Pyongyang he spent time mingling with Soviet officers, plying them with food and women, using his connections to place his followers in key positions across the public security organs. The

Russians needed a figurehead for their provisional government, but they picked Cho Man-sik instead. Known as the 'Gandhi of Korea', Cho was a Christian nationalist who for decades had promoted a non-violent path to independence. He was highly respected, but it soon became clear that he would only collaborate with the Soviets on his own terms. When he refused a trusteeship of five years under the control of the Soviet Union, it was the last straw. Cho was placed under house arrest in January 1946. Kim came to the fore instead, as Stalin ticked his name on a shortlist of potential candidates. The only other contender was Pak Hon-yong, an independence activist who had set up the Korean Communist Party in the south after liberation.[5]

Kim had made a poor impression in October 1945, but the Soviets helped him prop up his image. Pyongyang was festooned with portraits of Kim hanging alongside those of Stalin. His youth was praised, his mythical past was extolled. Kim worked on his smile, appearing kind and cheerful. He became modesty itself, telling people, 'I am not a general, but your friend.' One interviewer reported being struck by 'the light of genius' glittering in his eyes. A key moment came in August 1946, as Kim was acclaimed as 'the great leader', 'hero of the nation' and 'leader of all the Korean people' at the founding congress of the North Korean Workers' Party. The novelist Han Sorya, who would soon become the chief engineer of Kim's cult of personality, referred to him as 'our sun', unlike the Japanese sun towards which the colonial subjects had been forced to bow in the past.[6]

The moment Kim was approved by Moscow, the Soviet model was imposed at all levels of society. Industry was nationalised, drastic land reform implemented. Kim was at the centre of it all, criss-crossing the country to dispense advice to his subjects, from how to cultivate steep land to ways of increasing living standards. It was he who created a bumper harvest in 1946, and it was he who controlled the winter floods later that year. Rallies were held in the countryside, with villagers expressing their gratitude to General Kim through songs, speeches and letters. In the meantime, an estimated one million people, roughly 7 to 8 per cent of the population, voted with their feet, joining an exodus of wealth and talent to south Korea.[7]

His revolutionary credentials were eulogised. A short biography translated from the *Komsomolskaya Pravda* in 1946 harped on about the supernatural powers that ordinary villagers attributed to the guerrilla fighter who for so many years had eluded capture by the Japanese: he could fly through the air, tunnel his way through mountains. His parents were introduced to the population by Gitovich and Bursov, two Russians who interviewed Kim and his partisan fighters. His father was a devoted teacher and professional revolutionary who had been imprisoned twice, his mother a crafty accomplice who provided her son with weapons hidden around the house. But it was a Korean writer named Han Chae-tok who first hailed the 'triumphal return' of Kim to the motherland, portraying him as an 'all-Korean hero' who had stood at the forefront of the liberation movement from the age of seventeen onwards. His account appeared in book form in 1948.[8]

The raid in Pochonbo was elevated to legendary status, most of all in an epic published by Cho Gi-cheon, a poet sometimes referred to as 'Korea's Mayakovsky'. *Mount Paektu*, published in 1947, depicted the region as a mystical area abounding in fantastical tales, with stories of sleeping warriors waiting to rise and free their land and revolutionary leaders jumping from one mountain to the next.[9]

By 1948 an iron curtain was coming down, dividing the world into two camps. In Korea two very different governments had emerged on either side of the 38th parallel. Peaceful reunification looked increasingly unlikely. In the south Syngman Rhee, an opponent of communism, won the first presidential elections in May with the backing of the United States. A few months later, on 15 August 1948, exactly three years after the country's liberation from Japan, the Republic of Korea was declared in Seoul. In the north, Kim Il-sung proclaimed the Democratic Republic of North Korea on 9 September.

From general he became premier, reigning supreme. Another title that appeared after the establishment of the Democratic

Republic was *surong*, the equivalent of the term *vozhd* used for Stalin. His photograph now appeared as a frontispiece in books and journals. His speeches, which were numerous, were printed in the newspapers. On May Day tens of thousands of people assembled to praise Stalin and Kim. As the propaganda machine never tired of intoning, the people were united behind their leader.[10]

North Korea was a heavily militarised country, but as conflict with the south became increasingly likely, a Korean People's Army was established in February 1948, equipped and advised by Moscow. The Soviet troops withdrew by the end of the year. Two hundred tanks were delivered, together with lorries, artillery and light weapons.

As in all one-party states the army belonged to the party, not to the people. Its supreme commander was Kim Il-sung, and he was bent on extending the revolution, liberating the south from Syngman Rhee and his 'US reactionary faction' to unite the country. He approached Stalin in March 1949, but his master demurred. Kim had to watch in frustration as Mao took over China, bringing a quarter of humanity into the socialist camp while his own country remained partitioned.

Kim repeatedly badgered Stalin, who was in no hurry for an open conflict involving the United States. But by the end of 1949 he had begun to waver. The Americans had not intervened in the civil war in China and had all but abandoned Chiang Kai-shek in Taiwan. In January 1950, after the United States indicated that Korea no longer fell within their defence perimeter in the Pacific, Stalin gave the green light. But he refused to commit any troops: 'If you should get kicked in the teeth, I shall not lift a finger. You have to ask Mao for all the help.' Mao agreed, needing Stalin in turn to acquire the sea and air power necessary to invade Taiwan.[11]

On 25 June 1950 a comprehensive air and land invasion was launched from the north. The south was ill prepared, with fewer than 100,000 soldiers, as the Americans had deliberately denied Syngman Rhee armour, anti-tank weapons and artillery heavier than 105mm. His troops crumbled within weeks. For a brief moment, Kim Il-sung looked like a military genius. His portrait went up everywhere in the liberated areas.[12]

Kim, however, had miscalculated on a staggering scale. He and his advisers had initally counted on popular support, but most people in the south remained neutral. There were no cheering crowds waving red flags. The United States did not turn a blind eye, fearful of a larger conflict with the Soviet Union. Instead they rallied the United Nations, proclaiming that peace had been broken, and sent troops in support of South Korea. They turned the tide in August 1950. Two months later General Douglas MacArthur reached the 38th parallel. He could have stopped there, but decided instead to push all the way to the border with China, ignoring the most basic security concerns of the People's Republic.

It was a disaster for Kim. In October Mao came to the rescue, sending hundreds of thousands of troops across the border under the cover of night. They took the enemy by complete surprise. But after gaining a series of rapid victories, they, too, soon exhausted their supply lines. A blood-soaked stalemate emerged around the 38th parallel in the summer of 1951.

Kim had to find a scapegoat for the rout, and moved against the Number Two inside the party, a Korean born and raised in the Soviet Union named Ho Kai. Ho was an accomplished administrator who had built up the party machine from scratch. He had also become Kim's closest ally, acting as patron and guardian. This alone would have been reason enough to get rid of him, but Ho was also Moscow's man in Pyongyang. Now that the Chinese presence balanced that of the Soviets, Kim felt free to strike. First, he asked Ho to purge the party, then he turned around and accused him of having gone too far. Ho was humiliated in the presence of other leaders, stripped of his positions and expelled from the party. Kim reinstated hundreds of thousands of members who had been expelled. Many were barely literate villagers, and all of them embraced Kim as their saviour.[13]

War demanded unity and obedience to the leader whose cult was shored up in 1952, even as the bombing became more intense. On Kim's fortieth birthday, celebrated on 15 April, a short biography was published that became required reading for all and sundry. Study sites appeared across the country, as people in factories and schools marked Kim's birthday by 'enthusiastically indoctrinating themselves' with his thoughts. Memorial halls in his honour were established at Pochonbo and Mangyongdae, his birthplace on a hill just outside Pyongyang.[14]

Boundless enthusiasm from the masses went hand in hand with the ritual abasement of potential rivals. Three of the most prominent party leaders published paeans to Kim Il-sung, acclaiming him as a Great Leader on a par with Lenin and Stalin. The least effusive praise came from Pak Hon-yong, the founder of the Korean Communist Party in Seoul who had moved to North Korea in 1948 to become minister of foreign affairs.[15]

A ceasefire was finally proclaimed in July 1953, a few months after Stalin died. Stalin had prolonged the war by two years, pleased at the losses sustained by the imperialist camp. Kim had been merely a pawn in his great game of geopolitical chess.

The border remained the same, but up to three million people had lost their lives in one of the most vicious and deadly wars of modern times. Much of the peninsula was reduced to rubble, with little left standing in the north.

Kim proclaimed victory. From the beginning, the propaganda machine had presented the Fatherland Liberation War as a just war of defence, one in which the United States was the invader. The imperialist scheme to colonise the entire peninsula had been successfully foiled thanks to the brilliant foresight of the Great Leader. It was a great lie, but one made credible by endless indoctrination and complete isolation from the outside world. Over a decade, the one-party state extended control over what people could read, what they could say, where they could live and where they could travel. Security agents began keeping everyone under constant surveillance, sending dissenters to labour camps scattered across the remote, inhospitable mountains in the north.[16]

North Korea not only became a hermit kingdom, but also a society with a permanent siege mentality, living under the constant threat of invasion by hostile forces everywhere. It was a message endlessly repeated by the propaganda machine, but one widely shared by ordinary people who had endured years of devastation at the hands of the enemy.

North Korea was a society traumatised by war. The propaganda presented the Great Leader as a fatherly figure around whom his shell-shocked people could gather, looking for direction in their lives. Still, rivals inside the party were emboldened by the failed war. Kim was wary of Pak Hon-yong, the minister of foreign affairs who had been tepid in his praise a year earlier. Pak retained a large personal following among members who had worked in the underground resistance in Korea before 1945. Kim had them placed under arrest in March 1953. Always an eager student of Stalin, Kim orchestrated a show trial, as twelve of the accused obediently confessed to the most outlandish crimes in front of the international press. They were found guilty and sentenced to death. It was a great diversion from the destruction of war.[17]

Kim also followed Stalin in rebuilding his country. North Korea became the beneficiary of large amounts of aid from the socialist camp, all of which was spent on rapid industrialisation and the collectivisation of the countryside. But Kim, as always, was in a hurry, and by 1955 there was evidence of a widespread famine, with children frequently seen begging barefoot in the snow. Entire villages in the north huddled together, trying to hibernate through the winter months. Again, the Soviet Union and China stepped in, sending 200,000 tonnes of grain in emergency aid.[18]

Even as North Korea depended on the Soviet Union, portraits of Marx, Lenin and Stalin came down. There were none on display in the parade organised to celebrate National Day on 15 August 1954. On the other hand, complained the Russian ambassador, 'In every railway station, in every ministry, in every hotel there are images larger than life of Kim Il-sung.' His wisdom was celebrated in songs and poems. His slogans were plastered in bold script, hanging from banners in schools, factories and offices. Films celebrated not only the sites he had visited, but even a rock on which he had rested.[19]

Kim was ubiquitous. He was a restless, energetic leader, who concerned himself with every detail. There were inspections of schools, tours of cooperatives, visits to factories, even impromptu appearances at local meetings that he would chair, all of them reported in minute detail with numerous photographs in the newspapers. The expression 'on-the-spot guidance' began to emerge, as Kim dispensed advice on beekeeping, orchard maintenance, irrigation techniques, steel production and construction work. By one estimate he made more than 1,300 trips between 1954 and 1961. His teachings were published and closely studied across the nation. The Sinuiju Pulp Factory held daily meetings on the Great Leader's teaching after a visit in early 1956.[20]

He showed himself to countless workers and villagers, turning himself into a living legend. He was a listener, always concerned with the welfare of his people, questioning them closely about their lives, taking notes as he visited their homes and met their families. He bestowed benefits. Workers wrote to thank him for his leadership. He, in turn, wrote to congratulate them on their achievements.[21]

Beneath the gleaming surface of propaganda, however, fear accompanied the cult, as the slightest sign of disrespect towards the Great Leader was harshly punished. One victim was sentenced to five years for wrapping a book in a newspaper containing a photograph of Kim Il-sung. Another went to a labour camp for five years for touching up a poorly executed poster. A villager who complained about grain requisitions by pointing a finger at a portrait of the leader, shouting, 'You are tormenting the people in vain' was packed off for seven years. There were thousands of victims sentenced for similar crimes.[22]

The more visible the leader became, the more his peers were forced to dwell in his shadow. Constant adulation deflected potential criticism from his rivals inside the party. But in 1956, the moment Khrushchev denounced the cult of personality, they saw an opportunity to bring Kim down by a notch or two. Yi Sang-jo, North Korea's ambassador in Moscow, complained to officials in the Ministry of Foreign Affairs that his leader had surrounded himself with sycophants, accumulating ever more power while the official press extolled him as a genius who had led the revolutionary struggle from the age of twelve onwards. Kim, on a visit to Moscow a month later, was reprimanded by Khrushchev and asked to reform. He humbly accepted his recommendations.[23]

Emboldened, his critics at home confronted Kim at a meeting of the Central Committee in August 1956. They savaged his economic record, mocked the incompetence of his underlings and accused him of concentrating too much power in his own hands. Above all they criticised the cult of personality, invoking the Twentieth Congress to advocate reform. But over the years Kim had packed the Central Committee with young, loyal followers. They heckled his opponents, yelling and whistling as they delivered their speeches, then voted down their proposals.

Kim turned the showdown to his advantage. He denounced his rivals as 'factionalists', dismissing them from their posts or expelling them from the party. Many of them had been born in the Soviet Union or in China. Fearing for their lives, several fled the country, seeking refuge in their countries of birth. Their persecution rattled Moscow and Beijing, who realised that their influence in Pyongyang was on the wane. They sent a joint delegation to Korea to increase the pressure. Kim, again, humbly accepted their advice, convening another meeting of the Central Committee in September. He rehabilitated his rivals and made token gestures towards de-Stalinisation.

Kim was saved by the uprising in Budapest a month later in October 1956. As Soviet tanks extinguished Hungary's bid for freedom, reform in the socialist camp came to a halt. Kim felt vindicated and eliminated every one of his critics over the following two years. The families of those who had fled abroad vanished, probably executed.[24]

In October 1957, as leaders of the socialist camp met to celebrate the fortieth anniversary of the October Revolution, Mao took Kim aside to express his personal regret over the joint delegation. Both leaders were opposed to de-Stalinisation. Never one to miss a good opportunity, Kim asked Mao to withdraw his troops. Some 400,000 Chinese soldiers had stayed behind in North Korea after the end of the war, and they appeared as an occupation force amidst a population of ten million. They left in October 1958. Kim, at long last, was master of his country, having outmanoeuvred his two most powerful backers, the Soviet Union and the People's Republic.

In a nationwide witch-hunt reminiscent of the purge that followed the Hundred Flowers in China, tens of thousands of 'factionalists' and 'conspirators' of every hue were hauled before public denunciation meetings, accused, humiliated and sometimes beaten, occasionally executed in public. In the Academy of Science a suspect was denounced by his colleagues for twelve days for insisting, after the Twentieth Congress in Moscow, that the phrase 'Our beloved leader Kim Il-sung' be dropped from official publications. Countless others ended up in prison or labour camps.[25]

In 1957 the entire population was divided into three distinct groups according to their degree of loyalty towards the party. The system was called *songbun*, from the term *chengfen* used in the People's Republic of China where it had been devised in 1950. Below the 'core class' and the 'wavering class' was a 'hostile class' of people encompassing some 20 per cent of the entire population. Their class status determined everything, from the amount of food a family was allowed to claim to access to education and employment. In North Korea, as in China, the label was passed on from parents to their children. People whose only crime was to have a relative who had moved to South Korea were deported from cities to the countryside. Loyalty to the party soon enough became loyalty to the Great Leader.[26]

The Chairman had his Great Leap Forward, the Great Leader his Thousand Mile Horse. The Chollima Campaign, named after a mythical winged horse that could gallop a thousand miles in a day, was launched in the summer of 1958. It was designed to propel North Korea into the future, but without economic assistance from the Soviet Union or the People's Republic. Ideological incentives rather than material rewards, Kim believed, would motivate his people to work harder and achieve economic self-sufficiency. 'Rush at the speed of the chollima' was his slogan, as North Korea would catch up and outstrip Japan in industrial output within less than two years. As in the Soviet Union and China, workers who failed to comply were denounced as 'saboteurs'. With the Chollima Campaign came a new wave of repression, as some 100,000 people were exposed as 'hostile and reactionary elements' between October 1958 and May 1959 alone.[27]

As Kim's rivals vanished, the past was rewritten. Already in March 1955 the propaganda machine had begun airbrushing the Soviet Union and the People's Republic of China out of history, focusing instead on the contribution of the 'revolutionary masses' to the liberation of the country. In 1956 a revolutionary museum had opened its doors in Pyongyang. It had one section only, namely 5,000 square metres devoted to Kim Il-sung's anti-Japanese activities. By 1960 the museum had more than doubled in size, but across its many rooms only a couple of display cases were devoted to the Soviet Union. Twelve large statues of Kim, now heralded as the 'National Emancipator', greeted visitors during their visit.[28]

A year later the Fourth Party Congress in September 1961 marked a watershed for Kim Il-sung. He had successfully eliminated all opposition and entrenched his followers across the party. A few months earlier he had exploited the Sino-Soviet rift to court both the Soviet Union and China, signing two back-to-back treaties that provided enhanced protection against South Korea and the United States. Kim's struggle to consolidate his power seemed complete.[29]

For several years Kim rarely appeared in public, delegating most tasks to his underlings. But his presence was ubiquitous. His quotations were in every newspaper. Every publication in every domain, from civil engineering to molecular biology, came with an obligatory reference to his work. His speeches were anthologised and issued as his Collected Works. His Selected Works appeared in translation. Beneath his benevolent gaze his subjects studied his words in every office and classroom across the country. Marx, Engels and Lenin, on the other hand, were rarely seen or read.[30]

On 9 September 1963 North Korea held a huge parade to celebrate its fifteenth anniversary. Not a single mention was made of the Soviet Union in the opening speeches. The slogan was 'All

Through Our Own Effort', as a huge effigy of Kim Il-sung was carried through the streets of Pyongyang.[31]

Like all good dictators, however, Kim needed to establish himself as the founder of an ideology. His writings were widely studied, but he needed a philosophy, preferably one that added the suffix 'ism' to his name. In December 1955, even as the Soviet Union and China were sending emergency food to North Korea, Kim Il-sung had presented his Juche Thought. The word *juche*, loosely translated, means 'self-reliance'. Buried in jargon was a simple idea: people are the masters of their own destiny, and by becoming self-reliant they can achieve true socialism. Marxism-Leninism, which insisted that material conditions were the primary force of historical change, was turned upside down.[32]

For years Juche Thought was barely mentioned, even though the notion of economic self-sufficiency ran through the Chollima Campaign, while independence and self-reliance had always been among the most prominent slogans in North Korea. But in April 1965, as the Sino-Soviet rift was in full swing, Kim travelled to Indonesia on the occasion of the tenth anniversary of the Bandung Conference of African and Asian countries. It was Kim's first trip outside the socialist camp, and he used it to stake his claim as leader of the non-aligned countries of the Third World. In Jakarta he talked at length about the basic principles of Juche. He advocated a barely disguised position of independence from the Soviet Union and the People's Republic of China in the anti-imperialist struggle.[33]

At home Juche Thought served a very different purpose. In October 1966, after fifteen years of breakneck development in heavy industry, even some of Kim's own followers began asking for an improvement in the living standards of ordinary people. The country was again on the verge of starvation. The capital Pyongyang had not seen cooking oil or meat for months.[34]

Kim viewed these demands as a threat and demanded that Juche Thought become enshrined as the official ideology of North Korea. He wanted nothing less than a monolithic ideological system, the 'unity of ideology and will', in order to lead the revolution. He required unconditional obedience from every member in the party. In 1967 his critics were purged.[35]

As Kim's word became absolute the epithets used to describe him became ever more extravagant. He was hailed as the 'genius leader of a 40-million nation' and 'the outstanding leader of the international communist and workers movement'. He was the one who had liberated the fatherland from the yoke of colonial rule in August 1945, and he was the one who had inflicted a 'hundred and a thousand-fold retaliation' on the American imperialists, forcing them to their knees during the Korean War. He was the red beacon for the oppressed in Africa, Latin America and Asia. 'Kim Il-sung is the Red Sun', wrote a Nigerian poet in the *Pyongyang Times*.[36]

His cult extended to his family. A theatre troupe from the Ministry of Security performed a widely disseminated play about the 'heroic deeds' of his mother, described as 'the mother of Kim Il-sung and our mother'. His father was canonised as a saint of the revolution, while the revolutionary family circle extended to his grandfather, grandmother and one of his great-grandfathers.[37]

In 1967 May Day, celebrated for the first time in four years, was held under the banner of Juche Thought. There were no foreign flags. The pennants came in yellow, green and blue, the colours of the national flag, but not a single one in red. 'All Through Our Own Efforts' or 'Unity through Self-Reliance', proclaimed the banners in the parade, which was opened by several giant winged horses followed by endless portraits and effigies of the Great Leader. The event ended with the participants ceremoniously singing a Kim Il-sung song, then chanting his name for several minutes.[38]

There was no Cultural Revolution. Like other dictators, Kim Il-sung was baffled by the chaos it engendered in China. But with the elevation of Juche Thought came an attack on everything that smacked of bourgeois culture. Some 300,000 people with a family member considered 'politically unreliable' were removed from the capital Pyongyang. Love songs and love stories were banned. Popular theatre, with singers and musicians recounting folk tales, became taboo. Classical music, including Beethoven, was proscribed. Even *How the Steel Was Tempered*, a socialist-realist novel published in 1936 by Nikolai Ostrovsky, fell victim to the censors. A more sweeping approach followed in May 1968, as all foreign books were confiscated, while studying the original works of Marx and Engels was considered 'undesirable'. In meeting places, lecture halls and dedicated study rooms, sometimes described as 'cult rooms' by foreigners, captive audiences studied the works of Kim Il-sung, committing his work to memory to betoken their burning loyalty.[39]

Tension was ratcheted up, a martial atmosphere fostered. The parade in May 1967 was also a display of military prowess, with long formations of anti-tank guns, anti-aircraft artillery and grenade launchers rumbling through the capital. 'Let Us Free South Korea!' and 'Let Us Arm the Entire People' were slogans that set the tone. In an atmosphere of impending war, air-raid drills were held regularly in cities and villages, compelling even the sick and elderly to march for kilometres to seek shelter in underground tunnels.[40]

There is nothing like the threat of war to focus attention on the leader, as people close ranks and rally together, but the heightened tension was also the result of changes in the party membership that took place in 1962. With all his opponents purged, Kim promoted his own young generals to key positions. It was to some extent a reaction to a successful military coup in South Korea in May 1961. It was also part of a renewed desire to reunify the peninsula through military conquest. For several years his generals strengthened the military and armed the people, turning the country into an 'impregnable fortress'.

But in January 1968 they went too far. First, they sent a guerrilla unit to Seoul on a mission to assassinate the South Korean president Park Chung-hee. They failed, with several of the commandos killed on the spot. Then, on a whim, a few days later they seized an American intelligence vessel named the *Pueblo*. Its crew of eighty-three were abused and imprisoned for eleven months, bringing the country to the brink of war.[41]

In public Kim congratulated the officers responsible for the capture of the *Pueblo*, but after the crisis was solved through lengthy negotiations he quietly removed twelve of the highest ranking generals from his own partisan group. No dictator feels

secure with a powerful military group in command, even when
they have been loyal all their lives. It marked the end of the militant
policy of the 1960s.

In 1969 young followers devoted to economic development were
promoted instead. Kim's family members began filling some of the
most senior positions, now vacant. His younger brother advanced
to the fourth-ranking post. His wife took over as chair of the
Democratic Women's Union of Korea. When in May 1972 the East
Germans and Soviets compiled a list of Kim family members in
positions of power, they counted a dozen.[42]

On 15 April 1972 Kim turned sixty. Preparations for the event had
begun months earlier. In October 1971 the propaganda machine
announced that across the country monuments were to be built
in honour of the Great Leader. Shrines appeared to memorialise
revolutionary battlefields, and poems were inscribed in stone
to mark the ground he had stood on. New roads, bridges and
embankments were built. As a sign of gratitude for his on-the-
spot guidance, monuments were unveiled in every province and
every major city, factory, mine and agricultural cooperative. No
one wanted to lag, as people volunteered to work around the clock,
often by artificial light during the night. Their personal sacrifice
was a demonstration of genuine love for the Great Leader, a gift to
the one who had bestowed so much on his people.[43]

Kim's place of birth at Mangyongdae, already visited by
1.3 million students and workers on annual pilgrimages, was rebuilt
with markers commemorating historic moments in his life: the
place where he sat with his father, his sledding hill, his wrestling
grounds, his favourite fishing spot, his swing, even a tree under
which he had sat. On display were the wooden ploughs and rakes
used by his family, as well as the yellow bowl from which he had
eaten his rice. Further north in Pochonbo and Musan, two historic
sites where the Great Leader had fought the Japanese, twenty-three
historical monuments were erected.[44]

The scale of the public works was pharaonic. Vast resources
were diverted towards the anniversary projects, which required so

much cement that despite contractual obligations all deliveries to the Soviet Union were halted. Miners were enrolled to meet the deadline, plunging entire towns into darkness as the coal needed to fire power plants ran out.[45]

Pyongyang was transformed. The capital had been reduced to rubble during the Korean War, but urban planners used the opportunity to turn the city into a monument to the Great Leader. Over the years large boulevards lined with trees had appeared, interspersed with parks, fountains and flower beds. Work on a new Kim Il-sung Square had started in 1954 and was completed in time for the sixtieth birthday celebrations. On this vast space paved in granite stood a bronze statue of Kim Il-sung.

The most imposing tribute, however, appeared on the high hill of Mansudae, overlooking the city. Here the revolutionary museum that had boasted a mere 5,000 square metres some fifteen years earlier had been completely revamped, turned into a colossal monument covering an imposing 50,000 square metres with more than ninety exhibition rooms. In front of the museum stood a statue of the Great Leader, one hand on his hip, the other outstretched with open fingers, as if presenting the future. Towering twenty metres high, it was the largest statue ever built in the country, floodlit at night and visible for many kilometres outside the city.[46]

Weeks before the event a campaign entitled 'Loyalty Gifts' was inaugurated. It was an opportunity for everyone to demonstrate their love of the leader by voluntarily reaching even higher production quotas than usual. Real gifts also arrived in the capital ahead of the birthday, with ships sent by Koreans living in Japan. They were loaded with hundreds of imported vehicles, including Mercedes-Benz cars, together with lorries, bulldozers and excavators, also colour television sets, jewellery, silk and other luxuries.[47]

On 15 August the museum was inaugurated with great pomp, as some 300,000 visitors shuffled through its many rooms in respectful silence. Seven sections allowed them to follow the story of the Great Leader, from his struggle against the Japanese to his exploits in the international arena. Thousands of items were on display: Kim's gloves, shoes, belts, caps, sweaters and pens, maps and pamphlets, dioramas of famous battles, scale models of famous meetings, paintings of famous scenes. Statues stood everywhere, each one approved by Kim Il-sung himself.[48]

Badges were introduced. They had appeared two years earlier, but were now widely distributed. A first batch of 20,000 arrived from China in time for the celebrations, showing a stern-looking Great Leader against a red background. A more benevolent smile would only appear much later. At first they were known as 'party badges', displayed by high-ranking officials, but before long every subject was required to wear one, always on their left breast pocket.[49]

Six months later, in December 1972, a new constitution was passed. It enshrined Juche, in effect substituting the Great Leader's thought for Marxism-Leninism. A new position was also created. Besides chairman of the party, Kim was crowned president of the republic. As president he was simultaneously head of state and commander of the armed forces, with the power to issue edicts, grant pardons and conclude or abrogate treaties. The constitution not only ensconced Kim Il-sung at all levels of government, but also marked a subtle shift of power away from the party towards the state.[50]

North Korea had been a hermetically sealed country, with few visible foreigners besides embassy members from the socialist camp, all of them under surveillance. But Kim's sixtieth birthday was also a coming-out party, with delegations from thirty countries attending the ceremonies.[51]

For the first time an American correspondent was invited to visit North Korea. He had been carefully selected, having reported for many years from the Soviet Union and Albania. The morning after he landed, Harrison Salisbury was driven around Pyongyang in a brand-new Mercedes-Benz. He was taken to model schools, factories and farms. Everything impressed him, from the happy villagers working in the fields to the proud children in kindergartens who sang to the glory of the Great Leader: 'We Have Nothing to Envy in the Whole World'.[52]

Salisbury met the fatherly marshal, who welcomed him with outstretched hands. Like Stalin and Mao, he walked slowly, projecting a stately aura. And, like them, he knew how to smile and put his guests at ease, laughing and even chuckling at times, occasionally turning towards his colleagues for support in his statements. Salisbury concluded that Kim Il-sung was a 'monumentally astute and visionary statesman'.

The camera took photographs of the carefully choreographed meeting between Salisbury and Kim, although in the newspapers next day the interpreter who sat between them vanished, excised from the record. A week later another American journalist arrived, followed in turn by more visitors, as North Korea prudently opened its doors.[53]

In Jakarta in 1965 Kim had presented himself as an advocate for non-aligned nations, courting the Third World while the Soviet Union and the People's Republic were at loggerheads. After some 250,000 troops led by the Soviet Union invaded Czechoslovakia in the summer of 1968 to suppress the country's campaign for democratic reform, North Korea refused to attend the International Meeting of Communist and Workers' Parties in Moscow. Kim Il-sung invoked Juche Thought openly to confront Moscow, proclaiming that national revolution took precedence over international revolution. Newspaper articles, pamphlets and potted biographies of the Great Leader were published abroad, with full-page advertisements in leading newspapers in Sweden, Britain and the United States. The bulk of the propaganda effort was to present Kim Il-sung as a genius, a leader of international stature who had creatively developed Marxism-Leninism into a body of work that was an inspiration for revolutionary peoples around the world.[54]

Over the following years North Korea explored every opportunity to establish relationships with countries that had expressed reservations about the Soviet Union, from Yugoslavia in September 1971 to the Republic of Seychelles in August 1976. China's isolation during the Cultural Revolution was also exploited, as tens of thousands of people regularly lined the streets to welcome foreign dignitaries to Pyongyang. Kim himself went abroad, taking to international travel with the same energy with which he had toured his own country. In 1975 he undertook two major trips, granting liberal interviews to foreign correspondents in a dozen countries. He was trying to win friends abroad.[55]

Much of this charm offensive had to do with the United Nations, which finally admitted North Korea in 1975. But throughout the 1970s Kim continued to project himself as a leader of the Third World. North Korea financed more than 200 organisations in some fifty countries to study Juche Thought. An International Forum on Juche was held in Tokyo in 1974, at long last inaugurating the term Kim Il-sungism. The biggest event came in September 1977, when representatives from seventy-three countries were invited to Pyongyang to attend a series of seminars on Kim Il-sungism chaired by the Great Leader himself. The participants listened respectfully, not one of them raising a single question.[56]

By 1978 Kim Il-sung realised that his efforts to promote Juche Thought abroad had earned him derision rather than respect. The campaign came to a halt. Funding for study centres abroad ceased, interviews with foreign journalists were scaled down. North Korea's brief support of the Third World came to an end.[57]

At home Kim Il-sung was presented as a key player on the world stage, a great and influential statesman with a say in every international issue. In 1978 an International Friendship Exhibition Hall was opened in Myohyangsan, a sacred mountain some two hours north of Pyongyang. Built like a traditional temple, the sprawling complex displayed countless tokens of esteem received over the years by the Great Leader. There were armoured carriages sent by Stalin and Mao, black limousines from former Soviet premier Georgy Malenkov, a crocodile-skin briefcase from Fidel Castro of Cuba, a bear skin from Ceauşescu, an elephant tusk, a coffee maker, ashtrays, vases, lamps, pens, rugs, endless objects in endless rooms, all of them providing tangible proof of the endless respect for Kim Il-sung by leaders around the world. By 1981 roughly 90 per cent of the international news shown on television each evening consisted of reports about foreign seminars, conferences or publications on the Great Leader. The world revered him.[58]

Oaths of absolute loyalty to the leader became common after Kim Il-sung's sixtieth birthday. When he turned sixty-three, radio and television showed workers at the beginning of the day swearing an oath of loyalty and bowing in front of his portrait, a book of his quotations in one hand. They bowed again at the end of their shift. Party members also began swearing loyalty to his son, Kim Jong-il, a chubby young man aged just over thirty, in charge of the party secretariat.[59]

Enlarged photographs of Kim Jong-il, who always assumed the same poses as his father, now began appearing. On 16 February 1976 some 15,000 children and youngsters celebrated Kim Jong-il's thirty-fourth birthday at the Pyongyang stadium. Even more telling, perhaps, was the conspicuous absence of several top leaders from public functions in the following years. A number were purged in December 1977. Kim was removing those suspected of opposing the appointment of his son as heir apparent. In October 1980 Kim Jong-il was elected the fourth highest ranking member in the party.[60]

The son's first task was to demonstrate his loyalty to his father. He coordinated the construction of several monuments to mark the Great Leader's seventieth birthday in April 1982. Right across the river from Kim Il-sung Square a granite megalith was erected, towering 170 metres over the city. The Juche Tower was topped by a forty-five-tonne red flame sculpture that glowed at night. Further to the north of Pyongyang an Arch of Triumph was inaugurated, modelled after the Arc de Triomphe in Paris, each one of its 25,550 granite blocks representing a different day in the life of the one who had liberated the country. The term Kim-Il-sungism, under his guidance, replaced Juche Thought.

The Great Leader gradually withdrew from the scene. There were fewer on-the-spot guidance tours, fewer speeches and only rare interviews. He still travelled, making goodwill visits to the Soviet Union and China to restore amicable relationships. The cult took on a new dimension. In 1958 nineteen trees had been discovered with inscriptions carved by revolutionary fighters during the war of resistance against Japan. But in the middle of the 1980s a further 9,000 slogan trees came to light, all of them fabricated. Every tree was transformed into a shrine, with photos of the inscription on full display: 'Long Live Kim Il Song, President of Independent Korea', 'The Great Man sent by Heaven', 'Kim Il Song is the Leader of a World Revolution'. Party members and military units now undertook pilgrimages to these shrines. Several hundred trees eulogised a baby boy: 'Korea Rejoice! The Great Sun has been Born!' When Kim Jong-il, now known as the Dear Leader, celebrated his birthday in 1990, a mysterious rainbow was observed over the Paektu Mountain, the holy land in the north.[61]

The Great Leader died of a heart attack on 8 July 1994, aged eighty-two. Thirty-four hours later the population appeared in offices, schools and factories to listen to a lengthy obituary delivered by an announcer dressed in black. They all cried, although no one could tell who was sincere and who was not. Medical teams were on hand to help those who fainted. In the following days many of the mourners converged on Kim Il-sung's giant statue on Mansudae Hill. They tried to outdo one another in displays of grief, pounding their heads, collapsing in theatrical swoons, ripping off their clothes, waving their fists at the sky in feigned rage. They were encouraged to do so by endless broadcasts on television of heart-broken comrades: there were images of pilots weeping in the cockpit, sailors banging their heads against the masts of their ships. A ten-day mourning period was declared, with the secret police keeping watch on everyone, trying to measure their sincerity by observing their facial expression and listening to the tone of their voice. One five-year-old spat in her hand to wet her face with saliva, making it look as if she was crying. Under the watchful eye of the Dear Leader the Great Leader's body entered a giant mausoleum. But in life as in death Kim Il-sung retained his title of president. As new monuments known as 'eternal life towers', erected in all major towns, proclaimed, he 'lives forever'.[62]

6

Duvalier

Like the prow of a great stone ship, jutting out from the jungle on a mountain peak, the Citadelle Henri Christophe is the largest fortress in the Americas, designed to house up to 5,000 people. It was built between 1806 and 1820 by a former slave and key leader of the Haitian Rebellion. For years Henri Christophe had fought under Toussaint Louverture, the legendary black figure who transformed a slave rebellion in the French colony into a popular movement for independence. Toussaint Louverture died in 1802, but two years later his large and well-disciplined army succeeded in crushing the colonisers and establishing the world's first black republic. Soon afterwards his lieutenant Jean-Jacques Dessalines was made emperor. His reign did not last, as he was assassinated in 1806.[1]

A power struggle ensued, resulting in the division of the country into two halves. The south was dominated by *gens de couleur*, a term for people of mixed race who had been free before the abolition of slavery. Former slaves went to the north, where Henri Christophe established a kingdom in 1811. In the following years he proclaimed himself Henri I, King of Haiti, and used forced labour to build extravagant palaces and fortresses. Christophe created his own nobility, designing a coat of arms for his dukes, counts and barons. They, in turn, dutifully named his son Jacques-Victor Henri as prince and heir. But Henri I slowly descended into paranoia, seeing plots and conspiracies everywhere. Rather than risk a coup, he shot himself with a silver bullet at the age of fifty-three. His son was slain ten days later.

The north and the south were reunited, but the social divisions remained. The elite were proud of their links with France, and looked down on the majority of the population, poor villagers descended from African slaves. For more than a century self-proclaimed monarchs and emperors from both communities succeeded one another, most of them ruling through political violence. The economy made scant progress, hampered, in large measure, by a crippling indemnity exacted by France in 1825 in exchange for recognising independence. The debt was not paid off until 1947.

The United States occupied the island in 1915 and stayed for two decades, further deepening the racial divide. Among those who reacted against the American occupation was Jean Price-Mars, a respected teacher, diplomat and ethnographer who championed the island's African origins. He viewed Voodoo, a mixture of Roman Catholic rituals and African beliefs that had thrived on slave plantations, as an indigenous religion on a par with Christianity. After the Americans left some of his followers went further, developing a nationalist ideology that advocated overthrowing the elite and handing over control of the state to representatives of the majority population. They called it noirisme, from the French word *noir*, black, and argued that the social differences that had divided Haiti for so long were determined by deep evolutionary laws.

One such follower was François Duvalier. In an article published in 1939 entitled 'A Question of Anthro-Sociology: Racial Determinism', the young author insisted that biology determined psychology, as each racial group had its own 'collective personality'. The true Haitian soul was black, its religion was Voodoo. The noiristes advocated an authoritarian and exclusive state, one which would place power in the hands of an authentic black leader.[2]

As a child François Duvalier was shy and bookish. He had two influential teachers in high school. One was Jean Price-Mars, the influential enthnographer, the other Dumarsais Estimé, an outspoken opponent of the United States. Both inspired him to take pride in his country's African heritage. He tried his hand at journalism, railing against the elite, defending the cause of the poor villagers. He already equated blackness with oppression.[3]

After obtaining a degree in medicine from the University of Haiti in 1934 the twenty-seven-year old served in several local hospitals, occupying his spare time in researching Voodoo and writing about noirisme in the spirit of Price-Mars. He befriended Lorimer Denis, a humourless twenty-four-year-old who wore a hat and carried a cane, assuming the air of a Voodoo priest. Duvalier adopted his style, building a network of contacts with priests (houngans) and priestesses (mambos), seeing the religion as the very heart and soul of the Haitian peasantry. Together with Denis he worked for the Bureau of Ethnology, founded by his teacher Price-Mars in 1941 to counter a brutal campaign against Voodoo orchestrated by the state, as cult objects were destroyed and priests forced to renounce their beliefs.[4]

By the end of the Second World War Duvalier had spent two semesters in the United States studying public health. In 1945 he went back to the countryside to help fight tropical diseases. There he projected himself as a selfless man devoted to the poor peasants, a medical kit strapped to one shoulder, a syringe in one hand. 'He suffers their pain, he mourns their misfortune,' he later wrote about himself in the third person.[5]

In 1946 his former schoolmaster Dumarsais Estimé, a skilful civil servant who had risen through the ranks to become minister of education, was elected president and installed in the National Palace, a large, attractive edifice with a dome reminiscent of the White House built by the Americans in 1920. Duvalier was appointed director general of the National Public Health Service, becoming minister of health and labour three years later. But Estimé soon proved to be too radical for the elite: he expanded black representation in the civil service, introduced income-tax measures and promoted Voodoo as the indigenous religion of the majority population. In May 1950 a military junta under Paul Magloire, a burly military officer in charge of the police in Port-au-Prince, removed him from power. Duvalier lost his job, seething at the dominance of the elite. He learned a bitter lesson, namely never to trust the army.

He went back to practising medicine in the countryside, but soon joined the ranks of the opposition. After the government put a price on his head in 1954 he was forced to take to the hills with one of his most trusted friends, a young man named Clément Barbot. They were sought out by an American publicist, who was led blindfolded to their hiding place. Herbert Morrison found both men disguised as women, with Barbot concealing a machine gun inside the folds of his skirt. It was the beginning of the myth of Duvalier, the resistance fighter flitting from one hideout to another to avoid capture.[6]

In September 1956, after Paul Magloire granted an amnesty for all political opponents, Duvalier came out of hiding. A few months later Magloire lost the support of the army and fled the country with his family, leaving behind an empty treasury. By now there was a growing political desire for a break with the past, sufficiently widespread to pressure the military junta into orchestrating show elections. Antonio Kébreau, chairman of the Military Council, called for nominations to come forward.[7]

Duvalier declared his candidacy, together with a dozen other contenders. Ten months of political chaos followed, with crippling strikes, widespread violence and the fall of five provisional governments. By August 1957 two main candidates remained, François Duvalier and Louis Déjoie, a wealthy sugar planter and industrialist. Throughout the campaign Duvalier invoked the widely respected Dumarsais Estimé, promising to consolidate and enlarge the revolution his erstwhile schoolmaster had launched in 1946. He made promises to the workers and promises to the peasants. He used appeals to national unity and economic reconstruction. But most of all Duvalier adopted a mild-mannered, unassuming persona, radiating a doctor's concern for other people. He and his family were too poor to own a home, as the kind man was devoted to his patients. He worked tirelessly into the night. He was adored by his people. 'The peasants love their doctor, and I am their Papa Doc,' he gently pointed out. He came across as an inoffensive man.[8]

The quiet doctor seemed easy to control. After he agreed to appoint Kébreau as the army's chief-of-staff, the military junta took steps to weaken his main opponent. Army officers who supported Déjoie were dismissed, his supporters attacked, and finally campaigning in his favour was forbidden altogether.[9]

Duvalier was elected president on 22 September 1957. Twenty-two was his lucky number. 'My government will scrupulously protect the honour and the civil rights which constitute the joy of all free peoples. My government will guarantee liberty for the Haitian people,' he solemnly declared during his inauguration speech a month later.[10]

Duvalier's first act was to remove his political rivals, who challenged the outcome of the election. Within weeks the ranks of the civil service were purged. Duvalier appointed his followers, regardless of expertise or experience. Two months later his allies dominated the executive and judicial branches of government, while the legislature was under his thumb.[11]

Duvalier recruited Herbert Morrison as director of public relations. During the presidential campaign, Morrison had bought a second-hand camera and taken hundreds of photographs, promoting Duvalier abroad. Photos with the caption 'Champion of the Poor' had appeared with the president-elect posing next to a poor peasant. Now Morrison travelled the island with his camera, snapping pictures to portray Haiti as a beacon of democracy. On radio in New York a year later he described Duvalier as 'a humble country doctor, a dedicated, honest individual who is trying to help his people'. 'It's the first time in Haitian history,' he explained to his American audience, 'that the middle class and the suburban masses, the rural masses, have elected in a free election the man of their choice.'[12]

Clément Barbot was tasked with organising the secret police. Ordered to attack opponents of the regime, its agents did so with such brutality that it caused general indignation. Within weeks of the election boys as young as eleven were dragged off into the bushes and beaten with hickory sticks. Entire families ended up in prison.[13]

Antonio Kébreau, the army's chief-of-staff, intimidated, imprisoned and deported the regime's opponents. Labour unions were crushed and newspapers silenced, their premises occasionally burned to the ground. A radio station was wrecked. Suspects were accused of being communists and placed under arrest in the hundreds. A curfew imposed by the junta before the elections was maintained indefinitely.[14]

The seat of power, however, continued to be the army. The alliance between Duvalier and Kébreau was an uneasy one, born of mutual need. But as the junta helped him crush his opponents, they went too far, beating to death an American citizen who was a vocal supporter of Louis Déjoie. In December the American ambassador was recalled in protest. Duvalier exploited the affair, blaming the military for the violence. Kébreau was dismissed two months later.[15]

In the following months the army was whittled down in size, as many officers were discharged, transferred or released on early retirement, in particular the senior grades. A further opportunity to purge the ranks presented itself in the summer, after five American soldiers of fortune accompanied by two Haitian military officers landed near the capital, hoping to rally the population and besiege the presidential palace on 28 July 1958. All the insurgents were killed by troops loyal to the president.

The attempted coup was a blessing in disguise. A week later Duvalier addressed the nation on radio. 'I have conquered the nation. I have won power. I am the New Haiti. Those who seek to destroy me seek to destroy Haiti itself. It is through me that Haiti breathes; it is through her that I exist ... God and Destiny have chosen me.' All constitutional guarantees were suspended, while the president was given full powers to take all measures necessary to maintain national security. Less than 'a year after coming to power Duvalier reigned like an absolute monarch, with few limits placed on his power.[16]

In the name of national security, Duvalier further starved the army of funds, developing his own militia instead as a deliberate counter-balance to the regular forces. Like the secret police, they were supervised by Clément Barbot. At first the militia were called the *cagoulards*, named after the hooded fascists who terrorised France in the 1930s. But soon they became known as the tonton macoutes, a Creole term for bogeymen. Within a year Barbot claimed to have a force of 25,000 militia under his command, although they probably never numbered more than 10,000, with a hard core of about 2,000 in the capital. The macoutes dressed like gangsters, with shiny blue-serge suits, dark, steel-rimmed glasses and grey homburg hats. They carried a gun, tucked away in a belt or an armpit holster. Duvalier alone could enrol a macoute, granting him permission to carry a weapon. The macoutes, in turn, reported back to Duvalier. In the words of the *New Republic*, a macoute was 'an informer, neighbourhood boss, extortioner, bully and political pillar of the regime'. They were Duvalier's eyes and ears. Few were paid, and all used their power to extort, intimidate, harass, rape and murder.[17]

The macoutes crushed or interfered with every liberty but one. The new constitution proclaimed freedom of religion in April 1958. At the stroke of a pen, the dominant position of the Catholic Church was undermined. Voodoo was no longer banned. For more than two decades Duvalier had studied the religion, systematically developing links with the houngans. Now he made good use of his knowledge, recruiting them to become leaders of the macoutes in the countryside. They were widely consulted, invited to the palace and asked to perform religious ceremonies.[18]

Duvalier projected himself as a Voodoo spirit. Since his early friendship with Lorimer Denis he had affected the manners of a houngan, often dressing in black, carrying a cane and adopting a taciturn demeanour. His model was Baron Samedi, the spirit of the dead and guardian of cemeteries. In popular culture Baron Samedi was often depicted with a top hat and black tailcoat, wearing dark glasses, cotton plugs stuffed in his nostrils, resembling a corpse prepared for burial in the countryside.

Duvalier wore thick, dark spectacles, and occasionally appeared in public with a top hat and tailcoat. He would mumble mysteriously in a deep nasal tone, as if chanting incantations against his enemies.

He encouraged rumours about his links with the occult world. In 1958 the American anthropologist Harold Courlander came to pay his respects in the palace. He had known Duvalier from his early years at the Bureau of Ethnology. The visitor blinked in surprise as a guard led him into a pitch-dark room draped with black curtains. Duvalier, dressed in a black woollen suit, sat in front of a long table with dozens of black candles, surrounded by his macoutes wearing their dark glasses.[19]

One of the more persistent rumours began circulating after the macoutes intervened in the burial of a former rival in April 1959. They pulled the casket from the black hearse, loaded it into their own vehicle and drove off, leaving behind a crowd of stunned mourners. The official explanation was that the body had been removed to prevent a public rally at his graveside, but word soon spread that the president wanted to use his heart as a magic charm to strengthen his own power.[20]

There were plenty of other stories. The president sought council from the spirits while sitting in his bathtub, wearing the top hat of Baron Samedi. He studied goat entrails in the Salon Jaune of the National Palace. But Duvalier did not rely on rumour alone. Much as he purged the ranks of the government and the army, so he eliminated the houngans who refused to cooperate. 'Never forget,' he told them in 1959, 'that I am the supreme authority of the state. Henceforth I, I alone, I am your only master.'[21]

Haiti shares the island of Hispaniola with the Dominican Republic, which occupies the east. To the west, a mere fifty kilometres across the Windward Passage, lies the island of Cuba. In January 1959 Fidel Castro and his guerrilla fighters entered Havana. It was yet another stroke of luck for Duvalier, as the United States began courting him with financial assistance and military advice. The following month US$6 million was extended in aid, refloating a regime that was experiencing a severe economic crisis. In an interview with Peter Kihss in the *New York Times* Duvalier proclaimed that he was no dictator, but merely a doctor concerned about rebuilding his country.[22]

Still, the Voodoo spirits can be fickle. On 24 May 1959 Duvalier suffered a heart attack. Illness implied weakness, and rumours spread about his declining powers. His father's tomb was desecrated, the coffin destroyed and the remains scattered. His enemies were emboldened. Bombs exploded in the capital. Several politicians questioned his use of state funds. One senator even launched into a tirade against the regime. But even in this moment of extreme vulnerability Duvalier appeared to thrive, with the American ambassador visiting the palace on 2 June to demonstrate his support.[23]

A month later Duvalier signalled his resumption of power with a dramatic gesture, appearing with his family and advisers on the front steps of the National Palace to review a military parade. Thousands of enthusiastic supporters, carefully assembled by the macoutes, gave him a vociferous welcome. The president toured the streets of the capital the following day, accompanied by his director of public relations, Herbert Morrison, who took photographs of the event.[24]

Two months later Duvalier announced that a vast communist plot to overthrow the government had been uncovered. He demanded the power to rule by decree and suspend parliamentary immunity. He used his new prerogatives almost immediately, impeaching six senators who had taken advantage of his illness over the summer to criticise his rule.[25]

Duvalier now lived in self-isolation, surrounded by sycophants. His advisers assumed several official roles simultaneously, even though their authority was never specified, creating great confusion throughout the administration. Competence aroused his suspicion, even when it came from a loyal subordinate. As a result, he was involved in every decision, even though he seemed hardly interested in governance. He 'spends all of his time on the political manipulation of persons', wrote one American adviser.[26]

Tyrants trust no one, least of all their allies. Duvalier disposed of friends and foes alike, striking down anyone he thought was too ambitious or might develop a separate power base. No one was indispensable. During his illness his confidant and henchman Clément Barbot had maintained order. But as chief of the macoutes he was potentially dangerous. After Barbot held secret negotiations with the United States, on 15 July Duvalier summarily placed him and ten associates under arrest. Haiti's Number Two, like so many other close collaborators of dictators, had failed to gauge the full extent of his master's gift for dissimulation. Morrison, the president's publicity director, then fell under suspicion for his friendship with Barbot, but managed to escape to Miami. Two weeks later the president reviewed the macoutes in front of the palace, flanked by his high command. For the first time since their creation two years earlier the militia were officially recognised. Duvalier asked them to 'keep their eyes open'.[27]

One last bastion of resistance remained, namely the Church. They supported the students, who still had the courage to organise strikes, despite ferocious repression from the macoutes. In January 1961 Duvalier expelled the French bishop and four priests, earning him excommunication from the Vatican. His grip on the country was now almost complete.

The constitution imposed a six-year limit on the presidency. Two years before his term expired, Duvalier began preparing for his second mandate. As he turned fifty-four on 14 April 1961 newspapers hailed him as 'Supreme Leader', 'Spiritual Leader of the Nation', 'Venerated Leader', 'Apostle of the Collective Good' and 'Greatest Man in Our Modern History'. It set the tone for elections to a newly created legislative body two weeks later. Every candidate took pains to proclaim their fealty to Duvalier. The president's name appeared on every ballot. In Cap-Haïtien the macoutes rounded up people as they left church on Sunday morning, herding them into the polling stations. A seven-year-old child was made to vote. The following day the papers announced that the people had not only voted for the legislative candidates, but had also spontaneously approved a second term for President Duvalier.[28]

On Flag Day, when the creation of the Haitian flag by Jean-Jacques Dessalines was traditionally celebrated in the city of Arcahaie, Duvalier was welcomed by crowds of cheering villagers, watched over by the security forces with their guns in hand. In one extravagant speech after another the president was acclaimed by his underlings. The most extreme declamation came from Father Hubert Papailler, minister of national education, who explained that the people had taken the ballot boxes by assault in the hope that the present chief would reign not merely for six new years but 'perhaps as long as God, from Whom he holds his power'. Duvalier watched, inscrutable behind his dark glasses.[29]

Duvalier's inauguration took place on 22 May, an auspicious date containing the number twenty-two. For days on end the macoutes had scoured the countryside for volunteers, forcing men, women and children into a fleet of lorries. Those who resisted were whipped. No food was offered, even if the journey often took a full day. They were quartered in schools and warehouses, made to wait for the occasion. Every road out of the capital was barricaded. On the day some 50,000 people were escorted to the palace, where they dutifully showed their support, carrying banners, holding high portraits, cheering on command. 'You are Me, and I am You,' proclaimed Duvalier.[30]

The United States, with John F. Kennedy now in the White House, was repelled by the surprise elections. In mid-1962 economic aid was quietly suspended. Foreigners left in droves. As the economy deteriorated Duvalier used the United States as a scapegoat for all the ills that beset Haiti.

In April 1963, Duvalier released Clément Barbot from prison, even offering him a brand new car as a sign of reconciliation. Rather than display gratitude, his former henchman tried to kidnap Jean-Claude and Simone Duvalier, the president's two children. The president unleashed a reign of terror with the macoutes, who used the opportunity to settle accounts and eliminate their own enemies. Hundreds of suspects were killed, and many more vanished. In the capital bodies were left to rot by the roadside. In less than a week, the United States issued five formal protests over incidents involving US citizens.[31]

A few weeks later the United States increased pressure by declining official invitations to attend the first anniversary of Duvalier's re-election. The embassy began to evacuate its employees. Diplomatic relations were suspended. But Duvalier did not flinch, calculating that Washington needed an ally in its fight against Cuba. The celebrations went ahead on 22 May, with tens of thousands of assembled villagers dutifully dancing and singing his praises in front of the palace. Papa Doc appeared on the balcony, 'in a calm so complete that it seemed narcotic', according to one witness. 'Bullets and machine guns capable of frightening Duvalier do not exist,' he explained. 'I am already an immaterial being.' In New York, *Newsweek* declared him 'utterly, irretrievably mad'. But on 3 June the United States asked to resume normal diplomatic relations. In Haiti the radio crowed over Duvalier's 'triumph of statesmanship'.[32]

A further victory came in mid-July, when Barbot and his brother were finally hunted down in the countryside and shot. Photographs of their mangled bodies were published in the newspapers.

Every crisis seemed to make Duvalier stronger. After yet another ill-fated invasion attempt by one of his exiled enemies in August he suspended all civil rights for six months, including the right of assembly. It was a symbolic gesture, since there were no liberties left to suspend. On 17 September 1963 Haiti officially became a one-party state, as all political activities had to be carried out under the aegis of the 'Party of National Unity'. The party had never loomed very large, but a separate party machine provided another device for protecting the revolution. It also linked more people to Duvalier, reaching beyond the houngans and macoutes.[33]

'I am the revolution and the flag,' Duvalier declared over the following months. Neon lights in the centre of Port-au-Prince blinked the same message: 'I am the Haitian Flag, United and Indivisible. François Duvalier'. The square nearby was renamed 'Place de la Révolution Duvalier'. Plastic busts and portraits of the dictator, already prominently displayed in shops and offices, appeared in private homes. On radio, where his voice was heard regularly, Duvalier portrayed himself as the personification of God, exclaiming 'and the word was made flesh'. But there were no statues. Duvalier modestly declined after legislators passed a law to approve the building of monuments memorialising their leader. Like Hitler, he believed that statues were for the dead.[34]

The adulation had a goal. Duvalier wished to become president for life. In March 1964 leaders of the Church, commerce and industry were successively summoned to the palace to demonstrate their loyalty. After waiting for hours in stifling heat they were made to read prepared scripts in public, imploring the president to stay on forever. Duvalier was unfailingly gracious. He thanked all of them effusively, especially those known to be critical of him. For days on end the press published telegrams demanding a change in the constitution. Psalms were read and hymns sung. On 1 April the president himself appeared in public, declaring: 'I am an exceptional man, the kind the country could produce only once every 50 to 75 years.'[35]

Endless parades were held in the following months, as thousands of people were transported to the capital to beg their leader to stay on. A poster appeared, showing Christ with his hands on the shoulder of a seated Duvalier: 'I have chosen him.' The campaign culminated in a referendum held on 14 June. The ballot came with a printed 'Yes'. Out of a total population of four million, some 2,800,000 voted in favour and 3,234 against, representing a 99.89 per cent victory. A new constitution was drafted to conform to popular demand. On 22 June the president took a solemn oath before the entire diplomatic corps. He was an hour late and began reading a ninety-minute speech. His audience had to stand, but after a while a German diplomat, through sheer fatigue, took his seat. Duvalier stopped, turned around and instructed a protocol officer to ask him to rise again.[36]

A few weeks later, in honour of the President for Life, the state press released a booklet entitled *Catechism of the Revolution*. It contained catchy phrases designed to be committed to memory. Chapter One set the tone:

Q – Who is Duvalier?
A – Duvalier is the Greatest Patriot of all time, the Emancipator of the Masses, the Renovator of the Haitian

Nation, the Champion of National Dignity, Chief of the
Revolution and President for Life of Haiti.

Q – By which name can Duvalier also be identified?

A – Duvalier is also the worthy heir of blood of the
Dessalinien ideal, made President for Life to save us.[37]

Like the great independence fighter Jean-Jacques Dessalines,
who had declared himself emperor in 1804, François Duvalier now
had a life term. In September a decree ordered portraits of Duvalier
and his hero Dessalines to be displayed in every classroom in every
school, private, public or clerical.[38]

Haiti, by 1965, was in dire straits. American financial assistance,
which in 1960 had amounted to slightly less than half of the country's
public expenditures, had come to a complete halt. The country
was an exporter of coffee and sisal, but prices on the international
market had collapsed. Tourism had dwindled, largely as a result
of the reign of terror imposed by the macoutes. Commerce and
industry suffered from endless demands for contributions to
austerity funds, national bonds or government lotteries.[39]

None of the electoral promises to campaign against hunger,
poverty, illiteracy and injustice were fulfilled. Unemployment
was increasing, while illiteracy was higher than before. With 65
per cent of all funds devoted to state security, most public services
were neglected. Abandoned cars lay rusting in the streets. Once-
beautiful parks were overgrown with brush and weeds. Deaths
from starvation were reported from Cayes and Jeremie, two areas in
the southern peninsula where the harvest was usually abundant.[40]

Despite a climate of fear and insecurity, however, the death toll
was relatively low. As in North Korea, roughly 7 to 8 per cent of the
population were able to vote with their feet. Poor people illegally
crossed the border into the Dominican Republic or sailed across
the Windward Passage to Cuba. Those who were better off fled to
the Bahamas, hoping to enter the United States. By the middle of
the 1960s four out of five of the country's best lawyers, doctors,

engineers, teachers and other professionals lived in exile. Those who remained in Haiti were crushed into apathy.[41]

Duvalier himself lived like a recluse, rarely seen, occasionally heard, a prisoner in his own palace. He alone made all the decisions. Like Mussolini he occupied himself with every detail of government. He decided not only who was to be killed and who was to be spared, but also what kind of material should be used for a new road, who should be granted a university degree and which spelling should be used in Creole.[42]

But enthusiasm, even enforced at the barrel of a gun, was waning. The country was peaceful but prostrate. For the first time in many years the celebrations to mark 22 June, a date which replaced 22 May as the high point in the dictator's calendar, were toned down.[43]

In November 1965 Duvalier showed himself in broad daylight, visiting several shops in the capital. It was apparently a reaction to hostile broadcasts from New York, taunting him for being too afraid to leave the palace. His bullet-proof Mercedes-Benz was followed by half a dozen sedans packed with bodyguards to ensure his safety. A few days later the president visited several orphanages. His appearance, according to the official release published in the newspapers, provoked 'delirious enthusiasm'.[44]

On 2 January 1966 Duvalier struck a new tone in his New Year speech to the nation. It was time, he announced, to put an end to the explosive phase of the Duvalierist Revolution. Having swept away the 'political, social and economic superstructure of the former regime', the moment had come to begin rebuilding the economy. The curfew was ended. Roadblocks were removed, the streets cleaned up. The presidential palace received a fresh coat of paint. The macoutes were reined in.[45]

Duvalier refurbished his image, projecting himself as a benign and elderly statesman, the spiritual leader of the black world. In April the President for Life welcomed the King of Kings, Haile Selassie, Emperor of Ethiopia. Before he landed the airport was hastily renamed Aéroport François Duvalier. Its new access road was christened Avenue Haile Selassie. Coverage from the local press, radio and television was lavish and adulatory. Duvalier was unusually open with the international press that was invited to Haiti by the regime's new public-relations firm. In a series of interviews, he appeared cordial and self-assured, candidly admitting that there was indeed censorship in the media, which he deemed necessary to protect the people from false reporting. One correspondent described him as 'charming, cooperative and thoroughly relaxed'.[46]

More public appearances followed. In June he attended a football tournament with his son Jean-Claude. A few days later he took his daughter Marie-Denise to the opening ceremony of the annual congress of the Caribbean Travel Association. For the first time since 1963 he showed himself at a diplomatic function, toasting the British ambassador at a reception organised to mark the birthday of Queen Elizabeth II.[47]

Duvalier, his people were told, was a great statesman acclaimed by international figures. A local newspaper published a statement attributed to Haile Selassie. 'You must remain president, so that this people may continue to benefit from your goodness. I have understood, from visiting you, from having seen, why this people and this nation love you so much.' The quotation was a fabrication concocted by one of the president's ghost writers.[48]

Duvalier created the impression that he was a leader of international stature, a statesman with direct access to Washington and the Vatican. In June he gave a CBS interview to Martin Agronsky. Seated in his gold and blue throne at the National Palace, he intimated that he was in 'close touch' with President Johnson to discuss the renewal of American aid. But his contacts with the White House were 'privileged matter not to be discussed publicly'. Later that year the Vatican restored links with Haiti and granted Duvalier the right to appoint his own bishops. The President for Life appeared on radio and television to make the agreement appear the result of close collaboration between him and Pope Paul VI.[49]

Duvalier also worked on his image as a great writer, historian, ethnologist, poet and philosopher. Most of all, Duvalier was the father of Duvalierism, which found expression in the publication of his Essential Works. As he put it, 'when one is a leader one must have a doctrine. Without a doctrine you cannot direct a people.' The two first volumes appeared in May 1966, to much acclaim, greeted with glowing newspaper reviews, as well as endless laudatory letters written by prominent members of the community. Excerpts were read on radio in a five-hour programme, subsequently retransmitted by all stations in the capital. Duvalier, listeners were told, was a giant in the same category as Kipling, Valéry, Plato, St Augustine and de Gaulle. 'He is the greatest doctrine-giver of the century.'[50]

Gift sets were presented to schools and other educational institutions. The two hefty tomes were also awarded to outstanding students, who, apparently on command, wrote more adulatory letters, all published in the newspapers.[51]

A high point came in September as the legislative chamber passed a decree awarding Duvalier the title of Grand Master of Haitian Thought. They designated his birthday as Day of National Culture, and demanded that everyone should learn at least three-quarters of the Essential Works by heart, even though 90 per cent of the population were illiterate.[52]

Duvalier's sixtieth birthday was celebrated over four days, in a style befitting a dictator fully in control of his country. Mardi Gras, the Haitian carnival, was brought forward to heighten the festive mood. Beauty queens were flown in from Miami and the Dominican Republic. Poetry readings were held, with pride of place given to the works of François Duvalier. Leading politicians, soldiers, scholars, businessmen and civil servants presented tributes. A delegation of 2,000 uniformed schoolchildren paraded in front of the palace. The macoutes paraded, the soldiers paraded.[53]

The festivities were spoilt, however, after a bomb exploded inside an ice-cream cart, killing two and injuring forty. Suspecting a military coup, Duvalier reshuffled the leadership and had nineteen officers of the palace guard thrown into Fort Dimanche, a dungeon on the outskirts of the capital. For good measure two ministers were also placed under arrest. On 8 June Duvalier arrived at Fort Dimanche in full military uniform and army helmet, personally presiding over the execution of the nineteen suspects, tied to stakes on a rifle range.[54]

Two weeks later, on 22 June, as the country marked the third anniversary of Duvalier's election as President for Life, a captive audience of thousands was assembled in front of the palace. In a great show of force, Duvalier solemnly took a roll call of the nineteen officers, pausing theatrically after each name. 'All of them have been shot,' he announced in the end, sending shock waves through the crowd. 'I am an arm of steel, hitting inexorably,' he exclaimed. Then he described himself as the embodiment of the nation, on a par with other great leaders like Atatürk, Lenin, Nkrumah and Mao.[55]

The cult of personality was further cranked up over the following months, culminating in the tenth anniversary of the revolution. Gold coins in four denominations were minted, carrying the president's effigy. A compilation of his Essential Works was published as *Breviary of a Revolution*. Like the Little Red Book, which had just appeared, it came in a small format, easily tucked inside a pocket. The newspapers were filled with adulatory reports, 'sickeningly transparent and endlessly repeated' according to the American Embassy. A few days before the main event, Duvalier spoke to the nation, referring to himself as 'the God you have created'. Mass parades were held over the following two days. A François Duvalier Bridge, a François Duvalier Library, a François Duvalier Swimming Pool (Olympic size) and a François Duvalier International Air Terminal were opened.[56]

On 22 September the president spoke again, referring to himself in the third person. He listed his many achievements, and then concluded: 'We are superior blacks, because no other blacks in the world have accomplished an historical epic. This is why, without indulging in any narcissism and without any sense of superiority, we believe ourselves, we blacks of Haiti, superior to all other blacks in the world. This is why, my dear friends, I want to tell you today that your Chief is considered a Living Sun by blacks throughout the world. It is said that he has lighted the revolutionary conscience of the blacks of the American continent and of the universe.'[57]

Duvalier was a manipulator of men, not the masses. He may have been a champion of the poor, but he showed little interest in mobilising them, even for the greater glory of his own person. He rarely left the palace, and never travelled the country. The macoutes ensured that thousands turned up on the lawns of his palace to dutifully acclaim him several times a year, but otherwise the vast majority of people were left alone. There was no official ideology, no all-encompassing party, no attempt to institute thought control, even though dissent was prohibited. The radio occasionally broadcast his speeches, but until 1968 stations in the north of the country were too weak for reception. Newspapers carried his pronouncements, but were rarely seen in the impoverished countryside, where few could read.[58]

Duvalier was a dictator's dictator, a man who wielded naked power without the pretence of ideology, despite all the talk about revolution. He ruled alone, from his mahogany desk, an automatic pistol within reach, a few palace guards behind the nearest door. There was no junta, no faction, no clique, no true party except in name, only underlings vying for his attention, hoping to supplant each other by demonstrations of absolute loyalty. Duvalier, suspicious of everyone, was single-minded in exploiting their foibles, manipulating their emotions, testing their loyalty. It helped that he occasionally miscalculated, crushing friends and foes alike.[59]

His network of willing accomplices extended all the way to the countryside. Even in the most remote part of the country, the president was popular. No public official ever claimed a good decision as his own. Deputies filled meetings with accolades to their leader. Every positive development, including a successful rainy season, was held to radiate from Duvalier.[60]

It was a comparatively small network of loyalties, but it was enough to sustain his regime. The remaining four million mattered very little to him. They were accustomed to predatory governments. They lived in fear at worst, apathy and subservience at best.

Nonetheless, a small commando of professional soldiers, properly equipped and trained, could easily have toppled the regime. It never happened, largely thanks to the United States. After the disaster of April 1961, when a group of Cuban refugees trained by the CIA tried to land in the Bay of Pigs to overthrow Castro, there was no realistic chance of the United States trying to intervene in Haiti. And even if Washington viewed Duvalier with revulsion, he, unlike Castro, was an ally in the midst of the Cold War. Duvalier exploited the relationship to the fullest. He could be stubborn, unpredictable, irascible, but he never truly severed all the links. He knew how to insult the Americans even as he took advantage of their economic aid.[61]

Duvalier's best propaganda vehicle in Washington was communism. For a decade Duvalier played up the threat from the left, labelling his real and imagined enemies as underground agents of Cuba and Moscow.

In December 1968 two rival parties combined to form the United Party of Haitian Communists. They were committed to overthrowing Duvalier. In March 1969 they picked the only village in Haiti without a houngan and took down the regime's flag. Duvalier responded with a huge witch-hunt as dozens of people were shot or hanged in public, many more forced to flee into the mountains. Every book even vaguely related to communism became taboo, its mere possession a crime punishable by death. When Nelson Rockefeller, the governor of New York, visited Port-au-Prince three months later, Duvalier was able to assure him that the communist threat had been eliminated. It was the start of yet another rapprochement with the United States.[62]

However, the press photograph released for the occasion showed an ailing Duvalier leaning on Rockefeller for support. Papa Doc was frail, in declining health, looking much older than his sixty-two years. He began eliminating all opposition to his son being designated as his heir. In January 1971 Jean-Claude was named as his successor. A referendum was dutifully held, although among the 2,391,916 votes one was apparently negative. François Duvalier died of a heart attack three months later, on 21 April 1971. His reign was a few months short of that of Henri Christophe (1806–20). His son was installed in the first hour of 22 April, as ever a lucky date for the Duvalier family.[63]

Thousands of Haitians filed by their late ruler's body as he lay in state at the National Palace. Duvalier was dressed in his favourite black frock coat, resting in a glass-topped, silk-lined coffin. Losing a dictator can be as traumatic as having to live under one, but despite widespread apprehension that chaos would follow his disappearance, complete calm prevailed. His body was buried first in the National Cemetery, but later transferred to a grandiose mausoleum erected by his son. When Baby Doc himself fell from power in 1986 an angry crowd demolished Papa Doc's final resting place.

Ceauşescu

The Palace of the People, located in what was once a thriving residential area of Bucharest, is the largest administrative building in the world. In terms of volume it eclipses the Great Pyramid of Giza. Its kitsch, neoclassical structure contains more than a thousand rooms, filled with marble columns, ornate staircases and crystal chandeliers. Nicolae Ceauşescu, who laid the cornerstone in June 1985, announced that the project was a fitting tribute to the greatness of his time, officially known as 'the Ceauşescu Era'.

In reality it was a monument to himself. Ten square kilometres of housing were bulldozed to clear the ground, including twenty churches and six synagogues. Thousands of workers laboured around the clock. The project consumed a third of the national budget. Ceauşescu supervised every detail, making impromptu visits to give orders. An energetic but short man who was touchy about his height, he had the staircases rebuilt twice to match his step. Although he never saw the finished project, work resumed a few years after he was shot on Christmas Day 1989. It remains a work in progress.[1]

Nothing predisposed Ceauşescu to become a dictator. He showed no particular promise or flair as a child, leaving home at the age of eleven to work as an apprentice for a shoemaker. Four years later he was briefly arrested for distributing communist leaflets. Membership of the Romanian Communist Party, in 1933, languished in the hundreds. Communism was unpopular, as most

Romanians distrusted the Soviet Union. But Ceauşescu was a fiery, fanatical believer who found in ideology a seemingly simple key to a complicated world.

The police repeatedly picked him up and released him again on account of his youth. In 1936 he was sent to a political prison for two years. He was unpopular with other inmates, mocked for his lack of education, his stammer and his regional accent. He was impulsive, intensely competitive and often contemptuous of others. But he had the political astuteness to forge links with the leaders in the communist movement, including Gheorghe Gheorghiu-Dej, who took the young man under his wing. More stints in prison followed during the Second World War, when the country sided with Germany.[2]

The Red Army occupied Romania in 1944 and turned the country into a satellite state. Gheorghiu-Dej emerged as its first communist leader in 1947. He manoeuvred successfully against his rivals, all of whom were purged, arrested or murdered. Lucretiu Patrascanu, a founding member of the party, was executed in 1954. Hundreds of thousands of political prisoners were sent to internment camps.

By 1956 Gheorghiu-Dej was sufficiently entrenched to use Khrushchev's policies selectively. On the one hand, he strengthened his country's economic independence from the Soviet Union, moving trade towards the West. On the other, he continued to build a repressive system dominated by the Securitate, the secret police agency set up in 1948 with help from the Soviet Union. Gheorghiu-Dej relied on them to instil fear in the population.[3]

He also expanded his cult of personality. As portraits of Stalin were taken down, his own went up in every school, factory and office. Newspapers published photographs of villagers gathered around the radio to listen to his broadcasts. He travelled the country, acclaimed by his people, while his comrades receded into the background.[4]

Ceauşescu steadily rose through the ranks, ingratiating himself further with Gheorghiu-Dej. He vehemently attacked the regime's opponents, harassed critical intellectuals and helped push through the forced collectivisation of the countryside. Ceauşescu was a dedicated, modest, hard-working and loyal lieutenant. Like his master, he was critical of his country's dependence on the Kremlin but keen to maintain the rigid structures of the Stalinist one-party state.

In 1954 Gheorghiu-Dej trusted Ceauşescu enough to put him in charge of the secretariat of the Central Committee. All new appointments went through his office. Like Stalin in the early 1920s Ceauşescu cultivated his own underlings and made sure that they thrived.[5]

Gheorghiu-Dej died in 1965. The leadership was divided about the course of de-Stalinisation. Gheorghe Apostol, rumoured to have been chosen as successor by an ailing Gheorghiu-Dej, was considered too close to the Soviet Union. Gheorghe Maurer, a senior and highly respected party leader, rallied the leadership around Ceauşescu instead. The diminutive young man, hampered by a lack of verbal skills and organisational talent, seemed an ideal party figurehead.[6]

For two years after he was elected secretary general in March 1965, Ceauşescu bided his time, playing his part as spokesman of a collective leadership. But he made the most of his position, addressing crowds, visiting factories and establishing links with the military and the security forces. His trips abroad, on behalf of the party, received extensive press coverage. He also struck a defiant tone, rattling Moscow by inviting leaders critical of the Soviet Union. Zhou Enlai was welcomed in 1966, future president Richard Nixon in 1967.

On 26 January 1968 Ceauşescu turned fifty. A prudent man, he was anxious to avoid the impression that he sought a cult of personality. Nonetheless, two volumes of his speeches were published, to much acclaim. His colleagues, especially Apostol and Maurer, were keen to pay homage.[7]

Three months later, in April 1968, Ceauşescu felt secure enough to turn against his erstwhile master, denouncing Gheorghiu-Dej for the arrest, trial and execution of faithful party members. This move allowed him to eliminate one of his main rivals, Alexandru Draghici, who had been in charge of the secret police at the time.

Ion Iliescu, one of Ceauşescu's faithful followers, stepped into his shoes. But the case of Lucretiu Patrascanu, executed a few days before Ceauşescu joined the Central Committee in 1954, implicated the entire old guard. All of them were now tainted and made to grovel.[8]

Ceauşescu's moment came over the summer, when the Soviet Union invaded Czechoslovakia in order to suppress the country's uprising against communism. Troops from Bulgaria, Poland and Hungary pledged support, but none from Romania. As the tanks rolled into Prague, Ceauşescu called for a mass meeting in the Palace Square, in front of the Central Committee. He delivered an impassioned speech, condemning Leonid Brezhnev's actions as a 'great mistake and a grave danger to peace in Europe'. He became a national hero overnight, adored for his promise that no power would be allowed to 'violate the territory of our homeland'.[9]

Ceauşescu posed as a fearless hero, the man who dared to stand up to the Soviet Union. Foreign dignitaries queued up to visit him, portraying him as a proponent of socialism with a human face. Richard Nixon, now President of the United States, was given a lavish welcome in August 1969. Photographs were published of the most powerful man in the world leaning forward towards Ceauşescu, who was sitting back in a comfortable chair. 'He may be a Commie, but he is our Commie!' Nixon later proclaimed.[10]

A party congress was convened three days after Nixon left. Ceauşescu introduced a change in the party statutes, mandating his direct election by members of the congress. It meant that the Central Committee could no longer remove him. In one speech after another, delegates paid tribute to their leader. Of the old guard only one remained, namely Gheorghe Maurer, who continued to serve as Number Two. Ceauşescu was the undisputed leader, his men in charge of all the top party organs.[11]

Between July 1965 and January 1973, Ceauşescu undertook 147 whirlwind tours of the country. In January 1970 alone, he visited forty-five industrial enterprises and agricultural units, or so the party newspaper *Scinteia* claimed. Each one was elaborately staged, following a choreography that barely changed over the years. A motorcade draped in flowers arrived. The local population was assembled along the main road, waving red flags to greet their leader. Children offered flowers. Ceaușescu appeared on the balcony of the local party headquarters to address a crowd, often standing on a pedestal to appear taller. The crowd cheered enthusiastically, with the secret police in the background to ensure that everyone joined the chorus. Each visit was reported on the front page of every newspaper, contributing to Ceaușescu's image as a ubiquitous leader in close touch with his people. As a result, people tended to blame his subordinates, rather than him. 'If only Ceaușescu knew about the situation, he would attack the shopkeepers with an iron broom', people whispered during food shortages.[12]

Ceaușescu enjoyed the carefully rehearsed ritual, although nothing quite prepared him for the welcome he received when he visited China and Korea in June 1971. In Beijing the entire leadership met him and his delegation on the tarmac of the airport. Lining the roads were tens of thousands of cheering people. On Tiananmen Square a mass gymnastics display was held in his honour, as hundreds of participants dressed in different colours synchronised their movements to project welcoming messages: 'Long Live Romanian–Chinese Friendship!'[13]

Everywhere, Ceaușescu noted, people were hard at work. China was a country seemingly devoid of idleness. 'They are very well organised, and they are very disciplined,' he observed. In Pyongyang, the next leg of his trip, everything had been reconstructed from scratch following the devastation of the Korean War. The city had large, modern buildings. The shops were full of goods. Agriculture and industry thrived, thanks to a spirit of economic self-sufficiency. Unity, discipline, autarky, independence: all these goals seemed to come together when a population was mobilised around their leader.[14]

Like Hitler on his first trip to Italy, Ceaușescu did not seem to realise that much of what he had seen in China and Korea was mere show. He even denounced his own embassy staff in Beijing and Pyongyang, accusing them of having misled the Executive

Committee by reporting severe shortages when he himself had witnessed nothing but plenty for all.[15]

As soon as he returned to Bucharest, Ceaușescu launched his own mini Cultural Revolution. For a few brief years after 1965, when he had presented himself as a reformer, the ideological restrictions of the Stalinist era had been relaxed. Press censorship had eased, with writers granted some leeway. Foreign programmes were shown on television. Still, the thaw had been limited, as Ceaușescu had repeatedly emphasised that Marxism-Leninism remained 'the common denominator of our socialist art'.[16]

These limited freedoms now came to an end. In China Ceaușescu had witnessed how the old world had been eliminated, as every aspect of culture had been rebuilt along revolutionary lines. He wanted the same for his own country. On 6 July 1971 he made a speech to the Executive Committee which later became known as the July Theses. He railed against 'bourgeois ideological influences and retrograde ideas', demanding that they be eliminated from the press, radio, television, literature and even opera and ballet. He celebrated socialist realism and called for strict ideological conformity in every domain. Culture was to undergo a revolution, becoming the ideological tool to mould a 'New Man'.[17]

The leadership was purged. Ion Iliescu, promoted only three years before, was dismissed. On the flight back home there had apparently been a furious row over what they had seen in North Korea.[18]

As culture was regimented, the cult of personality spread. Even before his trip to East Asia, Ceaușescu had been eager to acquire a court biographer. He found a willing accomplice in Michel-Pierre Hamelet, a French journalist working for *Le Figaro* who had accompanied the General Secretary of the French Communist Party to Romania in 1967. Hamelet had been instantly captivated by his host: 'I was struck by the fire in his eyes, the mental energy they conveyed, the ironic smile that constantly illuminated his face.' He returned to Romania a few years later and was given every assistance to compile his biography. *Nicolae Ceaușescu* was published in 1971 in French, followed by Romanian, Hungarian and German translations the same year.

Hamelet portrayed Ceauşescu as a 'passionate humanist' who announced nothing less than 'the coming of a new era', one in which social relationships would be rebuilt according to a new ideology. He was a gifted child born in poverty. The boy went to school barefoot, too poor to buy books, but was always top of the class. Hamelet interviewed his teacher, who remembered that the boy excelled at mathematics but was, most of all, a true comrade to others. Identified by the police at the age of sixteen as a dangerous agitator, he was sent back to his village in shackles. But nothing could make him abandon the cause. He became an enemy of the state, a determined organiser of the communist movement, a passionate exponent of the tenets of Marxism-Leninism.[19]

Hamelet was not the only one recruited to promote the image of the peasant boy who through hard work, courage and sheer talent overcame adversity to become a socialist leader. In 1972 Donald Catchlov published *Romania's Ceauşescu* in London, further spreading the Ceauşescu myth. This was followed by Heinz Siegert's *Ceauşescu* in German in 1973 and Giancarlo Elia Valori's *Ceauşescu* in Italian in 1974. *The Demi-God of Romania* appeared in Greek in 1978.[20]

Ceauşescu, usually working through the Propaganda and Agitation Department, approved every detail himself, down to the number of copies to be printed. Generous funding was standard. In 1976, Mihai Steriade, author of a booklet entitled *The Presence and Prestige of a Humanist: Nicolae Ceauşescu*, asked for US$8,000 to assist him in 'propagating Romania' in Belgium. Ceauşescu personally revised the amount downwards to US$5,000.[21]

The Propaganda and Agitation Department, or Agitprop, also ensured that the image of the leader was promoted abroad through other means. In 1971, for instance, it paid the Italian newspaper *L'Unità* some US$5,000 to print a supplement on the anniversary of the Romanian Communist Party. It featured photographs of Ceauşescu as an international leader standing shoulder to shoulder with Mao, Nixon and de Gaulle. No Soviet leader was mentioned.[22]

Ceauşescu was leader of the party and head of state. But unlike other dictators, he was not content with holding symbolic power as head of state while in true control through the party machine. The authority of the State Council was expanded, as separate bodies headed by Ceauşescu bypassed the Council of Ministers. One of these was the Defence Council, another the Economic Council. In effect this meant that he had both the state and the party at his disposal and could play one against the other when he encountered opposition. He not only controlled all the levers of power, but also set himself up as the supreme authority on every topic, from window displays in department stores to the interior decoration of the National Theatre in Bucharest. He was impatient, and developed a penchant for reshuffling the ranks of the bureaucracy when they failed to implement his policies rapidly enough. Ceauşescu also frequently rotated cadres between the party and the state to ensure that no one could develop a power base. The frenzy only increased confusion and inefficiency.[23]

Nothing, however, was quite enough. In 1974 Ceauşescu decided to expand his position as president of the State Council to president of the republic, which would give him the power to appoint ministers by personal decree. At a preparatory meeting his underlings vied with each other to devise an ever more extravagant inauguration ceremony. Emil Bodnaras, vice-president of the State Council, suggested that a special copy of the constitution be printed with gold letterings. Another proposed firing a cannon salute, although Ceauşescu modestly declined.[24]

On 28 March, having been duly elected President of Romania, Ceauşescu was inducted with all the pomp and circumstance of a feudal monarch. The high point of the ceremony, transmitted by radio and television, was the presentation of a presidential sceptre. Salvador Dalí, the surrealist painter, was so struck by the event that he sent a congratulatory telegram. The message appeared the following day in *Scinteia*, the editor apparently unaware that it was satirical: 'I deeply appreciate the historical act of your introducing the presidential sceptre.'[25]

The same month Gheorghe Maurer, the faithful Number Two who had tried to provide a measure of moderation, was relieved of his duties. Ceauşescu now had no peers. A new press law imposing even more crushing censorship on written materials was immediately passed. Slander of party leaders was outlawed, as was any criticism of any party policy. At the end of the year the Eleventh Party Congress created a new body, concentrating all power in a Permanent Bureau of the Executive Council. Like other statutory bodies it possessed only an advisory capacity, as its dozen members listened respectfully to Ceauşescu. To mark the occasion *Scinteia* described the leader as 'Julius Caesar, Alexander of Macedonia, Pericles, Cromwell, Napoleon, Peter the Great and Lincoln', hailing him as 'our lay God, the heart of the party and the nation'. Ceauşescu had become the Conducator, a title derived from the verb *conduce*, or *ducere* in Latin. Like the Duce or the Führer he was the Supreme Leader of the nation.[26]

Ceauşescu was secretary general, president and supreme commander, but he craved official recognition as a leading ideologist. Two volumes of his selected writings and speeches had appeared in 1968. The pace accelerated in the following years, as Agitprop proposed a publication plan every year, supervised by Ceauşescu himself. His speeches were translated into half a dozen languages in 1971, followed by a steady output of his selected writings, which were available by 1976 in a variety of languages from Italian to Chinese.[27]

In 1976 Ceauşescu took over the Ideological Commission of the Central Committee. His subordinates queued up to hail him as a 'major thinker in contemporary Marxism', a brilliant ideologist who had 'rejuvenated and further developed Marxism'. Ceauşescu was 'Marxism-Leninism in action'. Authors, scholars and party activists were compelled to use his work as a major reference source.[28]

Ceauşescu's writings were a hodgepodge of contradictory ideas, but in a nutshell he clothed communism in nationalist garb. He posed as a champion of nationalist values while upholding the faith, calling it 'revolutionary patriotism'. His wisdom purportedly appealed to people around the world. As premier Manea Manescu observed after a lengthy trip to several Asian countries, 'Nicolae Ceauşescu enjoys enormous international prestige, profound esteem, and respect everywhere, even in the most remote parts of the world, where his name has become a symbol of fiery patriotism and internationalism, of the struggle for independence and national sovereignty.' He was a leader of world communism, an international figure of the working-class movement.[29]

On his sixtieth birthday in 1978, the entire nation rendered homage to its leader. Constantin Pirvulescu pronounced Ceauşescu 'the most genuine popular leader to emerge in the entire history of the Romanian people'. In their official message the Party, the State and the Nation announced that the new Ceauşescu Era he had created was 'an era that represents the most fruitful chapter in our entire thousand-year history, one rich in achievements and great success'.[30]

Since Ceauşescu was the nation's ideologist-in-chief, the main seats of learning held special ceremonies to recognise and celebrate his many scholarly achievements. Honorary degrees proliferated: one academy made him Doctor of Economics, another Doctor of Political Science. His support for Romania's sovereign existence was now termed the Ceauşescu Doctrine, delivering an oblique snub to the idea of limited sovereignty, known as the Brezhnev Doctrine, named after the man who had sent in the tanks to crush the popular rebellion in Prague a decade earlier. An exhibition was organised to display all the gifts Ceauşescu had received during his many travels abroad, illustrating the high esteem accorded him as an international statesman and leading theoretician of Marxism-Leninism.[31]

The celebrations lasted three weeks. There were poems, songs, plays, paintings, busts, tapestries and medals. His name was spelled out in capital letters. He was the torch, the flagbearer, the January star, the highest fir tree in the country. He was a hawk. He was 'the measure of all beings and things in this blessed country called Romania'. He was the Christ-like incarnation of the people, 'a body from the people's body, a soul from the people's soul'.[32]

Ceauşescu received, for the second time, the coveted title of Hero of the Socialist Republic of Romania. From Yugoslavia came the order of Hero of Socialist Labour. A magnanimous Brezhnev awarded him the Order of Lenin. But these accolades paled by comparison with the recognition he won from the West. A few months after his birthday, President Jimmy Carter of the United States wined and dined Ceauşescu and his wife in the White House. Yet surely the peak of his career was his state visit to Buckingham Palace in June 1978, organised by Sir Reggie Secondé, the British ambassador to Romania. Secondé had no illusions. In a confidential memo to the Foreign and Commonwealth Office he judged Ceauşescu 'as absolute a dictator as can be found in the world today'. The establishment in London welcomed the autocrat with open arms. One Romanian dissident staged a lonely protest, but the police promptly arrested him. Ceauşescu accompanied Queen Elizabeth II in her royal carriage, waving to the cheering crowds, and received the Order of the Bath. At Buckingham Palace his security guards tested the food before allowing it to be served. All the public events – the breakfasts, the lunches, dinners, and banquets – were broadcast on Romanian television around the clock. The visit crushed all who opposed their tyrant.[33]

Some resistance remained nonetheless. Ion Pacepa, a powerful Securitate general, defected to the United States a few weeks later, destroying the country's intelligence network and revealing the inner workings of the Ceauşescu court. Pacepa received a death sentence *in absentia*, with a bounty of US$2 million placed on his head. Ceauşescu grew even more suspicious of those around him. As his circle diminished, he relied instead on family members.[34]

Foremost among these was his wife Elena, a dour, uncultured but ambitious and determined woman who had been inspired by Madame Mao Zedong during her trip to China in 1971. She was Ceauşescu's constant companion, invariably at his side at party congresses, state ceremonies and official visits at home and abroad. She rose to the top of the political hierarchy within a few years, joining the powerful Permanent Bureau of the Executive Council in 1977.

Elena shared her husband's appetite for titles and honours. Despite minimal education, she was always referred to as

'Academician Doctor Engineer Elena Ceauşescu' and posed as the nation's premier scientist. By 1977 she had received twenty-four foreign decorations, ranging from Zaire's National Order of the Leopard, North Korea's Order of the National Flag and the Netherlands' Order of Orange-Nassau to Egypt's Order of Virtues. In 1975 the Soviet Union presented her with a medal to mark the Thirtieth Anniversary of the Victory over Fascism. Impressive though this portfolio was, it paled in comparison with the collection of her husband, who by 1977 had garnered some fifty international decorations, including France's prestigious Legion of Honour as well as endless Orders of the Red Flag from communist countries.[35]

In January 1979, several months after the Pacepa defection, Elena became chair of the Commission for State and Party Cadres, placing her in charge of all appointments. The new post coincided with her sixtieth birthday, lavishly celebrated over two days as every party member grovelled, extolling the First Lady as a 'star who stands beside a star in the eternal arch of heaven'. The First Lady undertook her new role with relish, insisting that every single one of the 2.9 million members was scrutinised, which put the party on probation. Blind obedience became the norm. Elena's brothers received important government positions, while her son Nicu was promoted to the Central Committee.

By the time the Twelfth Party Congress convened in November 1979 she was the powerful Number Two. One lonely voice still dared to confront the Ceauşescus. Constantin Pirvulescu, a founding member of the party who only a year earlier had celebrated his leader, accused Ceauşescu of ignoring the country's real problems to pursue his own glory. Members of the congress shouted him down, praising their leader's popularity abroad.[36]

The cult of personality effectively prevented anyone else from building an independent power base. More family members were appointed in the following decade. By the time the regime collapsed in 1989, according to some accounts no less than fifty relatives held influential positions.[37]

*

On his sixtieth birthday in January 1978 Nicolae Ceaușescu was compared to several national heroes from the past: Mircea the Elder, Stephen the Great, Michael the Brave, all rulers of medieval Wallachia.

Another model was Burebista, the king who destroyed the rule of the Celts, opposed the advance of the Romans and united the tribes of the Dacian kingdom from 61 to 41 BC. Dacia was described as a unique civilisation in an area that covered much of present-day Romania. Like Mussolini, Ceaușescu viewed himself as the reincarnation of a glorious, ancient tradition. He peered back into the nation's archaic past, discerning continuities between various historical stages that linked the kingdom of Dacia to the Socialist Republic of Romania, making him nothing less than the culmination of thousands of years of history.

The 2050th anniversary of the foundation of Dacia was celebrated with great pomp on 5 July 1980. The entire upper echelon of the party machine attended the ceremony, held in the Stadium of the Republic. Allegorical plays were staged and poems were read. Ceaușescu was portrayed as a direct descendant of Burebista, who soon became the favourite subject for artists in Romania. His profile was painted, carved and knitted, always with a noble profile and manly beard. The film *Burebista* was the year's leading artistic event. Linguists, historians and archaeologists published learned tomes on the Dacians.[38]

Ordinary people, however, seemed to lack enthusiasm. They avoided public celebrations. A few openly expressed their discontent with the regime, despite a ubiquitous police presence. 'Ceaușescu is very much discredited amongst the population,' wrote the French ambassador. The reason was clear. Everywhere there were long queues. At the butcher's shop nothing but lard, sausages, entrails and chicken feet were available. There was no fruit except for a few apples in the north and peaches in the south (but not the other way around). Ordinary wine was beyond the reach of all those who dined but in the most exclusive restaurants. The country faced a shortage of energy, as an overextended petrochemical industry consumed gargantuan quantities of petrol. Only one in every three light bulbs was turned on, while public transportation came to a halt on Sundays.[39]

Romania had entered a period of severe economic recession. A cornerstone of the Ceauşescu Doctrine was economic self-sufficiency. Like his predecessor Gheorghe-Dej, the Conducator emulated the Stalinist model even as he distanced himself from the Soviet Union. Wishing to create a heavy industrial base, he borrowed massively from Western countries to import the necessary technology, equipment and raw materials. But oil prices soared during the 1979 energy crisis, leading to much higher interest rates, which in turned forced the regime to borrow on an even larger scale.

In 1981, as foreign debt peaked at roughly US$12 billion, Romania could no longer keep up its interest payments. Ceauşescu, in a snap decision, decided to repay the entire debt in the shortest time possible by imposing an austerity programme. Imports were cut and exports increased. Meat deliveries to the Soviet Union more than trebled from 1983 to 1985. Maize, fruit, vegetables, wine, all were directed towards foreign markets. Food was rationed, with queues for such staples as bread and potatoes. Sometimes animal feed instead of flour was used for bread. Heavy cuts were also imposed on energy demands, with people living in the dark and shivering through the winter. There was no fuel for the tractors.[40]

The greater the misery, the louder the propaganda. As living standards declined, the Ceauşescu cult grew ever more extravagant. Anniversaries in uneven years were acclaimed with great exuberance, always a telling sign of a regime's desperation. In 1982 Nicolae Ceauşescu's sixty-fourth birthday was celebrated, followed by the seventeenth anniversary of the Ninth Party Congress held in 1965. A few months later, at the sixtieth anniversary of the founding of the Young Communists' League, party members and ordinary people had to praise the 'revolutionary youth' of the Conducator. The eighth anniversary of his election as President of Romania followed later that year. On each occasion floods of telegrams arrived from every corner of the realm, thanking the Conducator for the

Ceauşescu Era and the Romanian Miracle. Ceauşescu demanded constant demonstrations of gratitude from the very people he was ruining. He also took the opportunity these occasions offered to blame the government for all the shortcomings, absolving himself and his party.[41]

In June 1982, in the intervals of several celebrations, the Conducator chaired the Ideological Commission of the Central Committee. It substituted Nicolae Ceauşescu's writings for Marxism-Leninism, which was no longer mentioned.[42]

The cult probably attained its height in 1985, as the country celebrated twenty years of the Ceauşescu Era with concerts, festivals, conferences, ceremonies, all meticulously rehearsed and flawlessly executed. All hailed Ceauşescu as the 'most beloved son of the people'. In every city, exhibits of his collected writings were organised.[43]

Ceauşescu's portrait, displayed in party and state institutions as soon as he returned from Korea in 1971, was now everywhere. By law it had to hang on the walls in schools, factories and army barracks, as well as at border checkpoints. Ordinary people were also obliged to display his portrait on public ceremonies, state anniversaries, mass meetings and official visits. By law his portrait had to appear on the first page of every textbook, while every primary school textbook had to display a colour photograph of Nicolae and Elena Ceauşescu. On the express instructions of the Conducator, it was to show the First Couple 'surrounded by pioneers and falcons', meaning students in the uniforms of the two party organisations that were compulsory for children aged four to fourteen.[44]

Television was limited to a single channel that broadcast for only two hours a day. Half of the schedule was routinely devoted to Ceauşescu's activities and accomplishments. Under personal supervision from the Conducator, to mark 1985, special programmes were produced, including 'The Ninth Congress: The Congress of New Breakthroughs'; 'Twenty Years of Socialist Achievements'; 'The Nicolae Ceauşescu Era'; and 'Science during the Nicolae Ceauşescu Epoch'. Similar policies governed radio broadcasting, with praise of Ceauşescu aired throughout the day.[45]

The front pages of the tightly controlled newspapers invariably reported on Ceauşescu's many achievements. Bookshops, by law, had to showcase his speeches, which had expanded by 1986 from a modest two volumes to an impressive twenty-eight weighty tomes. News kiosks presented smaller selections of his works. Music stores offered recordings of his speeches.[46]

Every minor decision had to pass by the Ceauşescus. A simple change in street name had to be sanctioned by Nicolae, who would write 'de acord' in the margin. When two football teams played a match, Elena decided whether or not the game should be shown on television. Every detail of the cult was determined by the Ceauşescus, including the number of times their names were broadcast each day. But there were no statues. Like Hitler and Duvalier, Ceauşescu refused any statues in his honour, with the exception of a large bust in his home village. When artists asked him if they could incorporate his image in a monument to be built in Bucharest entitled 'Victory of Socialism', he repeatedly declined.[47]

Ceauşescu had something much larger in mind. Years earlier, Pyongyang, with its straight boulevards and immense government buildings, had offered a vision of communist utopia: a truly modern city devoid of any trace of the past. When an earthquake devastated parts of Bucharest in 1977 he saw it as an opportunity to raise a new capital on top of the old one. The systematic destruction of the city centre, dotted with centuries-old houses, churches and monasteries, began in 1982. After a couple of years nothing but a naked hill was left, which in turn was flattened to make way for the Palace of the People, a pharaonic project that kept tens of thousands of workers busy around the clock. It was never finished. A Boulevard of the Victory of Socialism, 3.5 kilometres in length, ninety-two metres in width, was built, flanked by apartment blocks inspired by North Korea.[48]

Two kilometres away from the palace, in a different district, a Museum of National History was planned, although only the façade was ever erected. On the edge of the capital an eighteenth-century monastic complex was bulldozed to provide room for a new Palace of Justice, a project for which the ground was never broken.

Keen to remodel the country along straight lines, Ceauşescu's hand reached far beyond the capital, in a project termed systematisation. Begun in 1972, this initiative entailed the wilful destruction of thousands of small villages, with their inhabitants forced to resettle into shoddily built apartment blocks, often without working lifts or running water. The project petered out with the energy crisis in 1979, although lack of funds was never an impediment for Ceauşescu. Even as Romania's economy crumbled he revived systematisation in 1988, earmarking between seven and eight thousand villages for destruction.[49]

One hamlet thrived. In Scornicesti, site of a nationwide pilgrimage, precisely one cottage was spared the wrecking ball, namely Nicolae Ceauşescu's birth house. The village boasted paved streets, new homes, a large stadium, a model factory and shops with seemingly endless supplies.[50]

The Securitate quelled every expression of discontent. Carrying submachine guns, they could be seen standing on every street in the capital, and at regular checkpoints every fifteen kilometres or so in the countryside. A network of spies and informants covered the country.

People did what was required, without much conviction. In 1985 the French ambassador was struck by a society which was perfectly regimented, stripped of 'any sense of spontaneity in the expression of feelings towards the leader'. At mass rallies those who stood in front, enthusiastically acclaiming the leader, were often security agents dressed in workers' clothing. Ordinary people further back merely went through the motions, as loudspeakers produced the required volume by playing tape-recorded cheers.[51]

People sang the leader's praises in public, but cursed him under their breath. One observer noted how pedestrians would stop to applaud him when he appeared in public to inspect a building site. The moment he was gone, the insults began. John Sweeney, a British journalist who visited the country in the summer of 1985, observed that 'the whole country was locked in a mute, passive sulk against the regime'. Yet he too later acknowledged that none of the foreigners writing about Romania at that time fully grasped the sheer misery of ordinary people, since their every step was closely monitored by security agents.[52]

Ordinary people may have detested the regime, but they were unlikely to rebel. The party enrolled four million members out of a population of twenty-two million, meaning that roughly one in six people in some way benefited from the regime, with their fate linked to that of Ceauşescu. They served him well, and he sustained them in turn, providing generous benefits that set them apart from the rest of the population.[53]

Paradoxically, though, it was the Soviet Union that made a popular uprising most unlikely. Ceauşescu had spoken out against sending troops into Czechoslovakia in 1968, thereafter crafting his image as the man who had dared to stand up to the Soviet Union. He periodically snubbed or insulted the Soviets, but Moscow tolerated his antics since he never constituted any real threat. He remained a rigid, doctrinaire communist. Ordinary people knew very well that the Soviet Union was still the vigilant guardian of socialism, and that under the Brezhnev Doctrine the Red Army might very well cross the border to suppress an upheaval. Their fear of Brezhnev surpassed their loathing of Ceauşescu.[54]

The rise of Mikhail Gorbachev cast Ceauşescu in a very different light. After the proponent of perestroika laid out a vision of democratisation in January 1987 the Conducator began posing as the defender of ideological purity. He rejected political reform as a mere delusion, vowing to follow the 'correct road to communism'. Instead of relaxing economic stringency he demanded an even greater 'spirit of sacrifice' and promptly imposed further austerity measures. These made his ramshackle economy even more dependent on the Soviet Union.[55]

As the West embraced Gorbachev its leaders ceased to ingratiate themselves with Ceauşescu. Invitations dwindled. Visitors were few and far between. Foreign journalists became more critical, emboldening dissidents at home. In March 1989 six elderly

statesmen published an open letter attacking the leader's cult of
personality and the pervasive surveillance of the population. The
signatories included Constantin Pirvulescu, now ninety-three
years old. He was detained, interrogated and placed under house
arrest again.

Ceaușescu's own health was declining. He was suffering from
diabetes, left untreated for many years because he was too paranoid
to trust anyone, including his own doctors. He had faith only in
his wife, but she, too, was paranoid, and also ignorant. Both were
convinced that destiny had chosen them to lead their country
to greatness. Detached from reality, living in splendid isolation,
surrounded by the sycophants and liars they had promoted over
the years, they had come to believe in their own cult.[56]

In November 1989 the Fourteenth Party Congress dutifully
elected Ceaușescu yet again as leader of the Romanian Communist
Party. He took the opportunity to castigate the revolutions that
were bringing down communist regimes in Eastern Europe. In
June the trade union Solidarity had won the elections in Poland,
leading to the fall of the communist party a few months later.
Gorbachev had not intervened. In October, Hungary adopted a
package of democratic reforms that effectively ended communism.
Again, Gorbachev remained quiet.[57]

On 17 December Romanian troops fired into a crowd of
demonstrators in Timisoara, where the government had ordered the
arrest of a local pastor preaching against the projected destruction of
dozens of historic churches and monasteries. The violent crackdown
triggered nationwide protests. On 21 December, Nicolae Ceaușescu
appeared on the balcony of the party headquarters in the centre
of Bucharest, flanked by the entire apparatus, to address a mass
rally organised in support of the regime. For once the assembled
crowd failed to cheer him. Within minutes, people at the back
began whistling and jeering. He raised his hand, demanding
silence, repeatedly tapping the microphone. The unrest continued.
Ceaușescu looked stunned. His wife leaned forward, lecturing the
crowd: 'Stay quiet! What is wrong with you?' Ceaușescu decided to
plough on with his speech, in a hoarse, frail voice trying to placate

the demonstrators by offering to increase the minimum wage. But he had faltered. With the fear gone, the rally turned into a riot.

The speech was broadcast live. As soon as the transmission went blank, everyone recognised that a revolution was unfolding. People everywhere joined the protests, attacking government premises, tearing up official portraits of Ceauşescu and burning his propaganda books. Ceauşescu ordered the Securitate to fight to the last man. Throughout the night they shot at demonstrators, but were unable to stem the tide.

The following day the army joined the revolution. As angry protesters began to lay siege to the party headquarters, Elena and Nicolae Ceauşescu were forced to flee by helicopter, landing in a field outside the capital. Later that day they were hunted down and placed under arrest. On Christmas Day Ion Iliescu, head of the National Salvation Front, a spontaneous organisation formed by communist party members who had turned against their leader, hastily organised a military tribunal to try the Ceauşescus. After the death penalty was delivered, the couple were led to a freezing courtyard next to a toilet block. Ceauşescu apparently sang the Internationale. The First Lady screamed 'Fuck you' as they were lined up against a wall and shot.[58]

8

Mengistu

On the outskirts of the ancient capital Axum, where in 1937 the Italians dismantled and carted off a huge obelisk as spoils of war, burned-out Soviet tanks still lie abandoned across dusty fields. In other parts of Ethiopia, too, one can find rusty memorials of a civil war that claimed at least 1.4 million lives. For almost two decades the Horn of Africa was ravaged by a revolution that overthrew the emperor in 1974.

Ethiopia was an ancient empire that had embraced Christianity in AD 330, a few decades after Rome, as ports along the Red Sea served as a sanctuary for believers in exile. The faith served as a centralising force. At the end of the nineteenth century Emperor Menelik II expanded the empire, transformed the country into a modern state and led his troops in a victory against Italy. The Battle of Adwa against the Italians ensured that Ethiopia was never colonised, except for a brief period from 1936 to 1941.

Haile Selassie, crowned in 1916, wielded absolute power for almost six decades, a record for any head of state. Lion of Judah, King of Kings, Elect of God, he incarnated divine will. Authority, in the Ethiopian Orthodox Church, had to be powerfully exerted from above, and by all accounts he was an autocrat, using his clout to keep the empire together – often by force. His image was everywhere, on coins, paintings, stamps, postcards and photographs, his name used for schools and hospitals. Unlike other branches of Christianity, the church in Ethiopia never attempted to regulate the production of icons.[1]

Outside Ethiopia Haile Selassie was worshipped by the Rastafarians, who saw in him God incarnate, the returning Messiah leading black people to a golden age of peace and prosperity. But he resisted any kind of social reform, and in the decades after the Second World War became increasingly unwilling to adapt to the modern world. In 1973 a devastating famine revealed glaring poverty in the countryside. Countless villagers starved to death. Prices of food and oil shot up in the cities, leading to widespread protests. Discipline among the military crumbled, as several army units mutinied. In February 1974 unrest spread to the navy, the air force and the police before finally reaching the imperial bodyguard on 1 March. In order to placate the army Haile Selassie appointed a caretaker government, tasked with giving the country a constitutional monarchy.[2]

A group of military leaders popularly known as the Derg soon took over. Derg, an Amharic word for 'committee', was the short name for the 'Coordinating Committee of the Armed Forces, Bodyguard, Police and Territorial Army' established to investigate the army's demands. In reality it was a junta, composed mainly of low-ranking officers representing different military units. Senior officers were kept at arm's length, tainted by their association with the emperor.[3]

In July the Derg dismissed the prime minister. They then abolished the emperor's Crown Council and proceeded to arrest his personal staff one by one. All the palaces were nationalised, together with every enterprise owned by the imperial family. On the evening of 11 September the Derg aired a documentary on the famine on state television, interspersed with scenes of royal extravagance. This destroyed what was left of the imperial image. The next day Haile Selassie was deposed, shoved into a Volkswagen and whisked away from the palace.[4]

The Derg, under the slogan 'Ethiopia First', initially appointed a widely respected general as their shortlived figurehead. Aman

Andom was an Eritrean, who favoured a negotiated settlement with the Eritrean Liberation Front, an organisation that had gained a new lease of life from the collapse of the empire, and demanded independence for their people. Eritrea, a vast and formidable maritime province with vital ports, extended for hundreds of kilometres along the Red Sea. Without it, Ethiopia would have no access to the sea. The junior officers of the Derg insisted that troops in the region be reinforced in preparation for a major offensive against the secessionists.

On 23 November Aman was relieved of his duties. The Derg used the opportunity to eliminate their most outspoken opponents. In a mass execution up to sixty of the country's former civil and military leaders were summarily shot. Aman died in a shootout with troops sent to arrest him at his residence.

In his place the Derg appointed General Teferi Banti, a hardliner on Eritrea. A more pliant figure, on public occasions he appeared accompanied by two of his vice-chairmen, Atnafu Abate and Mengistu Haile Mariam. Their first act was to introduce a new penal code, which allowed the Derg to court-martial anyone for speaking against their slogan 'Ethiopia First'.[5]

Of the three men in charge of the Derg, Mengistu was probably the least prepossessing figure. There were rumours about his birth, always considered important in a feudal society. Some claimed that his mother, a servant at court who died in 1949 when Mengistu was eight years old, was the illegitimate daughter of one of the crown counsellors to the emperor. Others, pointing to his dark skin tone, alleged that he came from a slave family in the south. Whatever the truth, his family did not belong to the Amhara, the ruling people from the central highlands of Ethiopia. He was brought up in subservience in a noble household, in the shadow of the imperial palace.[6]

Mengistu had minimal education and followed his father into the army a few years after his mother passed away. He attracted the attention of General Aman Andom, who took him under his wing. From errand boy in the general's office he climbed through the ranks to become sergeant. After graduating from a military academy, he was assigned to the commander of a division in Addis Ababa, but he had a rebellious streak which alienated his superior, who described him as a firebrand. In 1970 he was sent to the Aberdeen Proving Ground in Maryland in the United States for several months, acquiring additional training and a rudimentary knowledge of English.[7]

Although he preferred to remain in the background, in reality Mengistu dominated the Derg. It was he who sent troops to his former mentor's house, and he ensured that the revolution turned bloody with the Massacre of the Sixty. It was Mengistu, again, who proclaimed 'Ethiopian Socialism' on 20 December 1974. Within months dozens of companies were nationalised, while all land was declared public property. Feudalism, Mengistu proclaimed in a mass rally, would be permanently relegated to the museum, as a 'new order' was being created. Some fifty-six teachers and students were sent to the countryside to 'spread the revolution'.[8]

The Derg ran the country from the Grand Palace, a sprawling complex of residential quarters, halls and chapels on top of one of Addis Ababa's seven hills, its red roofs contrasting with the glossy green of surrounding eucalyptus trees. They met in the Throne Hall, where the emperor had held important ceremonies and royal banquets. In a building nearby Haile Selassie spent his last days under house arrest. In August 1975 he died in mysterious circumstances, apparently from complications of prostate surgery, aged eighty-three. A persistent rumour made the rounds, alleging that Mengistu had a pillow placed over Haile Selassie's head. Years later it was revealed that he had the emperor's remains buried underneath his office, placing his desk right above the corpse.[9]

From the Grand Palace the Derg ruled through force and fear. A month after the emperor passed away they declared a state of emergency and prohibited any form of opposition to the revolution, from the distribution of placards down to uttering 'unlawful words in public or any other place'. They also embraced Marxism-Leninism, making it compulsory in schools, factories and offices. In the largely illiterate countryside, political commissars indoctrinated the villagers, forced to join collective peasant associations.[10]

In September 1976 Mengistu was ambushed as he returned home. The attempt on his life failed, but he seized the opportunity to eradicate his rivals. He appeared the following day at a mass rally held on the central square of the capital, renamed Revolution Square, defiantly urging 'vigilance to safeguard the revolution'. In the following weeks, dozens of opponents were killed in ruthless sweeps organised by the army. Behind the scenes members of the Derg themselves were ambushed, with dead bodies occasionally being borne out of the Throne Hall.[11]

Mengistu had betrayed his erstwhile mentor, General Aman Andom. On 3 February 1977 he turned against Teferi Banti, the Derg's figurehead, accusing him of having plotted a counter-revolutionary coup. With seven other Derg members, Teferi was placed under arrest in the Grand Palace. 'I will see your death, but you won't see mine,' Mengistu told them as they were taken away to the basement of the palace. Most were shot with a muffled gun, the others strangled. From a committee of more than a hundred members, no more than sixty remained on the Derg.[12]

A terse and chilling announcement crackled over Radio Ethiopia. Mengistu was now the sole chairman of the Derg. The Soviet ambassador congratulated him personally the following day.[13]

Mengistu was the architect of the Derg. With great tact and patience, he had transformed a loose coalition of junior officers into an organised structure taking the lead in the revolution. He had spent three years working behind the scenes, carefully inflecting the balance of power in his favour. He knew how to wait, and he knew how to pounce. One of his greatest skills was his ability to hide his feelings. He was humble. He could be all smiles, his voice ringing with sincerity when required. As one of his followers put it, he was like water and fire, both lamb and tiger.[14]

Mengistu had other qualities. He was blessed with an unusually good memory, never forgetting a face. He had an enormous appetite for work, preparing for every meeting in meticulous detail. He was a compelling speaker who knew how to assess the mood of an audience and turn it to his own advantage. He proposed a simple but appealing vision of national revival and social revolution, mixed with crude Marxist slogans. He carried conviction, in particular among junior officers of the Derg: 'When you see him you will start to believe in him', one of his followers later remembered. He was also a great listener, constantly trying to know more about the power dynamics around him. He was a shrewd manipulator of people and events. Most of all he was more determined than his junior colleagues on the Derg.[15]

On 5 February Mengistu appeared on Revolution Square to announce that a counter-revolutionary plot had been nipped in the bud. 'Our enemies were preparing us for lunch, but we had them for breakfast,' he told the assembled masses. At the end of his speech he theatrically smashed a bottle filled with red ink, defiantly declaring that the blood of all those who opposed the revolution would be spilt. As the crowd cheered him on, he pledged to arm the oppressed.[16]

A Red Terror followed. Within weeks urban neighbourhood committees and peasant associations were given weapons. They rooted out real and imagined enemies of the Derg, mainly competing Marxist-inspired student organisations. One of these was the Ethiopian People's Revolutionary Party, which had initially rallied behind the junta but soon accused the Derg of having betrayed the revolution. Tensions had spilled over into open conflict.

In Addis Ababa house-by-house searches were carried out. Sometimes cameras and typewriters were treated as evidence of spying activities. Suspects were arrested in the hundreds and executed on the outskirts of the capital. They included children as young as eleven. Their bodies could be seen lying in the gutter. Others were chased down the streets and shot in broad daylight. Doctors were so afraid that they refused to treat those suspected of being 'counter-revolutionaries'. Anyone could become an enemy, as people used the terror to settle grudges, denouncing their neighbours in the midst of the political chaos.[17]

Mengistu ordered state television to broadcast footage of the racked bodies of political prisoners who had been tortured to death. The gruesome images that flickered across the nation were evidence of his determination, designed to intimidate a population of thirty-two million. The worst of the terror abated after several months, but the blood continued to flow for several years, claiming tens of thousands of lives.[18]

Even as he cracked down at home Mengistu attempted to consolidate his power by courting the Soviet Union. In May 1977 all links with the United States were severed. In a dramatic show of alignment with the Soviet Union, Mengistu flew to Moscow a few days later, welcomed at the airport by a delegation of high-ranking generals. Atnafu Abate, the second vice-chairman of the Derg, voiced reservations about the rapprochement. He was accused of counter-revolutionary crimes and executed later that year, making Mengistu the undisputed leader.[19]

The Soviet Union, however, also backed Somalia, a strip of desert with three million people led by a military junta under Siad Barre. Barre, too, had a vision, hoping to create a Greater Somalia that would encompass Ogaden, a plateau of barren hills and dense shrubs to the east of Ethiopia conquered by Menelik II in the nineteenth century. Briefly, after the Second World War, the region joined Somalia, but Haile Selassie had successfully pleaded with the United Nations to obtain its return to the empire.

In July 1977, sensing weakness across the border, Siad Barre invaded Ogaden. His troops advanced rapidly in parts of the region where Somali nomads were dominant. Mengistu was forced on the defensive, hastily raising recruits to fight the war. Barre, like Mengistu, depended on the Soviet Union. Both men flew to Moscow. The Soviets tried to reconcile the enemies, but when this proved impossible they threw their weight behind Ethiopia, a country with ten times the population of Somalia. A huge airlift of military supplies, tanks, guns, rockets, artillery, mortars and missiles began arriving in Addis Ababa in December, followed by several thousand Russian and Cuban advisers. This assistance tipped the balance in favour of Ethiopia. In March 1978 the last Somali troops began to withdraw, ending the Ogaden War.

Mengistu now began polishing his image. In April 1978 he visited Cuba, where he was cheered by thousands of people lining the twenty-five-kilometre road between the airport and the main protocol house, despite a three-hour delay and sporadic rain.[20]

Some observers saw in this event the beginning of a cult of personality. Several weeks later, as he visited Ogaden, vast crowds welcomed Mengistu wherever he went. In Dire Dawa, a city which had held out against the Somali army, he was greeted by up to 100,000 residents, 'singing joyously and chanting revolutionary slogans'. The newspapers were filled with photographs of Chairman Mengistu receiving bouquets from children, laying foundation stones or reviewing his troops. He was seen off by a band, a guard of honour and the entire upper crust of the regional leadership.[21]

Mengistu modelled himself on Fidel Castro, appearing in combat fatigues, army boots and beret, a revolver on his hip. He aligned his titles to resemble those of his Cuban counterpart, being identified in the press as 'Commander in Chief of the Revolutionary Army' and in addition Chairman of the Provisional Military Administrative Council and Chairman of the Council of Ministers.

Most of all, he replicated imperial gestures. The Grand Palace, where his office was located, was maintained and run as if Haile Selassie were still in residence, with chained cheetahs, lion statues and liveried footmen. Mengistu's state gifts were displayed side by side with those given to the emperor. He sat alone, on a gilded chair or a raised dais. His portraits replaced those of the emperor, sometimes in the old frames with a crown on top. The buildings and gardens, where lions could be heard growling, were fenced with iron grillwork, decorated with Menelik II's initial, the Ethiopian letter M.[22]

Under the emperor leadership had always been highly personalised, a style that accorded much better with popular expectation than the faceless, shadowy character of the Derg in the first years of the revolution. Newspapers habitually reproduced photographs of the emperor receiving foreign visitors or lecturing groups of students in the upper left corner of the front page. Mengistu now filled the same spot.[23]

Much as the emperor had kept his provincial governors on their toes by travelling to the outer parts of his realm, so Mengistu toured the country. In the first months of 1979 he spent several weeks visiting the southern and western administrative regions. On every occasion local representatives tried to outdo each other in praising the Chairman. Negussie Fanta, chief administrator of Welega, hailed his 'far-sighted and wise revolutionary leadership'; others expressed 'heartfelt love' for the Chairman. Like the emperor Mengistu would dispense advice, giving 'confidential revolutionary guidance' to local officials, hospital directors, agricultural experts and industrial plant managers alike.[24]

The praise was prompted by fear. Mengistu was known for visiting the front to humiliate his generals, confiscating their medals and demoting them by a rank or two in front of their soldiers. A few were executed on the spot.[25]

By 1979 every public visit was a well-rehearsed ritual. Attendance was mandatory for the local population, who were told to cheer their leader, shout his slogans and carry his portrait. Mengistu would descend from the skies by helicopter, as a band played revolutionary songs. When he visited a tractor factory in Gojam, some 600 kilometres away from the capital, loudspeakers announced the arrival of the 'visionary, revolutionary and communist leader Comrade Mengistu'. Children gave flowers. Mengistu visited the factory, and then the canteen. Everywhere he saw portraits of himself. Speeches were made, hands shaken, presents given and photographs taken. Sometimes poems were read. When Mengistu visited a historical monastery in Tigray, a priest composed the following lines: 'Here comes the black star; He glows like a sunrise and shines like a sun; Here comes the black star like a shooting star.'[26]

Since 1974 Mengistu had murdered dozens of Derg members. Those who survived lived in fear. He, in turn, wondered which one would turn against him. He could never be sure of their total loyalty, while they were equally apprehensive about his intentions. They all knew, through experience, that he could be their best friend in the morning only to devour them in the evening. Whether or not they genuinely admired him, they were forced to hail him in public. All were transformed into liars, which made organising a coup much more difficult.

Derg members learned not to question Mengistu's directives, quoting from his speeches instead. A small booklet with selected quotations made the rounds. It became standard to begin a public address by invoking Mengistu's words of wisdom. On important occasions one of Mengistu's speech writers, Baalu Girma, was asked to provide an appropriate excerpt. A journalist with a master's degree from Michigan State University, Baalu had previously written speeches for the emperor. He became permanent secretary of the Ministry of Information in 1977, guaranteeing that fulsome praise for the leader was diffused far and wide.[27]

In the early years of the revolution Mengistu had prevented the printing and hanging of portraits of Aman Andom and Teferi Banti, the two Derg figureheads. After victory in the Ogaden War his own portrait went up in every government bureau, in every community office, in every factory and enterprise, whether private or public. His picture could even be seen in restaurants and bars. This, too, was prompted by fear. Local cadres were responsible for making sure that he was everywhere, and they kept lists of establishments that failed to comply.[28]

Mengistu's image, besides those of Marx, Engels and Lenin, was held at mass rallies, regularly organised from 1976 onwards. The highpoint of the revolutionary calendar was Revolution Day, also called National Day, which happened to coincide with the second day of the Ethiopian calendar, falling on either 11 or 12 September. In the past throngs of people had converged on Addis Ababa to celebrate religious holidays. Now they were mobilised by the urban neighbourhood committees, who levied fines on those who failed to turn up. Everything was carefully stage-managed, with thousands obliged to march and carry floats before the leader, who beamed from his gilded chair on a rostrum in Revolution Square. Red was the dominant colour, with stars, banners, sickles and hammers everywhere. In 1977 150,000 people participated in the event. At the end of the Chairmans' speech, a cannon fired banners into the air, which unfurled and drifted down, attached to small parachutes. Planes flew overhead in formation.[29]

As in every Marxist-Leninist regime, the second most important event was May Day. But there were other occasions, prompted by the whim of the leader. Unity rallies, victory rallies, war rallies and peace rallies occurred with depressing frequency. In 1979 20,000 children were made to goose-step in front of him at the stadium in Addis Ababa to mark International Year of the Child. In his spare time Mengistu occasionally toyed with his soldiers at the Grand Palace, making them stand to attention and parade around the grounds.[30]

Ethiopia, by 1979, had no constitution, no parliament and no party. All power was effectively vested in Mengistu. He relied on the Derg. They, in turn, depended on an army of roughly 280,000 soldiers as well as a loose network of urban neighbourhood committees and peasant associations. But what was lacking was a disciplined and loyal organisation capable of establishing a true dictatorship of the proletariat, guiding the country in its transformation towards socialism.[31]

In December 1979 Mengistu established a preparatory organisation called the Commission for the Organisation of the Workers' Party of Ethiopia, known by its acronym COPWE. Its purpose was to spread Marxism-Leninism and create from scratch a communist vanguard party, modelled on the Communist Party of the Soviet Union. Mengistu was responsible for determining the rules and conditions of recruitment, and personally appointed every member of the Central Committee, the Executive Committee (equivalent to a Politburo) and the Secretariat. All were his loyal supporters, and some his close confidants. None had any substantial following of their own, and a few were widely distrusted for having betrayed their colleagues during the Red Terror. As its Chairman, Mengistu mediated between the commission and the government. The commission vowed to 'take all measures necessary to avert any situation which threatens the revolution'. One of its first acts was to prohibit all other political organisations.[32]

During its first years the commission built up more than 6,000 cells, carefully screening every potential candidate. Like the Central Committee the cells were dominated by members from the military and the police. There was, of course, a price to pay. Since loyalty mattered more than belief, many of the party members had no more than a smattering of Marxism-Leninism. They were sent to the Soviet Union or Eastern Europe to learn the ropes, but remained 'largely innocent of ideology', to quote the historian Christopher Clapham.[33]

The commission asserted control over every organ of authority, including the urban neighbourhood committees and the peasant associations. They established new organisations that mirrored those of the Soviet Union, from a Revolutionary Ethiopia Women's Association to a Revolutionary Ethiopia Youth Organisation.

As the commission extended its grip over the country ever more radical programmes were carried out in the name of socialism. Mengistu did not need Marx to understand that collectivisation allowed him to extract a much greater surplus from the countryside. Within a few years some seven million households were organised into peasant associations, which were now organs of the state. These associations imposed grain quotas on the villagers, forcing them to sell their crops to the state at prices determined by the state. They taxed them relentlessly and conscripted them to work without pay on infrastructure projects far from home. They turned them into tenants of the state.[34]

In May 1982, at long last, *Das Kapital* was published in Amharic. Half a year later the East Germans donated a giant block of red granite depicting Karl Marx to guard the entrance to the University of Addis Ababa. Lenin followed in 1983, mass-produced in the Soviet Union, standing seven metres tall right before the United Nations Economic Commission for Africa, his gaze fixed firmly on the horizon, one leg arched forward on the path towards the future.[35]

After five years of preparatory work Mengistu felt ready formally to establish the Workers' Party of Ethiopia. A new chapter in the People's Revolution was reached in July 1984 as party branches were established in the provinces, all dutifully hailing Mengistu's 'vital and decisive leadership'. His portrait now hung in the middle, with Marx, Engels and Lenin to the left, a red star to his right.[36]

The real event was scheduled to coincide with the tenth anniversary of the revolution, falling in September 1984. Mengistu had visited Pyongyang two years earlier and was determined to emulate the scale on which the North Koreans marked their National Day. He returned from Pyongyang with a team of advisers who primped and preened the capital for the event, erecting hundreds of triumphal arches, obelisks and hoardings to extol Mengistu and Marxism. All commercial signs were removed, while huge revolutionary slogans crowned every modern building. Slum areas were blocked from view by kilometres of corrugated iron fences painted the obligatory red.[37]

A huge Party Congress Hall, in the socialist-realist style cherished by so many communist dictators, opened a week before the celebrations. In 1979 the commission had moved into an elegant art deco building once occupied by parliament. The outside was repainted in an earthy red shade, the iron gates refitted with a hammer and sickle. The new building, in contrast, stood as a monument to the achievements of the revolution. In the main conference room each of the 3,500 seats came equipped with the latest technology to provide simultaneous translation. Everything apart from the stone cladding on the outside of the building had been built to the highest specifications and imported from Finland. The bill was settled in cash.[38]

At their first meeting on 10 September members of the Workers' Party of Ethiopia unanimously elected their 'visionary leader' as General Secretary of the Central Committee and pledged their people to implement the slogan 'Forward with the Revolutionary Leadership of Comrade Mengistu Haile Mariam'. A member of the Politburo stepped forward, solemnly reading a biography of the Chairman, comparing the life of 'the saviour of Ethiopia, brilliant, generous' to the second coming of Christ. Mengistu, who had checked every word of the speech, was all humility, mumbling modestly that he did not deserve the praise.[39]

Even more impressive than the Party Congress Hall was the Tiglachin Monument, or Our Struggle Monument, a soaring stele designed by the North Koreans. It stood fifty metres tall, topped by a red star. On two sides of the stele intricately carved bronze reliefs illustrated the history of the revolution, from the downfall of the emperor to Mengistu Haile Mariam, leading his people towards a socialist future.[40]

In early September the main avenues of Addis Ababa were closed for several days, as North Korean advisers drilled large crowds for the parade. People who failed to turn up and march on command were beaten, imprisoned or starved, as food was rationed.

The big event took place on National Day, as some 70,000 students, villagers and troops marched past the reviewing stand on Revolution Square, carrying giant posters of Marx, Lenin and Mengistu, and shouting revolutionary slogans: 'Forward with the Revolutionary Leadership of Comrade Mengistu Haile Mariam'. Mengistu stood to attention. In a display of military might, hundreds of tanks, armoured personnel carriers and rocket launchers rumbled through the square. But the main attraction must have been a float with a giant statue of Mengistu, his left fist clenched in the air. It was decorated with yet another slogan, reading 'Without the Wise and Revolutionary Leadership of Mengistu Haile Mariam our Struggle Cannot Succeed'.[41]

A few years after the revolution all religious objects from the Ethnology Museum had been removed and placed in storage, but little had appeared about the new regime itself. As part of the tenth anniversary, a special exhibition opened its doors, at long last presenting a unified vision of the past. From paleoanthropological times to the Battle of Adwa and the overthrow of the emperor, the country was presented as an uninterrupted line of evolution, a story of progress and redemption culminating in the figure of Mengistu.[42]

By most estimates the celebrations cost between US$50 and 100 million.[43] Even before they began millions of people were starving. Ethiopia was a poor country, and rigid socialist economics did not help. Forced conscription and civil war further undermined a fragile countryside. Per capita cereal production declined by 15 per cent from 1974 to 1984, although more grain was requisitioned to pay for a higher military budget. The first signs of famine appeared in 1983, as parts of the country suffered from an unusually severe drought. By the summer of 1984 thousands of people were dying in the Wollo region alone, with towns overrun by starving villagers begging in the streets or waiting to die beside barren fields. The regime covered up the crisis, taking foreign reporters to see collective farms where people prospered. Since the famine affected the rebellious north, the regime also took advantage of the crisis by letting local people who sympathised with the rebels starve to death. By the time Mengistu addressed the crowd for five hours on the tenth anniversary of the revolution in September 1984 some seven million people were on the verge of starvation.[44]

The famine sparked international attention after harrowing images of wizened children on saline drips were broadcast on BBC news in October 1984. It galvanised a global campaign to raise millions in aid. In February 1985 Mengistu finally appeared on state television, declaring that the country faced a grave crisis resulting from drought. He proposed a solution, calling for the resettlement of famished villagers from the north to the more fertile plains of the south. Under the cover of aid the regime forcibly moved entire population groups out of rebellious areas to distant parts of the country. More than half a million people were relocated, often impelled by threat of violence. Worse was to come, as resettlement was followed by another scheme, known as 'villagisation'. It was collectivisation under another name, with scattered households herded into planned villages where the state controlled everything. By most estimates at least half a million people died in the 1983–5 famine.[45]

Much food aid was redirected from civilians to soldiers. Civil war had raged since 1977, as a variety of liberation movements were established in the wake of the revolution. Among them were the Oromo Liberation Front, the Tigrayan People's Liberation Front and the Afar Liberation Front, all located in Ethiopia's barren north. But the Derg's foremost enemy was the Eritrean People's

Liberation Front. At the height of the war against Somalia in the summer of 1977 Mengistu had called for a 'total people's war' against all aggressors. After he won the Ogaden War with backing from Cuba and the Soviet Union he had hoped to crush decisively the secessionist movements in the north. But operation Red Star, a huge military campaign in 1982 involving more than half the country's army, was a complete failure. Unlike the plateau in the east, the north offered ideal terrain for guerrilla fighters, with soaring mountains, treacherous cliffs and desolate plains covered with rocks.[46]

Mengistu assumed personal command of the operation, temporarily moving most of his cabinet to Asmara, the capital of Eritrea. But the very qualities that had helped him to win control of the Derg in the revolution's early years now militated against him. He went to war without a clear strategy, believing that his formidable army would prevail through sheer strength of numbers. When his troops failed to dislodge the insurgents from their mountainous strongholds he accused his generals of incompetence and treason, having them arbitrarily executed. He trusted no one, establishing a surveillance network of political commissars around the high command. Since loyalty was prized more than competence, flatterers and opportunists were promoted.[47]

The Red Star operation became a war of attrition, as hundreds of thousands of young men and boys were forcibly conscripted into the armed forces. They were barely fed and often beaten before being thrown into battle against some of the most hardened insurgents in the world. By the middle of the 1980s civil war and famine had become permanent features of the regime.[48]

Despite an army of 300,000 and twelve billion dollars in Soviet military aid, the regime began to collapse under the onslaught of different rebel movements. In March 1988 the Eritrean rebels scored a decisive victory at Afabet, a strategic garrison town reinforced by trenches and bunkers in the middle of the Sahel. It was the largest battle in Africa since El Alamein. Some 20,000 soldiers were killed or captured, changing the balance of war. A few months later, with Mengistu absent in East Germany seeking more arms, his senior officers attempted a coup. It failed, but increased the rate of desertions among the rank and file. When the Eritreans stormed the port of Massawa on the Red Sea in February 1990 even Moscow lost faith, determined to pull out of the conflict. Gorbachev urged Mengistu to reform.

The assorted guerrilla fighters were now on the move, spearheaded by the Eritrean People's Liberation Front, and reaching the outskirts of Addis Ababa by the end of 1990. Over the following months Mengistu increasingly lost touch with reality, alternating between declarations of defiance and dark hints of suicide. On 16 April 1991 he spoke on the radio, ranting against traitors and foreign plotters. Three days later he proclaimed a general mobilisation 'to safeguard the integrity of the motherland'. In a frenzied move, he clung on to all his titles but replaced several of his most senior ministers, all to no avail. On 21 May he escaped, slipping out of the capital to board a small plane and fly across the border to Nairobi. From there he went to Zimbabwe, where President Robert Mugabe granted him asylum.[49]

Within weeks the regime melted away. Even before Mengistu's escape his forces had vanished into the landscape as the rebels moved south. His posters were vandalised, some riddled with gunshot. Lenin was toppled from his pedestal. His sayings disappeared from the masthead of the party newspaper. On Revolution Square the slogans and stars were covered in paint. Nothing but rusty scaffolding remained where Mengistu had once been displayed.[50]

Mengistu left behind a legacy of devastation caused by war, famine and collectivisation, but no enduring institutions and no lasting ideology. He arrogated all power to himself, ensuring that no decision was made without his consent. Even the party he so painstakingly built up was no more than an instrument of personal rule. Since he embodied the revolution it vanished the moment he fled.

Afterword

In a garage run by the municipality of Addis Ababa, Lenin is lying on his back, surrounded by weeds and empty oil drums. Few people come to visit him. Those who do are warned by local workers not to wake him.[1]

He is large and weighty, and bringing him down from his pedestal was hard work. Heavy machinery had been required, as ropes could not even make him shake. He was not, of course, the first one to go. After the Berlin Wall came down in November 1989, Lenin was dismantled a thousand times, sometimes attacked with hammers or decapitated, occasionally mothballed. Other despots, too, were toppled. Across Albania jubilant crowds tackled statues of Enver Hoxha, who had controlled the country for forty years. For decades portraits, posters, slogans, busts and statues had gone up, but the tide had turned.

It took many observers by surprise. Dictators, the thinking went, were unshakable, like their statues. They had captured the souls of their subjects and moulded their thinking. They had cast a spell on them. But there never was a spell. There was fear, and when it evaporated the entire edifice collapsed. In the case of Ceaușescu, the moment he faltered when challenged by demonstrators in front of the party headquarters on 21 December 1989 can be pinned down almost to the minute. That moment took several decades to arrive.

There is no cult without fear. At the height of the twentieth century, hundreds of millions of people across the globe had no choice but to acquiesce in the glorification of their leaders, who backed up their rule with the threat of violence. Under Mao or Kim, mocking the leader's name was enough to warrant assignment to a labour camp. Failure to cry, cheer or shout on command carried a heavy penalty. Under Mussolini or Ceaușescu, editors received daily instructions on what should be mentioned and what was proscribed. Writers, poets and painters, under Stalin, trembled at the thought that their praise might not appear sufficiently sincere.

When the term 'cult of personality' is bandied about to characterise any and every effort to glorify a leader, this trivialises what occurred in modern dictatorships. When democratically elected presidents or prime ministers groom their image, or pose in front of children who sing their praises, or engrave their name on gold coins, or surround themselves with flatterers, they engage in political theatre. It may be repulsive, or appear narcissistic and even sinister, but it is not a cult. To have followers proclaim that their leader is a genius is not a cult either. In the first stage of a cult, a leader needs to have enough clout to abase his opponents and force them to salute him in public. But with a fully developed cult of personality no one can any longer be quite certain any more who supports and who opposes the dictator.

One such is Kim Jong-un, from the third generation of his family, in control of North Korea since 2011. In 2015, after having executed some seventy high-ranking officials, including several generals and his uncle-in-law, he handed out badges bearing his portrait to his inner circle. Statues dedicated to the family went up in every province the same year. Like Kim Il-sung, Kim Jong-un tours the country, offering on-the-spot guidance with his entourage eagerly writing down his every word. He walks like his grandfather, he smiles like his grandfather, he even looks like his grandfather.[2]

Kim is but one of many dictators who have thrived, despite the spread of democracy since 1989. Assad *fils* stepped in the shoes of Assad *père* in 2000. In an echo of the 'humble country doctor' François Duvalier, Bashar al-Assad at first presented himself as a 'mild-mannered ophthalmologist'. Then the doctor spread a culture of fear, covering Syria with his image while suppressing dissent with an iron fist.[3]

New dictators have appeared. In the early years of the twenty-first century Turkey appeared to be a democracy in the making, with a vibrant civil society and a relatively open press. Then along came Recep Tayyip Erdogan. Elected president in 2014, he began building up his image as the country's strongman. In 2016 he used a failed coup as a pretext to clamp down on all opposition, suspending, dismissing or imprisoning tens of thousands of people, including journalists, academics, lawyers and civil servants. And even as he purged his opponents he glorified himself. His speeches were broadcast several times a day on television, his face plastered on numerous walls, while his supporters likened him to a second prophet. Turkey is still a far cry from the fully fledged dictatorships that dominated the twentieth century, but those, too, took time to build up.[4]

In the wake of the Cultural Revolution the communist party in China amended its constitution explicitly to forbid 'all forms of personality cult', making slow but inexorable progress towards greater accountability. But the regime has been turning back towards dictatorship. After Xi Jinping was elected General Secretary of the party in 2012 his first act was to humiliate and imprison some of his most powerful rivals. Then he disciplined or purged hundreds of thousands of party members, all in the name of a campaign against corruption. As the regime makes a concerted effort to obliterate a fledging civil society, lawyers, human rights activists, journalists and religious leaders are confined, exiled, and imprisoned in the thousands.[5]

The propaganda machine has consistently idolised Xi. In the capital of Hebei province alone some 4,500 loudspeakers were installed in November 2017, before a major party congress, calling on all people to 'unite tightly around President Xi'. The party organ gave him seven titles, from Creative Leader, Core of the Party and Servant Pursuing Happiness for the People, to Leader of a Great Country and Architect of Modernisation in the New Era. 'To follow you is to follow the sun' went a new song launched in Beijing. Trinkets, badges and posters with his portrait are ubiquitous. His thoughts became compulsory reading for schoolchildren the same year. Fear goes hand in hand with praise, as even mocking the Chairman of Everything in a private message online can be treated as a heinous crime punishable by two years in prison. In March 2018 he became Chairman for life, as the National People's Congress voted to abolish limits on his term.[6]

Nonetheless, dictators today, with the exception of Kim Jong-un, are a long way from instilling the fear their predecessors inflicted on their populations at the height of the twentieth century. Yet hardly a month goes by without a new book announcing 'The Death of Democracy' or 'The End of Liberalism'. Undeniably, for more than a decade democracy has been degraded in many places around the world, while levels of freedom have receded even in some of the most entrenched parliamentary democracies. Eternal vigilance, as the saying goes, is the price of liberty, as power can easily be stolen.

Vigilance, however, is not the same as gloom. Even a modicum of historical perspective indicates that today dictatorship is on the decline when compared to the twentieth century. Most of all, dictators who surround themselves with a cult of personality tend to drift off into a world of their own, confirmed in their delusions by the followers who surround them. They end up making all major decisions on their own. They see enemies everywhere, at home and abroad. As hubris and paranoia take over, they seek more power to protect the power they already have. But since so much hinges on the judgements they make, even a minor miscalculation can cause the regime to falter, with devastating consequences. In the end, the biggest threat to dictators comes not just from the people, but from themselves.

Select Bibliography

ARCHIVES

ACS	Archivio Centrale dello Stato, Rome
ANR	Arhivele Naționale ale României, Bucharest
BArch	Bundesarchiv, Berlin
GDPA	Guangdong sheng Dang'anguan, Guangzhou
GSPA	Gansu sheng Dang'anguan, Lanzhou
HBPA	Hebei sheng Dang'anguan, Shijiazhuang
Hoover	Hoover Institution Library and Archives, Palo Alto
MfAA	Politisches Archiv des Auswärtigen Amts, Berlin
MAE	Ministère des Affaires Etrangères, Paris
NARA	National Archives at College Park, Washington
NMA	Nanjing shi Dang'anguan, Nanjing
OSA	Open Society Archives, Central European University, Budapest
PRO	The National Archives, London
RGANI	Rossiiskii Gosudarstvennyi Arkhiv Novei'shei Istorii, Moscow
RGASPI	Rossiiskii Gosudarstvennyi Arkhiv Sotsial'no-Politicheskoi Istorii, Moscow
SMA	Shanghai shi Dang'anguan, Shanghai

SECONDARY SOURCES

Abbott, Elizabeth, *Haiti: The Duvaliers and Their Legacy*, New York: McGraw-Hill, 1988.

Altman, Linda Jacobs, *Shattered Youth in Nazi Germany: Primary Sources from the Holocaust*, Berkeley Heights, NJ: Enslow Publishers, 2010.

Andrieu, Jacques, 'Mais que se sont donc dit Mao et Malraux? Aux sources du maoïsme occidental', *Perspectives chinoises*, no. 37 (Sept. 1996), pp. 50–63.

Applebaum, Anne, *Iron Curtain: The Crushing of Eastern Europe, 1944–1956*, New York: Doubleday, 2012.

Arendt, Hannah, *The Origins of Totalitarianism*, New York: Harvest Book, 1973.

Armstrong, Charles, *The North Korean Revolution: 1945–50*, Ithaca, NY: Cornell University Press, 2002.

Baberowski, Jörg, *Scorched Earth: Stalin's Reign of Terror*, New Haven, CT: Yale University Press, 2016.

Baczko, Bronisław, 'La fabrication d'un charisme', *Revue européenne des sciences sociales*, 19, no. 57 (1981), pp. 29–44.

Balázs, Apor, Jan C. Behrends, Polly Jones and E. A. Rees (eds), *The Leader Cult in Communist Dictatorships: Stalin and the Eastern Bloc*, Houndmills, Basingstoke: Palgrave Macmillan, 2004.

Barber, John, 'The Image of Stalin in Soviet Propaganda and Public Opinion during World War 2' in John Garrard and Carol Garrard (eds), *World War 2 and the Soviet People*, New York: St Martin's Press, 1990, pp. 38–49.

Baxa, Paul, '"Il nostro Duce": Mussolini's Visit to Trieste in 1938 and the Workings of the Cult of the Duce', *Modern Italy*, 18, no. 2 (May 2013), pp. 117–28.

Behrends, Jan C., 'Exporting the Leader: The Stalin Cult in Poland and East Germany (1944/45–1956)' in Apor Balázs, Jan C. Behrends, Polly Jones and E. A. Rees (eds), *The Leader Cult in Communist Dictatorships: Stalin and the Eastern Bloc*, Houndmills, Basingstoke: Palgrave Macmillan, 2004, pp. 161–78.

Beevor, Antony, *The Fall of Berlin 1945*, London: Penguin Books, 2002.

Berman, Stephen Jay, 'Duvalier and the Press', MA in Journalism dissertation, University of Southern California, 1974.

Ben-Ghiat, Ruth, *Fascist Modernities: Italy, 1922–1945*, Berkeley, CA: University of California Press, 2001.

Berneri, Camillo, *Mussolini grande attore*, Pistoia: Edizioni dell'Archivio Famiglia Berneri, 1st edn 1934, 2nd edn 1983.

Bessel, Richard, 'The Rise of the NSDAP and the Myth of Nazi Propaganda', *Wiener Library Bulletin*, 33, 1980, pp. 20–29.

Bessel, Richard, 'Charismatisches Führertum? Hitler's Image in der deutschen Bevölkerung' in Martin Loiperdinger, Rudolf Herz and Ulrich Pohlmann (eds), *Führerbilder: Hitler, Mussolini, Roosevelt, Stalin in Fotografie und Film*, Munich: Piper, 1995, pp. 14–26.

Bevan, Robert, *The Destruction of Memory: Architecture at War*, London: Reaktion Books, 2006.

Binet, Laurence (ed.), *Famine et transferts forcés de populations en Ethiopie 1984–1986*, Paris: Médecins Sans Frontières, 2013.

Biondi, Dino, *La fabbrica del Duce*, Florence: Vallecchi, 1967.

Blake, Robert and Wm Roger Louis (eds), *Churchill*, Oxford: Clarendon Press, 2002.

Bonnell, Victoria E., *Iconography of Power: Soviet Political Posters Under Lenin and Stalin*, Berkeley, CA: University of California Press, 1998.

Bonsaver, Guido, *Censorship and Literature in Fascist Italy*, Toronto: University of Toronto Press, 2007.

Boterbloem, Kees, *Life and Times of Andrei Zhdanov, 1896–1948*, Montreal: McGill-Queen's Press, 2004.

Bramsted, Ernest K., *Goebbels and National Socialist Propaganda 1925–1945*, East Lansing: Michigan State University Press, 1965.

Brandenberger, David, 'Stalin as Symbol: A Case Study of the Personality Cult and its Construction' in Sarah Davies and James Harris (eds), *Stalin: A New History*, Cambridge: Cambridge University Press, 2005, pp. 249–70.

Brooks, Jeffrey, *Thank You, Comrade Stalin!: Soviet Public Culture from Revolution to Cold War*, Princeton: Princeton University Press, 2000.

Bühmann, Henning, 'Der Hitlerkult. Ein Forschungsbericht' in Klaus Heller and Jan Plamper (eds), *Personenkulte im Stalinismus: Personality Cults in Stalinism*, Göttingen: Vandenhoeck and Ruprecht, 2004, pp. 109–57.

Burke, Peter, *The Fabrication of Louis XIV*, New Haven, CT: Yale University Press, 1992.

Calvino, Italo, 'Il Duce's Portraits', *New Yorker*, 6 Jan. 2003, p. 34.

Campbell, Ian, *The Addis Ababa Massacre: Italy's National Shame*, London: Hurst, 2017.

Cannistraro, Philip, *La fabbrica del consenso: Fascismo e mass media*, Bari: Laterza, 1975.

Chang, Jung and Jon Halliday, *Mao: The Unknown Story*, London: Jonathan Cape, 2005.

Chaussy, Ulrich and Christoph Püschner, *Nachbar Hitler: Führerkult und Heimatzerstörung am Obersalzberg*, Berlin: Christoph Links · Verlag, 2007.

Chinese Propaganda Posters: From the Collection of Michael Wolf, Cologne: Taschen, 2003.

Chen Jian, *China's Road to the Korean War*, New York: Columbia University Press, 1996.

Chirot, Daniel, *Modern Tyrants: The Power and Prevalence of Evil in Our Age*, Princeton: Princeton University Press, 1996.

Clapham, Christopher, *Transformation and Continuity in Revolutionary Ethiopia*, Cambridge: Cambridge University Press, 1988.

Cohen, Arthur A., *The Communism of Mao Tse-tung*, Chicago: University of Chicago Press, 1964.

Cohen, Yves, 'The Cult of Number One in an Age of Leaders', *Kritika: Explorations in Russian and Eurasian History*, vol. 8, no. 3 (Summer 2007), pp. 597–634.

Coox, Alvin D., *Nomonhan: Japan Against Russia 1939*, Palo Alto, CA: Stanford University Press, 1988.

Corner, Paul, *The Fascist Party and Popular Opinion in Mussolini's Italy*, Oxford: Oxford University Press, 2012.

Corvaja, Santi, *Hitler and Mussolini: The Secret Meetings*, New York: Enigma Books, 2008.

Courtois, Stéphane et al. (eds), *The Black Book of Communism: Crimes, Terror, Repression*, Cambridge, MA: Harvard University Press, 1999.

Cushway, Eric H., 'The Ideology of François Duvalier', MA dissertation, University of Alberta, 1976.

David-Fox, Michael, *Showcasing the Great Experiment: Cultural Diplomacy and Western Visitors to the Soviet Union, 1921–1941*, Oxford: Oxford University Press, 2011.

Davies, Sarah, *Popular Opinion in Stalin's Russia: Terror, Propaganda and Dissent, 1934–1941*, Cambridge: Cambridge University Press, 1997.

de Waal, Alex, *Evil Days: Thirty Years of War and Famine in Ethiopia*, New York: Human Rights Watch, 1991.

de Felice, Renzo, *Mussolini il Fascista*, vol. 1, *La conquista del potere, 1921–1925*, Turin: Giulio Einaudi, 1966.

Dee, Bleecker, 'Duvalier's Haiti: A Case Study of National
Disintegration', doctoral dissertation, University of Florida, 1967.

Deletant, Dennis, *Ceauşescu and the Securitate*, London: Hurst, 1995.

Deletant, Dennis, *Communist Terror in Romania: Gheorghiu-Dej and the
Police State, 1948–1965*, New York: St Martin's Press, 1999.

Demick, Barbara, *Nothing to Envy: Ordinary Lives in North Korea*, New
York: Spiegel and Grau, 2009.

Diederich, Bernard and Al Burt, *Papa Doc: Haiti and its Dictator*, London:
Bodley Head, 1969.

Diederich, Bernard, *The Price of Blood: History of Repression and
Rebellion in Haiti Under Dr. François Duvalier, 1957–1961*, Princeton,
NJ: Markus Wiener, 2011.

Diggins, John Patrick, *Mussolini and Fascism: The View from America*,
Princeton: Princeton University Press, 1972.

Dikötter, Frank, *Mao's Great Famine: The History of China's Most
Devastating Catastrophe, 1958–1962*, London: Bloomsbury, 2010.

Dikötter, Frank, *The Tragedy of Liberation: A History of the Chinese
Revolution, 1945–1957*, London: Bloomsbury, 2013.

Dikötter, Frank, *The Cultural Revolution: A People's History, 1962–1976*,
London: Bloomsbury, 2016.

Diller, Ansgar, *Rundfunkpolitik im Dritten Reich*, Munich: Deutscher
Taschenbuch Verlag, 1980.

Donham, Donald L., 'Revolution and Modernity in Maale: Ethiopia,
1974 to 1987', *Comparative Studies in Society and History*, 34, no. 1
(Jan. 1992), pp. 28–57.

Duggan, Christopher, *Fascist Voices: An Intimate History of Mussolini's
Italy*, Oxford: Oxford University Press, 2013.

Durandin, Catherine, *Ceauşescu, vérités et mensonges d'un roi communiste*,
Paris: Albin Michel, 1990.

Ennker, Benno, 'The Origins and Intentions of the Lenin Cult' in Ian
D. Thatcher (ed.), *Regime and Society in Twentieth-Century Russia*,
Houndmills, Basingstoke: Macmillan Press, 1999, pp. 118–28.

Evans, Richard J., 'Coercion and Consent in Nazi Germany',
Proceedings of the British Academy, 151, 2006, pp. 53–81.

Evans, Richard J., *The Third Reich in Power*, London: Penguin Books,
2006.

Evans, Richard J., *The Third Reich at War*, London: Penguin, 2009.

Eyal, Jonathan, 'Why Romania Could Not Avoid Bloodshed'
   in Gwyn Prins (ed.), *Spring in Winter: The 1989 Revolutions*,
   Manchester: Manchester University Press, 1990, pp. 139–62.
Falasca-Zamponi, Simonetta, *Fascist Spectacle: The Aesthetics of Power in
   Mussolini's Italy*, Berkeley, CA: University of California Press, 2000.
Farnsworth, Robert M., *From Vagabond to Journalist: Edgar Snow in
   Asia, 1928–1941*, Columbia, MO: University of Missouri Press, 1996.
Feigon, Lee, *Mao: A Reinterpretation*, Chicago: Ivan R. Dee, 2002.
Fest, Joachim C., *Hitler*, Boston, MA: Houghton Mifflin
   Harcourt, 2002.
Festorazzi, Roberto, *Starace. Il mastino della rivoluzione fascista*, Milan:
   Ugo Mursia, 2002.
Figes, Orlando, *The Whisperers: Private Life in Stalin's Russia*, New York:
   Picador, 2007.
Fisher, Mary Ellen, *Nicolae Ceauşescu: A Study in Political Leadership*,
   Boulder, CO: Lynne Rienner Publishers, 1989.
Fitzpatrick, Sheila, *Everyday Stalinism. Ordinary Life in Extraordinary
   Times: Soviet Russia in the 1930s*, Oxford: Oxford University Press,
   1999.
Foot, John, *Italy's Divided Memory*, Houndmills, Basingstoke: Palgrave
   Macmillan, 2009.
Franz-Willing, Georg, *Die Hitlerbewegung. Der Ursprung, 1919–1922*,
   Hamburg: R.v. Decker's Verlag G. Schenck, 1962, 2nd edn 1972.
Fritz, Stephen G., *Ostkrieg: Hitler's War of Extermination in the East*,
   Lexington, KT: University Press of Kentucky, 2011.
Gabanyi, Anneli Ute, *The Ceauşescu Cult: Propaganda and Power
   Policy in Communist Romania*, Bucharest: The Romanian Cultural
   Foundation Publishing House, 2000.
Gao Hua, *Hong taiyang shi zenyang shengqi de. Yan'an zhengfeng yundong
   de lailong qumai* (How did the red sun rise over Yan'an? A history of
   the Rectification Movement), Hong Kong: Chinese University Press,
   2000.
GaoWenqian, *Zhou Enlai: The Last Perfect Revolutionary*, New York:
   PublicAffairs, 2007.
Gentile, Emilio, *The Sacralisation of Politics in Fascist Italy*, Cambridge,
   MA: Harvard University Press, 1996.
Giorgis, Dawit Wolde, *Red Tears: War, Famine and Revolution in
   Ethiopia*, Trenton, NJ: Red Sea Press, 1989.

Girard, Philippe, *Haiti: The Tumultuous History – From Pearl of the Caribbean to Broken Nation*, New York: St Martin's Press, 2010.

Glantz, David, *Stumbling Colossus: The Red Army on the Eve of World War*, Lawrence, KA: University Press of Kansas, 1998.

Goncharov, Sergei N., John W. Lewis and Xue Litai, *Uncertain Partners: Stalin, Mao, and the Korean War*, Stanford, CA: Stanford University Press, 1993.

Grangereau, Philippe, *Au pays du grand mensonge. Voyage en Corée*, Paris: Payot, 2003.

Gundle, Stephen, Christopher Duggan and Giuliana Pieri (eds), *The Cult of the Duce: Mussolini and the Italians*, Manchester: Manchester University Press, 2013.

Haffner, Sebastian, *The Meaning of Hitler*, London: Phoenix Press, 1979.

Han, Hongkoo, 'Wounded Nationalism: The Minsaengdan Incident and Kim Il-sung in Eastern Manchuria', University of Washington, doctoral disertation, 1999.

Harden, Blaine, *The Great Leader and the Fighter Pilot: A True Story About the Birth of Tyranny in North Korea*, New York: Penguin Books, 2016.

Hasler, August Bernhard, 'Das Duce-Bild in der faschistischen Literatur', *Quellen und Forschungen aus italienischen Archiven und Bibliotheken*, vol. 60, 1980, pp. 421–506.

Hastings, Max, *The Korean War*, New York: Simon & Schuster, 1987.

Hatch, David Allen, 'The Cult of Personality of Kim Il-Song: Functional Analysis of a State Myth', doctoral dissertation, Washington, DC: The American University, 1986.

Hayes, Romain, *Subhas Chandra Bose in Nazi Germany: Politics, Intelligence, and Propaganda, 1941–1943*, London, Hurst, 2011.

Heinl, Robert D. and Nancy Gordon Heinl, *Written in Blood: The Story of the Haitian People, 1492–1995*, Lanham, MD: University Press of America, 1998.

Held, Joseph (ed.), *The Cult of Power: Dictators in the Twentieth Century*, Boulder, CO: East European Quarterly Press, 1983.

Heller, Klaus and Jan Plamper (eds), *Personenkulte im Stalinismus: Personality Cults in Stalinism*, Göttingen: Vandenhoeck and Ruprecht, 2004.

Henze, Paul B., *Layers of Time: A History of Ethiopia*, London: Hurst, 2000.

Herbst, Ludolf, *Hitler's Charisma. Die Erfindung eines deutschen Messias*, Frankfurt am Main: S. Fischer Verlag, 2010.

Herz, Rudolf, *Hoffmann & Hitler: Fotografie als Medium des Führer Mythos*, Munich: Klinkhardt and Biermann, 1994.

Hollander, Paul, *Political Pilgrims: Western Intellectuals in Search of the Good Society*, London: Routledge, 2017.

Hollander, Paul, *From Benito Mussolini to Hugo Chavez: Intellectuals and a Century of Political Hero Worship*, Cambridge: Cambridge University Press, 2017.

Hoyt, Edwin P., *Mussolini's Empire: The Rise and Fall of the Fascist Vision*, New York: Wiley, 1994.

Hughes-Hallett, Lucy, *Gabriele d'Annunzio: Poet, Seducer, and Preacher of War*, London: 4th Estate, 2013.

Hung Chang-tai, 'Mao's Parades: State Spectacles in China in the 1950s', *China Quarterly*, no. 190 (June 2007), pp. 411–31.

Hunter, Helen-Louise, *Kim Il-song's North Korea*, Westport, CT: Praeger Publishers, 1999.

Hupp, Kimberly, ' "Uncle Joe": What Americans thought of Joseph Stalin before and after World War II', doctoral dissertation, University of Toledo, 2009.

Iezzi, Frank, 'Benito Mussolini, Crowd Psychologist', *Quarterly Journal of Speech*, 45, no. 2 (April 1959), pp. 167–9.

Imbriani, Angelo M., *Gli italiani e il Duce: Il mito e l'immagine di Mussolini negli ultimi anni del fascismo (1938–1943)*, Naples: Liguori, 1992.

Jin Dalu, *Feichang yu zhengchang: Shanghai 'wenge' shiqi de shehui bianqian* (The extraordinary and the ordinary: Social change in Shanghai during the Cultural Revolution), Shanghai: Shanghai cishu chubanshe, 2011.

Johnson, Paul Christopher, 'Secretism and the Apotheosis of Duvalier', *Journal of the American Academy of Religion*, 74, no. 2 (June 2006), pp. 420–45.

Kallis, Aristotle, *The Third Rome, 1922–43: The Making of the Fascist Capital*, Houndmills, Basingstoke: Palgrave Macmillan, 2014.

Kebede, Messay, *Ideology and Elite Conflicts: Autopsy of the Ethiopian Revolution*, Lanham, MD: Lexington Books, 2011.

Keil, Thomas J., *Romania's Tortured Road toward Modernity*, New York: Columbia University Press, 2006.

Keller, Edmund J., *Revolutionary Ethiopia*, Bloomington, IN: Indiana University Press, 1988.

Kershaw, Ian, *Hitler, 1889–1936: Hubris*, London: Allen Lane, 1998.

Kershaw, Ian, *The 'Hitler Myth': Image and Reality in the Third Reich*, Oxford: Oxford University Press, 2001.

King, David, *The Commissar Vanishes: The Falsification of Photographs and Art in Stalin's Russia*, New York: Metropolitan Books, 1997.

Kirkpatrick, Ivone, *Mussolini: Study of a Demagogue*, New York: Hawthorn Books, 1964.

Klibansky, Raymond (ed.), *Benito Mussolini's Memoirs 1942–1943*, New York: Howard Fertig, 1975.

König, Wolfgang, 'Der Volksempfänger und die Radioindustrie. Ein Beitrag zum Verhältnis von Wirtschaft und Politik im Nationalsozialismus' in *Vierteljahrschrift für Sozial- und Wirtschaftsgeschichte*, 90, no. 3 (2003), pp. 269–89.

Koon, Tracy H., *Believe, Obey, Fight: Political Socialization of Youth in Fascist Italy, 1922–1943*, Chapel Hill, NC: University of North Carolina Press, 1985.

Kopperschmidt, Josef (ed.), *Hitler der Redner*, Munich: Wilhelm Fink Verlag, 2003.

Korn, David A., *Ethiopia, the United States and the Soviet Union*, Carbondale, IL: Southern Illinois University Press, 1986.

Kotkin, Stephen, *Stalin: Paradoxes of Power, 1878–1928*, New York: Penguin Press, 2014.

Kotkin, Stephen, *Stalin: Waiting for Hitler, 1929–1941*, New York: Penguin Press, 2017.

Kraus, Richard Curt, *Brushes with Power: Modern Politics and the Chinese Art of Calligraphy*, Berkeley, CA: University of California Press, 1991.

Ladany, Laszlo, *The Communist Party of China and Marxism, 1921–1985: A Self-Portrait*, London: Hurst, 1988.

Lankov, Andrei, *Crisis in North Korea: The Failure of De-Stalinization, 1956*, Honolulu: University of Hawai'i Press, 2005.

Lankov, Andrei, *From Stalin to Kim Il Sung: The Formation of North Korea, 1945–1960*, New Brunswick, NJ: Rutgers University Press, 2002.

Lankov, Andrei, *North of the DMZ: Essays on Daily Life in North Korea*, Jefferson, NC: McFarland, 2007.

Lankov, Andrei, *The Real North Korea: Life and Politics in the Failed Stalinist Utopia*, Oxford: Oxford University Press, 2013.

Leese, Daniel, *Mao Cult: Rhetoric and Ritual in China's Cultural Revolution*, Cambridge: Cambridge University Press, 2011.

Li Rui, *Dayuejin qin liji* (A witness account of the Great Leap Forward), Haikou: Nanfang chubanshe, 1999.

Li Rui, *Lushan huiyi shilu* (A true record of the Lushan plenum), Hong Kong: Tiandi tushu youxian gongsi, 2nd edn, 2009.

Li Zhisui, *The Private Life of Chairman Mao: The Memoirs of Mao's Personal Physician*, New York: Random House, 1994.

Lim Un, *The Founding of a Dynasty in North Korea: An Authentic Biography of Kim Il-song*, Tokyo: Jiyu-sha, 1982.

Locard, Henri, *Pol Pot's Little Red Book: The Sayings of Angkar*, Bangkok: Silkworm Books, 2004.

Lundahl, Mats, 'Papa Doc: Innovator in the Predatory State', *Scandia*, 50, no. 1 (1984), pp. 39–78.

MacFarquhar, Roderick and Michael Schoenhals, *Mao's Last Revolution*, Cambridge, MA: Harvard University Press, 2006.

Machiavelli, Niccolo, *The Prince*, translated by Tim Parks, London: Penguin Books, 2009.

Mack Smith, Denis, *Mussolini*, London: Weidenfeld & Nicolson, 1981.

Mack Smith, Denis, 'Mussolini: Reservations about Renzo De Felice's Biography', *Modern Italy*, 5, no. 2 (2000), pp. 193–210.

Marcus, Harold G., *A History of Ethiopia*, Berkeley, CA: University of California Press, 1994.

Marquis, John, *Papa Doc: Portrait of a Haitian Tyrant 1907–1971*, Kingston: LMH Publishing Limited, 2007.

Martin, Bradley K., *Under the Loving Care of the Fatherly Leader: North Korea and the Kim Dynasty*, New York: Thomas Dunne Books, 2004.

McNeal, Robert H., *Stalin: Man and Rule*, New York: New York University Press, 1988.

Medvedev, Roy, *Let History Judge: The Origins and Consequences of Stalinism*, New York: Knopf, 1972.

Melograni, Piero, 'The Cult of the Duce in Mussolini's Italy', *Journal of Contemporary History*, 11, no. 4 (Oct. 1976), pp. 221–37.

Merridale, Catherine, *Ivan's War: The Red Army 1939–45*, London: Faber and Faber, 2005.

Mocanescu, Alice, 'Surviving 1956: Gheorge Gheorghiu-Dej and the "Cult of Personality" in Romania' in Apor Balázs, Jan C. Behrends, Polly Jones and E. A. Rees (eds), *The Leader Cult in Communist Dictatorships: Stalin and the Eastern Bloc*, Houndmills, Basingstoke: Palgrave Macmillan, 2004, pp. 246–60.

Moorhouse, Roger, 'Germania: Hitler's Dream Capital', *History Today*, 62, issue 3 (March 2012).

Moseley, Ray, *Mussolini: The Last 600 Days of Il Duce*, Lanham, MD: Taylor Trade Publishing, 2004.

Munro, Martin, *Tropical Apocalypse: Haiti and the Caribbean End*, Charlottesville, VA: University of Virginia Press, 2015.

Murck, Alfreda (ed.), *Mao's Golden Mangoes and the Cultural Revolution*, Zurich: Scheidegger and Spiess, 2013.

Myers, Brian R., 'The Watershed that Wasn't': Re-Evaluating Kim Il-sung's "Juche Speech" of 1955', *Acta Koreana*, 9, no. 1 (Jan. 2006), pp. 89–115.

Nagorski, Andrew, *The Greatest Battle: Stalin, Hitler, and the Desperate Struggle for Moscow that Changed the Course of World War II*, New York: Simon & Schuster, 2008.

Nagorski, Andrew, *Hitlerland: American Eyewitnesses to the Nazi Rise to Power*, New York: Simon & Schuster, 2012.

Nathan, Andrew J., 'Foreword' in Li Zhisui, *The Private Life of Chairman Mao: The Memoirs of Mao's Personal Physician*, New York: Random House, 1994, pp. vii–xiv.

Neiberg, Michael, *Potsdam: The End of World War II and the Remaking of Europe*, New York: Basic Books, 2015.

Nicholls, David, 'Haiti: The Rise and Fall of Duvalierism', *Third World Quarterly*, vol. 8, no. 4 (Oct. 1986), pp. 1239–52.

Nitz, Wenke, *Führer und Duce: Politische Machtinszenierungen im nationalsozialistischen Deutschland und im faschistischen Italien*, Cologne: Böhlau Verlag, 2013.

Oberdorfer, Don, *The Two Koreas: A Contemporary History*, Reading, MA: Addison-Wesley, 1997.

Overy, Richard, *Russia's War: A History of the Soviet Effort: 1941–1945*, Harmondsworth: Penguin Books, 1997.

Pacepa, Mihai, *Red Horizons: The True Story of Nicolae and Elena Ceauşescus' Crimes, Lifestyle, and Corruption*, Washington, DC: Regnery Publishing, 1990.

Pantsov, Alexander V. and Steven I. Levine, *Mao: The Real Story*, New York: Simon & Schuster, 2012.

Paul, Gerhard, *Aufstand der Bilder. Die NS-Propaganda vor 1933*, Bonn: Dietz, 1990.

Person, James F., 'North Korea's chuch'e philosophy' in Michael J. Seth, *Routledge Handbook of Modern Korean History*, London: Routledge, 2016, pp. 705–98.

Pipes, Richard, *The Russian Revolution*, New York: Vintage Books, 1991.

Pipes, Richard, *Communism: A History of the Intellectual and Political Movement*, London: Phoenix Press, 2002.

Pisch, Anita, 'The Personality Cult of Stalin in Soviet Posters, 1929–1953: Archetypes, Inventions and Fabrications', doctoral dissertation, Australian National University, 2014.

Plamper, Jan, *The Stalin Cult: A Study in the Alchemy of Power*, New Haven: Yale University Press, 2012.

Plewnia, Margarete, *Auf dem Weg zu Hitler: Der 'völkische' Publizist Dietrich Eckart*, Bremen: Schünemann Universitätsverlag, 1970.

Plöckinger, Othmar, *Geschichte eines Buches. Adolf Hitler's 'Mein Kampf' 1922–1945*, Munich: Oldenbourg Verlag, 2006.

Polyné, Millery, *From Douglass to Duvalier: U. S. African Americans, Haiti, and Pan Americanism, 1870–1964*, Gainesville, FL: University of Florida Press, 2010.

Rabinbach, Anson and Sander L. Gilman (eds), *The Third Reich Sourcebook*, Berkeley, CA: University of California Press, 2013.

Radchenko, Sergey and David Wolff, 'To the Summit via Proxy-Summits: New Evidence from Soviet and Chinese Archives on Mao's Long March to Moscow, 1949', *Cold War International History Project Bulletin*, no. 16 (winter 2008), pp. 105–82.

Reid, Richard J., *Frontiers of Violence in North-East Africa: Genealogies of Conflict since c.1800*, Oxford: Oxford University Press, 2011.

Rivoire, Mario, *Vita e morte del fascismo*, Milan: Edizioni Europee, 1947.

Rees, E. A., 'Leader Cults: Varieties, Preconditions and Functions' in Apor Balázs, Jan C. Behrends, Polly Jones and E. A. Rees (eds), *The Leader Cult in Communist Dictatorships: Stalin and the Eastern Bloc*, Houndmills, Basingstoke: Palgrave Macmillan, 2004, pp. 3–26.

Rolf, Malte, 'A Hall of Mirrors: Sovietizing Culture under Stalinism',
    Slavic Review, 68, no. 3 (Fall 2009), pp. 601–30.
Rolf, Malte, 'Working towards the Centre: Leader Cults and Spatial
    Politics' in Apor Balázs, Jan C. Behrends, Polly Jones and E. A. Rees
    (eds), *The Leader Cult in Communist Dictatorships: Stalin and the
    Eastern Bloc*, Basingstoke: Palgrave Macmillan, 2004, pp. 141–59.
Rotberg, Robert I., *Haiti: The Politics of Squalor*, Boston: Houghton
    Mifflin, 1971.
Ryang, Sonia, *Writing Selves in Diaspora: Ethnography of Autobiographics
    of Korean Women in Japan and the United States*, Lanham,
    MD: Lexington Books, 2008.
Salisbury, Harrison, *The 900 Days: The Siege of Leningrad*, New York,
    Cambridge, MA: Da Capo Press, 1985.
Santoro, Lorenzo, *Roberto Farinacci e il Partito Nazionale Fascista 1923–
    1926*, Soveria Mannelli: Rubbettino, 2008.
Scalapino, Robert A. and Chong-sik Lee, *Communism in Korea. Part
    I: The Movement*, Berkeley, CA: University of California Press, 1972.
Schlenker, Ines, *Hitler's Salon: The Große Deutsche Kunstausstellung at
    the Haus der Deutschen Kunst in Munich 1937–1944*, Bern: Peter Lang
    AG, 2007.
Schmitz, David F., *The United States and Fascist Italy, 1922–1940*, Chapel
    Hill, NC: University of North Carolina Press, 1988.
Schmölders, Claudia, *Hitler's Face: The Biography of an Image*,
    Philadelphia: University of Pennsylvania Press, 2005.
Schneider, Wolfgang, *Alltag unter Hitler*, Berlin: Rowohlt Berlin
    Verlag, 2000.
Schram, Stuart R., 'Party Leader or True Ruler? Foundations and
    Significance of Mao Zedong's Personal Power' in Stuart R.
    Schram (ed.), *Foundations and Limits of State Power in China*,
    London: School of Oriental and African Studies, 1987, pp. 203–56.
Schrift, Melissa, *Biography of a Chairman Mao Badge: The Creation and
    Mass Consumption of a Personality Cult*, New Brunswick, NJ: Rutgers
    University Press, 2001.
Sedita, Giovanni, *Gli intellettuali di Mussolini: La cultura finanziata dal
    fascismo*, Florence: Casa Editrice Le Lettere, 2010.
Sebag Montefiore, Simon, *Stalin: The Court of the Red Tsar*,
    New York: Knopf, 2004.

Semmens, Kristin, *Seeing Hitler's Germany: Tourism in the Third Reich*, Houndmills, Basingstoke: Palgrave Macmillan, 2005.

Service, Robert, *Stalin: A Biography*, Basingstoke: Macmillan, 2004.

Siani-Davies, Peter, *The Romanian Revolution of December 1989*, Ithaca, NY: Cornell University Press, 2007.

Sobanet, Andrew, 'Henri Barbusse, Official Biographer of Joseph Stalin', *French Cultural Studies*, 24, no. 4 (Nov. 2013), pp. 359–75.

Sohier, Estelle, 'Politiques de l'image et pouvoir royal en Éthiopie de Menilek II à Haylä Sellasé (1880–1936)', doctoral dissertation, University of Paris 1, 2007.

Sösemann, Bernd, 'Die Macht der allgegenwärtigen Suggestion. Die Wochensprüche der NSDAP als Propagandamittel', *Jahrbuch 1989*, Berlin: Berliner Wissenschaftliche Gesellschaft, 1990, pp. 227–48.

Sösemann, Bernd, *Propaganda: Medien und Öffentlichkeit in der NS-Diktatur*, Stuttgart: Franz Steiner Verlag, 2011.

Stratigakos, Despina, *Hitler at Home*, New Haven, CT: Yale University Press, 2015.

Suh, Dae-sook, *Kim Il-sung: The North Korean Leader*, New York: Columbia University Press, 1988.

Sun, Judy and Greg Wang, 'Human Resource Development in China and North Korea' in Thomas N. Garavan, Alma M. McCarthy and Michael J. Morley (eds), *Global Human Resource Development: Regional and Country Perspectives*, London: Routledge, 2016, pp. 86–103.

Sweeney, John, *The Life and Evil Times of Nicolae Ceausescu*, London: Hutchinson, 1991.

Szalontai, Balázs, *Kim Il Sung in the Khrushchev Era: Soviet-DPRK Relations and the Roots of North Korean Despotism, 1953–1964*, Stanford: Stanford University Press, 2006.

Tareke, Gebru, *The Ethiopian Revolution: War in the Horn of Africa*, New Haven, CT: Yale University Press, 2009.

Taubman, William, *Khrushchev: The Man and his Era*, London, Free Press, 2003.

Taylor, Jay, *The Generalissimo: Chiang Kai-shek and the Struggle for Modern China*, Cambridge, MA: Harvard University Press, 2009.

Tiruneh, Andargatchew, *The Ethiopian Revolution 1974–87*, Cambridge: Cambridge University Press, 1993.

Tismaneanu, Vladimir, *Stalinism for All Seasons: A Political History of Romanian Communism*, Berkeley, CA: University of California Press, 2003.

Tola, Babile, *To Kill a Generation: The Red Terror in Ethiopia*, Washington: Free Ethiopia Press, 1989.

Tucker, Robert C., 'The Rise of Stalin's Personality Cult', *American Historical Review*, 84, no. 2 (April 1979), pp. 347–66.

Tucker, Robert C., 'Memoir of a Stalin Biographer', *Princeton Alumni Weekly*, no. 83, 3 Nov. 1982, pp. 21–31.

Ventresca, Robert A., *Soldier of Christ: The Life of Pope Pius XII*, Cambridge, MA: Harvard University Press, 2013.

Ullrich, Volker, *Hitler: Ascent 1889–1939*, New York: Alfred Knopf, 2016.

Vasilieva, Larissa, *Kremlin Wives*, New York: Arcade Publishing, 1992.

Wang, Helen, *Chairman Mao Badges: Symbols and Slogans of the Cultural Revolution*, London: British Museum, 2008.

Wedeen, Lisa, *Ambiguities of Domination: Politics, Rhetoric, and Symbolism in Contemporary Syria*, Chicago: University of Chicago Press, 1999.

Weintraub, Stanley, *Journey to Heartbreak: The Crucible Years of Bernard Shaw*, New York: Weybright and Talley, 1971.

Weintraub, Stanley, 'GBS and the Despots', *Times Literary Supplement*, 22 Aug. 2011.

Werth, Alexander, *Russia at War, 1941–1945: A History*, New York: Skyhorse Publishing, 2011.

White, Lynn T. III, *Policies of Chaos: The Organizational Causes of Violence in China's Cultural Revolution*, Princeton: Princeton University Press, 1989.

Wilson, Verity, 'Dress and the Cultural Revolution' in Valerie Steele and John S. Major (eds), *China Chic: East Meets West*, New Haven, CT: Yale University Press, 1999, pp. 167–86.

Wingrove, Paul, 'Mao in Moscow, 1949–50: Some New Archival Evidence', *Journal of Communist Studies and Transition Politics*, 11, no. 4 (Dec. 1995), pp. 309–34.

Wolff, David, '"One Finger's Worth of Historical Events": New Russian and Chinese Evidence on the Sino-Soviet Alliance and Split, 1948–1959', *Cold War International History Project Bulletin*, Working Paper no. 30 (Aug. 2002), pp. 1–74.

Wylie, Raymond F., *The Emergence of Maoism: Mao Tse-tung, Ch'en Po-ta, and the Search for Chinese Theory, 1935–1945*, Palo Alto, CA: Stanford University Press, 1980.

Yurchak, Alexei, 'Bodies of Lenin: The Hidden Science of Communist Sovereignty', *Representations*, no. 129 (Winter 2015), pp. 116–57.

Zeleke, Elleni Centime, 'Addis Ababa as Modernist Ruin', *Callaloo*, 33, no. 1 (Spring 2010), pp. 117–35.

Zewde, Bahru, *A History of Modern Ethiopia*, London: James Currey, 2001.

Notes

PREFACE

1 W. M. Thackeray, *The Paris Sketch Book*, London: Collins' Clear-Type Press, 1840, p. 369.
2 Peter Burke, *The Fabrication of Louis XIV*, New Haven, CT: Yale University Press, 1992.
3 See, for instance, the discussion in the exemplary work of Lisa Wedeen, *Ambiguities of Domination: Politics, Rhetoric, and Symbolism in Contemporary Syria*, Chicago: University of Chicago Press, 1999; see also Yves Cohen, 'The Cult of Number One in an Age of Leaders', *Kritika: Explorations in Russian and Eurasian History*, vol. 8, no. 3 (Summer 2007), pp. 597–634.
4 Andrew J. Nathan, 'Foreword' in Li Zhisui, *The Private Life of Chairman Mao: The Memoirs of Mao's Personal Physician*, New York: Random House, 1994, p. x.
5 Ian Kershaw, *The 'Hitler Myth': Image and Reality in the Third Reich*, Oxford: Oxford University Press, 2001.
6 Stephen F. Cohen, *Rethinking the Soviet Experience: Politics and History since 1917*, Oxford: Oxford University Press, 1985, p. 101.
7 Paul Hollander, *Political Pilgrims: Western Intellectuals in Search of the Good Society*, London: Routledge, 2017; Paul Hollander, *From Benito Mussolini to Hugo Chavez: Intellectuals and a Century of Political Hero Worship*, Cambridge: Cambridge University Press, 2017.
8 Henri Locard, *Pol Pot's Little Red Book: The Sayings of Angkar*, Bangkok: Silkworm Books, 2004, p. 99.

CHAPTER 1 MUSSOLINI

1 Aristotle Kallis, *The Third Rome, 1922–43: The Making of the Fascist Capital*, Houndmills, Basingstoke: Palgrave Macmillan, 2014, p. 245.

2 Christopher Duggan, 'The Internalisation of the Cult of the Duce: The Evidence of Diaries and Letters' in Stephen Gundle, Christopher Duggan and Giuliana Pieri (eds), *The Cult of the Duce: Mussolini and the Italians*, Manchester: Manchester University Press, 2013, p. 130.

3 ACS, SPD, CO, b. 2762, f. 509819.

4 ACS, SPD, b. 386, f. 142471, 29 April 1933, b. 386, f. 142484, 6 June 1933; b. 2773, Dec. 1938.

5 Herman Finer, *Mussolini's Italy*, New York: Holt and Co., 1935, p. 298.

6 Denis Mack Smith, 'Mussolini, Artist in Propaganda: The Downfall of Fascism', *History Today*, 9 no. 4 (April 1959), p. 224.

7 Peter Neville, *Mussolini*, Abingdon: Routledge, 2015, p. 46.

8 Ivone Kirkpatrick, *Mussolini: Study of a Demagogue*, New York: Hawthorn Books, 1964, p. 89; Denis Mack Smith, *Mussolini*, London: Weidenfeld & Nicolson, 1981, p. 39.

9 Emilio Gentile quoted in Lucy Hughes-Hallett, *Gabriele d'Annunzio: Poet, Seducer, and Preacher of War*, London: 4th Estate, 2013, loc. 179.

10 Kirkpatrick, *Mussolini*, pp. 98–9.

11 Mack Smith, *Mussolini*, p. 54.

12 Ibid., pp. 54–5; Kirkpatrick, *Mussolini*, p. 151; *The Times*, 28 October 1929, p. 14.

13 Kirkpatrick, *Mussolini*, p. 156; George Slocombe, *The Tumult and the Shouting*, Kingswood: Windmill Press, 1936, p. 148.

14 Kirkpatrick, *Mussolini*, p. 176.

15 Ibid., pp. 107 and 200–202.

16 Quinto Navarra, *Memorie del cameriere di Mussolini*, Milan: Longanesi, 1972, pp. 17–18; Dino Biondi, *La fabbrica del Duce*, Florence: Vallecchi, 1967, p. 96.

17 Navarra, *Memorie del cameriere di Mussolini*, p. 173.

18 Guido Bonsaver, *Censorship and Literature in Fascist Italy*, Toronto: University of Toronto Press, 2007, pp. 19–20.

19 Mussolini's speech to the Chamber, 3 January 1925, Patrick G. Zander, *The Rise of Fascism: History, Documents, and Key Questions*, Santa Barbara, CA: ABC-Clio, 2016, p. 140.

20 Bonsaver, *Censorship and Literature in Fascist Italy*, pp. 20–21; Mack Smith, *Mussolini*, p. 87.

21 William Bolitho, *Italy under Mussolini*, New York: Macmillan, 1926, p. 107; Mussolini's quotation about the state is famous, and appeared for the first time in 'Per la medaglia dei benemeriti del comune di Milano', 28 October 1925, Benito Mussolini, *Opera Omnia*, Florence: La Fenice, 1956, vol. 21, p. 425.

22 Bolitho, *Italy under Mussolini*, p. 107.

23 Kirkpatrick, *Mussolini*, p. 244; Mack Smith, *Mussolini*, p. 102.

24 ACS, SPD, Carteggio Ordinario, b. 234, f. 2795, pp. 19731–6, May 1923; Lorenzo Santoro, *Roberto Farinacci e il Partito Nazionale Fascista 1923–1926*, Soveria Mannelli: Rubbettino, 2008, pp. 197–8.

25 Mack Smith, *Mussolini*, pp. 102–3; Mario Rivoire, *Vita e morte del fascismo*, Milan: Edizioni Europee, 1947, p. 107.

26 Augusto Turati, *Una rivoluzione e un capo*, Rome: Libreria del Littorio, 1927, pp. 35 and 143; Partito Nazionale Fascista, *Le origini e lo sviluppo del fascismo, attraverso gli scritti e la parola del Duce e le deliberazioni del P.N.F. dall'intervento alla marcia su Roma*, Rome: Libreria del Littorio, 1928, p. xiii.

27 Navarra, *Memorie del cameriere di Mussolini*, pp. 197–9.

28 Percy Winner, 'Mussolini: A Character Study', *Current History*, 28, no. 4 (July 1928), p. 526; Bolitho, *Italy under Mussolini*, p. 62; Slocombe, *The Tumult and the Shouting*, p. 149.

29 Camillo Berneri, *Mussolini grande attore*, Pistoia: Edizioni dell'Archivio Famiglia Berneri, 1st edn 1934, second edn 1983, pp. 25–6; Mack Smith, *Mussolini*, p. 124.

30 William Sloane Kennedy, *Italy in Chains*, West Yarmouth, MA: Stonecraft Press, 1927, p. 18; Henri Béraud, *Ce que j'ai vu à Rome*, Paris: Les Editions de France, 1929, p. 38; Rivoire, *Vita e morte del fascismo*, p. 99.

31 Adrian Lyttelton, *The Seizure of Power: Fascism in Italy, 1919–1929*, London: Weidenfeld & Nicolson, 2nd edn, 1987, p. 401.

32 Béraud, *Ce que j'ai vu à Rome*, pp. 37–42; on the image of Mussolini, see also Simonetta Falasca-Zamponi, *Fascist Spectacle: The Aesthetics of Power in Mussolini's Italy*, Berkeley, CA: University of California Press, 2000.

33 Margherita Sarfatti, *The Life of Benito Mussolini*, London: Butterworth, 1925, pp. 29–30, 44 and 230.

34 Berneri, *Mussolini grande attore*, pp. 26–8; Vincenzo de Gaetano, *Il libro dell'Avanguardista*, Catania: Società Tip. Editrice Siciliana, 1927, pp. 45–6; also Sckem Gremigni, *Duce d'Italia*, Milano, Istituto di Propaganda d'Arte e Cultura, 1927.

35 Navarra, *Memorie del cameriere di Mussolini*, pp. 110–12, 124–5 and 135; Emil Ludwig, *Talks with Mussolini*, Boston: Little, Brown, and Co., 1933, p. 80; Kirkpatrick, *Mussolini*, p. 159.

36 Winner, 'Mussolini: A Character Study', p. 525.

37 René Benjamin, *Mussolini et son peuple*, Paris: Librairie Plon, 1937, p. 235; Maurice Bedel, *Fascisme An VII*, Paris: Gallimard, 1929, pp. 18–19; Berneri, *Mussolini grande attore*, p. 43.

38 Navarra, *Memorie del cameriere di Mussolini*, p. 161; Romain Hayes, *Subhas Chandra Bose in Nazi Germany: Politics, Intelligence and Propaganda, 1941–1943*, London, Hurst, 2011, pp. 9–10; Robert Blake and Wm Roger Louis (eds), *Churchill*, Oxford: Clarendon Press, 2002, p. 258; Edwin P. Hoyt, *Mussolini's Empire: The Rise and Fall of the Fascist Vision*, New York: Wiley, 1994, p. 115; see also John Patrick Diggins, *Mussolini and Fascism: The View from America*, Princeton: Princeton University Press, 1972; David F. Schmitz, *The United States and Fascist Italy, 1922–1940*, Chapel Hill, NC: University of North Carolina Press, 1988.

39 Roberto Festorazzi, *Starace. Il mastino della rivoluzione fascista*, Milan: Ugo Mursia, 2002, p. 71.

40 Piero Melograni, 'The Cult of the Duce in Mussolini's Italy', *Journal of Contemporary History*, 11, no. 4 (Oct. 1976), pp. 221–4; see also Winner, 'Mussolini: A Character Study', p. 518.

41 Berneri, *Mussolini grande attore*, p. 54; Kirkpatrick, *Mussolini*, p. 161.

42 Tracy H. Koon, *Believe, Obey, Fight: Political Socialization of Youth in Fascist Italy, 1922–1943*, Chapel Hill, NC: University of North Carolina Press, 1985, pp. 111–12; Mack Smith, *Mussolini*, pp. 175–6; G. Franco Romagnoli, *The Bicycle Runner: A Memoir of Love, Loyalty, and the Italian Resistance*, New York: St Martin's Press, 2009, p. 48.

43 A list of subsidised newspapers appears in ACS, MCP, Reports, b. 7, f. 73; the mottos are in ACS, MCP, Gabinetto, b. 44, f. 259, 'Motti del Duce'; on the flow of information between Ciano and Goebbels see Wenke Nitz, *Führer und Duce: Politische Machtinszenierungen im nationalsozialistischen Deutschland und im faschistischen Italien*, Cologne: Böhlau Verlag, 2013, p. 112.

44 Bonsaver, *Censorship and Literature in Fascist Italy*, pp. 61 and 124; Giovanni Sedita estimates that 632 million lire were used to subsidise both newspapers and individuals; Giovanni Sedita, *Gli intellettuali di Mussolini: La cultura finanziata dal fascismo*, Florence: Casa Editrice Le Lettere, 2010, p. 17; Asvero Gravelli, *Uno e Molti: Interpretazioni spirituali di Mussolini*, Rome: Nuova Europa, 1938, pp. 29 and 31; the subsidy received by the author is listed in an appendix published in Sedita, *Gli intellettuali di Mussolini*, p. 202.

45 Philip Cannistraro, *La fabbrica del consenso: Fascismo e mass media*, Bari: Laterza, 1975, pp. 228–41.

46 Navarra, *Memorie del cameriere di Mussolini*, pp. 114–15.

47 Franco Ciarlantini, *De Mussolini onzer verbeelding*, Amsterdam: De Amsterdamsche Keurkamer, 1934, p. 145.

48 Paul Baxa, '"Il nostro Duce": Mussolini's Visit to Trieste in 1938 and the Workings of the Cult of the Duce', *Modern Italy*, 18, no. 2 (May 2013), pp. 121–6; Frank Iezzi, 'Benito Mussolini, Crowd Psychologist', *Quarterly Journal of Speech*, 45, no. 2 (April 1959), p. 167.

49 Iezzi, 'Benito Mussolini, Crowd Psychologist', pp. 167–9.

50 Stephen Gundle, 'Mussolini's Appearances in the Regions' in Gundle, Duggan and Pieri (eds), *The Cult of the Duce*, pp. 115–17.

51 Koon, *Believe, Obey, Fight*, p. 30; Dino Alfieri and Luigi Freddi (eds), *Mostra della Rivoluzione Fascista*, Rome: National Fascist Party, 1933, p. 9; Dino Alfieri, *Exhibition of the Fascist Revolution: 1st Decennial of the March on Rome*, Bergamo: Istituto Italiano d'Arti Grafiche, 1933.

52 Edoardo Bedeschi, *La giovinezza del Duce: Libro per la gioventù italiana*, 2nd edn, Turin: Società Editrice Internazionale, 1940, p. 122; August Bernhard Hasler, 'Das Duce-Bild in der faschistischen Literatur', *Quellen und Forschungen aus italienischen Archiven und Bibliotheken*, vol. 60, 1980, p. 497; Sofia Serenelli, 'A Town for the Cult of the Duce: Predappio as a Site of Pilgrimage' in Gundle, Duggan and Pieri (eds), *The Cult of the Duce*, pp. 95 and 101–2.

53 ACS, SPD CO, b. 869, f. 500027/IV, 'Omaggi mandati a V.T.'.

54 Kirkpatrick, *Mussolini*, p. 170; many of the fasces can still be found today; see Max Page, *Why Preservation Matters*, New Haven, CT: Yale University Press, 2016, pp. 137–8; Ludwig, *Talks with Mussolini*, p. 121.

55 Mack Smith, *Mussolini*, p. 136; Kirkpatrick, *Mussolini*, pp. 275–6; see also Eugene Pooley, 'Mussolini and the City of Rome' in Gundle, Duggan and Pieri (eds), *The Cult of the Duce*, pp. 209–24.

56 Michael Mann, *The Dark Side of Democracy: Explaining Ethnic Cleansing*, Cambridge: Cambridge University Press, 2015, p. 309; Dominik J. Schaller, 'Genocide and Mass Violence in the "Heart of Darkness": Africa in the Colonial Period' in Donald Bloxham and A. Dirk Moses, *The Oxford Handbook of Genocide Studies*, Oxford: Oxford University Press, 2010, p. 358; see also Mack Smith, *Mussolini*, p. 171.

57 Kirkpatrick, *Mussolini*, pp. 288–9.

58 Jean Ajalbert, *L'Italie en silence et Rome sans amour*, Paris: Albin Michel, 1935, pp. 227–8.

59 Mack Smith, *Mussolini*, pp. 190 and 197.

60 Ruth Ben-Ghiat, *Fascist Modernities: Italy, 1922–1945*, Berkeley, CA: University of California Press, 2001, p. 216; Ian Campbell, *The Addis Ababa Massacre: Italy's National Shame*, London: Hurst, 2017; the incident with Graziani is recounted in Navarra, *Memorie del cameriere di Mussolini*, p. 202.

61 To give but one example, the journalist Henry Soullier received thousands of Swiss francs to visit Addis Ababa; ACS, MCP, Gabinetto, b. 10.

62 Romagnoli, *The Bicycle Runner*, p. 48; ACS, SPD, Carteggio Ordinario, b. 386, f. 142470, 23 Aug. 1936.

63 Kirkpatrick, *Mussolini*, pp. 331–2.

64 Santi Corvaja, *Hitler and Mussolini: The Secret Meetings*, New York: Enigma Books, 2008, pp. 27–8; Alfred Rosenberg, *Das politische Tagebuch Alfred Rosenbergs aus den Jahren 1934/35 und 1939/40: Nach der photographischen Wiedergabe der Handschrift aus den Nürnberger Akten*, Munich: Deutscher Taschenbuch Verlag, 1964, p. 28.

65 Kirkpatrick, *Mussolini*, pp. 350–54.

66 Galeazzo Ciano, *The Ciano Diaries, 1939–1943*, Safety Harbor, FL: Simon Publications, 2001, pp. 43–4 and 53.

67 Mack Smith, *Mussolini*, pp. 230 and 249.

68 Ciano, *The Ciano Diaries, 1939–1943*, p. 138.

69 Ibid., p. 223, see also p. 222; Mack Smith, *Mussolini*, pp. 237 and 240–43.

70 Renzo de Felice, *Mussolini il Fascista*, vol. 1, *La conquista del potere, 1921–1925*, Turin: Giulio Einaudi, 1966, p. 470; on his isolation see Navarra, *Memorie del cameriere di Mussolini*, pp. 45–6, and Kirkpatrick, *Mussolini*, p. 167.

71 Navarra, *Memorie del cameriere di Mussolini*, pp. 140 and 203; Ciano, *The Ciano Diaries, 1939–1943*, pp. 18–19.

72 Mack Smith, *Mussolini*, pp. 240–47.

73 Melograni, 'The Cult of the Duce in Mussolini's Italy', p. 221.

74 Duggan, 'The Internalisation of the Cult of the Duce', pp. 132–3.

75 Emilio Gentile, *The Sacralisation of Politics in Fascist Italy*, Cambridge, MA: Harvard University Press, 1996, pp. 151–2.

76 Emilio Lussu, *Enter Mussolini: Observations and Adventures of an Anti-Fascist*, London: Methuen & Co., 1936, p. 169; Romagnoli, *The Bicycle Runner*, p. 67.

77 Christopher Duggan, *Fascist Voices: An Intimate History of Mussolini's Italy*, Oxford: Oxford University Press, 2013, pp. 177 and 257–8; Ajalbert, *L'Italie en silence et Rome sans amour*, p. 231; Paul Corner, *The Fascist Party and Popular Opinion in Mussolini's Italy*, Oxford: Oxford University Press, 2012, pp. 200 and 250.

78 Mack Smith, *Mussolini*, p. 239.

79 Ciano, *The Ciano Diaries, 1939–1943*, p. 264.

80 ACS, MCP, Gabinetto, b. 43, pp. 39 ff, 20 Nov. 1940, Mack Smith, *Mussolini*, p. 260; ACS, MCP, Gabinetto, b. 44, f. 258, p. 29 on fighting clandestine radio.

81 Kirkpatrick, *Mussolini*, pp. 494–5; Ciano, *The Ciano Diaries, 1939–1943*, p. 583.

82 Kirkpatrick, *Mussolini*, p. 515.

83 Winner, 'Mussolini: A Character Study', p. 526; ACS, MCP, Gabinetto, b. 44, f. 258, 12 March 1943, p. 5.

84 Angelo M. Imbriani, *Gli italiani e il Duce: Il mito e l'immagine di Mussolini negli ultimi anni del fascismo (1938–1943)*, Naples: Liguori, 1992, pp. 171–6.

85 Robert A. Ventresca, *Soldier of Christ: The Life of Pope Pius XII*, Cambridge, MA: Harvard University Press, 2013, p. 192.

86 Imbriani, *Gli italiani e il Duce*, pp. 184–5.

87 Mack Smith, *Mussolini*, p. 298.

88 Gentile, *The Sacralisation of Politics in Fascist Italy*, p. 152; Italo Calvino, 'Il Duce's Portraits', *New Yorker*, 6 Jan. 2003, p. 34; John

Foot, *Italy's Divided Memory*, Houndmills, Basingstoke: Palgrave Macmillan, 2009, p. 67.

89 Ray Moseley, *Mussolini: The Last 600 Days of Il Duce*, Lanham, MD: Taylor Trade Publishing, 2004, p. 2.

90 Romagnoli, *The Bicycle Runner*, p. 259.

CHAPTER 2 HITLER

1 H. R. Trevor-Roper (ed.), *Hitler's Table Talk 1941–1944*, New York: Enigma Books, 2000, p. 10.

2 Margarete Plewnia, *Auf dem Weg zu Hitler: Der 'völkische' Publizist Dietrich Eckart*, Bremen: Schünemann Universitätsverlag, 1970, p. 84.

3 Adolf Hitler, *Mein Kampf*, Munich: Franz Eher Verlag, 1943, p. 235.

4 Ernst Hanfstaengl, *Unheard Witness*, Philadelphia: Lippincott, 1957, pp. 34–7; size of the audience in Volker Ullrich, *Hitler: Ascent 1889–1939*, New York: Alfred Knopf, 2016, p. 95.

5 Plewnia, *Auf dem Weg zu Hitler*, pp. 69 and 84–90.

6 Ian Kershaw, *Hitler, 1889–1936: Hubris*, London: Allen Lane, 1998, pp. 162–3; Plewnia, *Auf dem Weg zu Hitler*, p. 81.

7 Georg Franz-Willing, *Die Hitlerbewegung. Der Ursprung, 1919–1922*, Hamburg: R.v. Decker's Verlag G. Schenck, 1962, 2nd edn 1972, pp. 124–8 and 218–19.

8 Hanfstaengl, *Unheard Witness*, p. 70; Rudolf Herz, *Hoffmann & Hitler: Fotografie als Medium des Führer Mythos*, Munich: Klinkhardt and Biermann, 1994, pp. 92–3 and 99.

9 Plewnia, *Auf dem Weg zu Hitler*, p. 90; Ullrich, *Hitler*, p. 113; Ludolf Herbst, *Hitlers Charisma. Die Erfindung eines deutschen Messias*, Frankfurt am Main: S. Fischer Verlag, 2010, pp. 147–9.

10 Hanfstaengl, *Hitler*, p. 86.

11 William L. Shirer, *The Rise and Fall of the Third Reich: A History of Nazi Germany*, New York: Simon & Schuster, 50th anniversary reissue, 2011, pp. 75–6.

12 Adolf Hitler, *Mein Kampf*, p. 116; the term *Traumlaller* appears in Georg Schott, *Das Volksbuch vom Hitler*, Munich: Herrmann Wiechmann, 1924 and 1938, p. 10.

13 Ullrich, *Hitler*, p. 189.

14 Heinrich Hoffmann, *Hitler Was My Friend: The Memoirs of Hitler's Photographer*, London: Burke, 1955, pp. 60–61.

15 Claudia Schmölders, *Hitler's Face: The Biography of an Image*, Philadelphia: University of Pennsylvania Press, 2009, p. 87; Herz, *Hoffmann & Hitler*, pp. 162–9.

16 Hoffmann, *Hitler Was My Friend*, pp. 61–3.

17 Ullrich, *Hitler*, pp. 199–202.

18 Joseph Goebbels, *Tagebücher 1924–1945*, edited by Ralf Georg Reuth, Munich: Piper Verlag, 1992, vol. 1, p. 200; Ullrich, *Hitler*, p. 208.

19 Ullrich, *Hitler*, p. 217.

20 Hitler, *Mein Kampf*, p. 96; Joseph Goebbels, *Die zweite Revolution: Briefe an Zeitgenossen*, Zwickau: Streiter-Verlag, 1928, pp. 5–8; 'Der Führer', 22 April 1929, reproduced in Joseph Goebbels, *Der Angriff*, Munich: Franz Eher Verlag, 1935, pp. 214–16; see also Ernest K. Bramsted, *Goebbels and National Socialist Propaganda 1925–1945*, East Lansing, MI: Michigan State University Press, 1965, pp. 195–201.

21 Ullrich, *Hitler*, pp. 222–3.

22 Herbst, *Hitlers Charisma*, p. 215; *The Times*, 10 June 1931, p. 17; Richard Bessel, 'The Rise of the NSDAP and the Myth of Nazi Propaganda', *Wiener Library Bulletin*, 33, 1980, pp. 20–29.

23 Ullrich, *Hitler*, pp. 281–2.

24 Heinrich Hoffmann, *Hitler wie ihn keiner kennt*, Munich: Heinrich Hoffmann, 1935 (1st edn 1932); see also Herz, *Hoffmann & Hitler*, pp. 245–8.

25 Bramsted, *Goebbels and National Socialist Propaganda*, pp. 202–4; Emil Ludwig, *Three Portraits: Hitler, Mussolini, Stalin*, New York: Longmans, Green and Co., 1940, p. 27.

26 Gerhard Paul, *Aufstand der Bilder. Die NS-Propaganda vor 1933*, Bonn: Dietz, 1990, pp. 204–7.

27 Ullrich, *Hitler*, pp. 330–31.

28 Richard J. Evans, 'Coercion and Consent in Nazi Germany', *Proceedings of the British Academy*, 151, 2006, pp. 53–81.

29 Ibid.

30 BArch, R43II/979, 31 March, 2 and 10 April 1933.

31 BArch, R43II/979, 18 Feb., 7, 8, 11 March 1933; R43II/976, 7 April and 3 July 1933.

32 BArch, NS6/215, p. 16, Circular by Martin Bormann, 6 Oct. 1933.

33 Konrad Repgen and Hans Booms, *Akten der Reichskanzlei: Regierung Hitler 1933–1938*, Boppard: Harald Boldt Verlag, 1983, part 1, vol. 1,

p. 467; BArch, R43II/959, 5 and 13 April 1933, 29 Aug. 1933, pp. 25–6 and 48.

34 Richard Bessel, 'Charismatisches Führertum? Hitlers Image in der deutschen Bevölkerung' in Martin Loiperdinger, Rudolf Herz and Ulrich Pohlmann (eds), *Führerbilder: Hitler, Mussolini, Roosevelt, Stalin in Fotografie und Film*, Munich: Piper, 1995, pp. 16–17.

35 Ullrich, *Hitler*, p. 474.

36 *Deutschland-Berichte der Sozaldemokratischen Partei Deutschlands (Sopade) 1934–1940*, Salzhausen: Verlag Petra Nettelbeck, 1980, vol. 1, 1934, pp. 275–7; see also John Brown, *I Saw for Myself*, London: Selwyn and Blount, 1935, p. 35.

37 Victor Klemperer, *I Will Bear Witness: A Diary of the Nazi Years 1933–1941*, New York: The Modern Library, 1999, p. 82.

38 The speech can be found in Rudolf Hess, 'Der Eid auf Adolf Hitler', *Reden*, Munich: Franz Eher Verlag, 1938, pp. 9–14, and reactions to it in *Deutschland-Berichte der Sopade*, 1934, pp. 470–72.

39 Hitler, *Mein Kampf*, p. 387.

40 BArch, NS22/425, 30 Aug. 1934, p. 149; two weeks later, after it was reported that some of the portraits were being destroyed, a new circular allowed images of other leaders provided that Hitler's portrait prevailed in proportion and size; see p. 148, 14 Sept. 1934; on slogans in the 1935 rally see Louis Bertrand, *Hitler*, Paris: Arthème Fayard, 1936, p. 45.

41 *Deutschland-Berichte der Sopade*, 1934, pp. 10–11, 471–2, 482 and 730–31.

42 Joseph Goebbels, *'Unser Hitler!' Signale der neuen Zeit. 25 ausgewählte Reden von Dr. Joseph Goebbels*, Munich: NSDAP, 1934, pp. 141–9; see also Bramsted, *Goebbels and National Socialist Propaganda 1925–1945*, pp. 204–5.

43 Bernd Sösemann, 'Die Macht der allgegenwärtigen Suggestion. Die Wochensprüche der NSDAP als Propagandamittel', *Jahrbuch 1989*, Berlin: Berliner Wissenschaftliche Gesellschaft, 1990, pp. 227–48; Victor Klemperer, *To the Bitter End: The Diaries of Victor Klemperer 1942–1945*, London: Weidenfeld & Nicolson, 1999, p. 106.

44 Wolfgang Schneider, *Alltag unter Hitler*, Berlin: Rowohlt Berlin Verlag, 2000, p. 83; BArch, R58/542, p. 30, *Frankfurter Zeitung*, 25 Aug. 1938; p. 32, *Berliner Börsen Zeitung*, 7 Sept. 1938; p. 38, *Völkischer Beobachter*, 6 Nov. 1938.

45 Othmar Plöckinger, *Geschichte eines Buches. Adolf Hitlers "Mein Kampf" 1922–1945*, Munich: Oldenbourg Verlag, 2006, pp. 414–15; BArch, R4901/4370, 6 Feb. and 5 April 1937.

46 Ansgar Diller, *Rundfunkpolitik im Dritten Reich*, Munich: Deutscher Taschenbuch Verlag, 1980, pp. 62–3.

47 Goebbels, *Tagebücher 1924–1945*, p. 772.

48 On the numbers and cost of radio sets, see Wolfgang König, 'Der Volksempfänger und die Radioindustrie. Ein Beitrag zum Verhältnis von Wirtschaft und Politik im Nationalsozialismus' in *Vierteljahrschrift für Sozial- und Wirtschaftsgeschichte*, 90, no. 3 (2003), p. 273; *Deutschland-Berichte der Sopade*, 1934, pp. 275–7; 1936, p. 414; 1938, p. 1326; Klemperer, *I Will Bear Witness*, p. 155.

49 Stephan Dolezel and Martin Loiperdinger, 'Hitler in Parteitagsfilm und Wochenschau' in Loiperdinger, Herz and Pohlmann, *Führerbilder*, p. 81.

50 On mobile cinemas, see Richard J. Evans, *The Third Reich in Power*, London: Penguin Books, 2006, p. 210.

51 Hoffmann, *Hitler Was My Friend*, p. 70; Herz, *Hoffmann & Hitler*, p. 244.

52 Ines Schlenker, *Hitler's Salon: The Große Deutsche Kunstausstellung at the Haus der Deutschen Kunst in Munich 1937–1944*, Bern: Peter Lang AG, 2007, p. 136.

53 A. W. Kersbergen, *Onderwijs en nationaalsocialisme*, Assen: Van Gorcum, 1938, p. 21.

54 Annemarie Stiehler, *Die Geschichte von Adolf Hitler den deutschen Kindern erzählt*, Berlin-Lichterfelde: Verlag des Hauslehrers, 1936, p. 95; Kersbergen, *Onderwijs en nationaalsocialisme*, p. 22.

55 Paul Jennrich, *Unser Hitler. Ein Jugend- und Volksbuch*, Halle (Saale), Pädagogischer Verlag Hermann Schroedel, 1933, p. 75; Linda Jacobs Altman, *Shattered Youth in Nazi Germany: Primary Sources from the Holocaust*, Berkeley Heights, NJ: Enslow Publishers, 2010, p. 95.

56 Rudolf Hoke and Ilse Reiter (eds), *Quellensammlung zur österreichischen und deutschen Rechtsgeschichte*, Vienna: Böhlau Verlag, 1993, p. 544.

57 Despina Stratigakos, *Hitler at Home*, New Haven, CT: Yale University Press, 2015, pp. 24–46.

58 Albert Speer, *Inside the Third Reich*, New York: Macmillan, 1970, p. 103; Christa Schroeder, *Er war mein Chef: Aus dem Nachlaß der Sekretärin von Adolf Hitler*, Munich: Langen Müller, 1985, p. 71.

59 Stratigakos, *Hitler at Home*, p. 59.

60 Ibid., p. 84.

61 Kristin Semmens, *Seeing Hitler's Germany: Tourism in the Third Reich*, Houndmills, Basingstoke: Palgrave Macmillan, 2005, pp. 56–68; BArch, R43II/957a, 10 Oct. 1938, pp. 40–41.

62 Ulrich Chaussy and Christoph Püschner, *Nachbar Hitler. Führerkult und Heimatzerstörung am Obersalzberg*, Berlin: Christoph Links Verlag, 2007, pp. 141–2; David Lloyd George, 'I Talked to Hitler' in Anson Rabinbach and Sander L. Gilman (eds), *The Third Reich Sourcebook*, Berkeley, CA: University of California Press, 2013, p. 77–8.

63 Chaussy and Püschner, *Nachbar Hitler*, p. 142.

64 Andrew Nagorski, *Hitlerland: American Eyewitnesses to the Nazi Rise to Power*, New York: Simon & Schuster, 2012, pp. 84–6.

65 Kershaw, *Hubris*, p. 590; Max Domarus, *Hitler: Reden und Proklamationen 1932–1945*, Leonberg: Pamminger, 1988, p. 606.

66 *Deutschland-Berichte der Sopade*, 1936, pp. 68–70; W. E. B. Du Bois, 'What of the Color-Line?' in Oliver Lubrich (ed.), *Travels in the Reich, 1933–1945: Foreign Authors Report from Germany*, Chicago: University of Chicago Press, 2010, p. 143.

67 *Deutschland-Berichte der Sopade*, 1936, pp. 68–70, 141, 409, 414 and 419; Domarus, *Hitler*, p. 643.

68 William L. Shirer, *Berlin Diary*, New York: Alfred Knopf, 1942, p. 86.

69 *Deutschland-Berichte der Sopade*, 1937, pp. 139–40, 143–6, 603, 606, 1224 and 1531.

70 Ibid., pp. 1528 and 1531.

71 Ullrich, *Hitler*, p. 736; Kershaw, *Hitler: Nemesis*, pp. 110–12.

72 Klemperer, *I Will Bear Witness*, p. 29; Goebbels, 'Geburtstag des Führers', 19 April 1939, *Die Zeit ohne Beispiel*, Munich: Franz Eher Verlag, 1942, p. 102; *The Times*, 20 April 1939.

73 'Aggrandizer's Anniversary', *Time* magazine, 1 May 1939; Speer, *Inside the Third Reich*, p. 149.

74 'Aggrandizer's Anniversary', *Time* magazine, 1 May 1939.

75 Roger Moorhouse, 'Germania: Hitler's Dream Capital', *History Today*, 62, issue 3 (March 2012); Speer, *Inside the Third Reich*, p. 69.

76 Goebbels, *Tagebücher 1924–1945*, pp. 1319–20; Sebastian Haffner, *The Meaning of Hitler*, London: Phoenix Press, 1979, p. 34; Kershaw, *Hitler: Nemesis*, p. 184.

77 Klemperer, *I Will Bear Witness*, p. 305; *Deutschland-Berichte der Sopade*, 1938, pp. 406–7; Speer, *Inside the Third Reich*, p. 148.

78 *Deutschland-Berichte der Sopade*, 1939, p. 450; BArch, R43II/963, 15 Feb. 1939, p. 56.

79 *Deutschland-Berichte der Sopade*, 1938, pp. 1056–7.

80 *Deutschland-Berichte der Sopade*, 1939, p. 442.

81 Evans, *The Third Reich in Power*, p. 704.

82 Shirer, *Berlin Diary*, p. 201; Hoffman, *Hitler Was My Friend*, p. 115.

83 Hoffman, *Hitler Was My Friend*, p. 115.

84 Shirer, *Berlin Diary*, p. 205; Klemperer, *I Will Bear Witness*, p. 315; C. W. Guillebaud, 'How Germany Finances The War', *Spectator*, 29 December 1939, p. 8.

85 Shirer, *Berlin Diary*, p. 241.

86 Ibid., p. 320.

87 Shirer, *Berlin Diary*, p. 336; Goebbels, *Tagebücher 1924–1945*, p. 1450; Hitler's instructions are in BArch, R55/20007, July 1940, pp. 8–9; see also Stephen G. Fritz, *Ostkrieg: Hitler's War of Extermination in the East*, Lexington, KT: University Press of Kentucky, 2011, p. 31.

88 Richard J. Evans, *The Third Reich at War*, London: Penguin, 2009, pp. 136–8.

89 Shirer, *Berlin Diary*, pp. 454–5.

90 Ernst Hanfstaengl, his publicist in the United States, repeatedly mentioned Hitler's lack of strategic vision when it came to the United States; see Hanfstaengl, *Unheard Witness*, pp. 37 and 66.

91 Evans, *The Third Reich at War*, p. 424.

92 Ibid., p. 507; Schroeder, *Er war mein Chef*, pp. 74–5.

93 Bramsted, *Goebbels and the National Socialist Propaganda 1925–1945*, pp. 223–4.

94 Evans, *The Third Reich at War*, pp. 421–2.

95 Ibid., pp. 422–3; Ulrich von Hassell, *The von Hassell Diaries: The Story of the Forces against Hitler inside Germany, 1938–1945*, Boulder, CO: Westview Press, 1994, p. 304.

96 BArch, NS18/842, 17 July 1942, p. 38.

97 Hoffmann, *Hitler Was My Friend*, p. 227; Speer, *Inside the Third Reich*, p. 473.

98 Evans, *The Third Reich at War: 1939–1945*, p. 714; Klemperer, *To the Bitter End*, p. 387.

99 Speer, *Inside the Third Reich*, p. 473.

100 Evans, *The Third Reich at War*, p. 732; Hans J. Mallaquoi, *Destined to Witness: Growing up Black in Nazi Germany*, New York: HarperCollins, 2001, p. 251; Klemperer, *To the Bitter End*, p. 458; see also Joachim C. Fest, *Hitler*, Boston, MA: Houghton Mifflin Harcourt, 2002, pp. 753–4.

101 Antony Beevor, *The Fall of Berlin 1945*, London: Penguin Books, 2002, p. 415.

CHAPTER 3 STALIN

1 Henri Béraud, *Ce que j'ai vu à Moscou*, Paris: Les Editions de France, 1925, pp. 46–7.

2 Richard Pipes, *The Russian Revolution*, New York: Vintage Books, 1991, pp. 808–12.

3 Ibid., p. 814.

4 Ibid., p. 815.

5 Robert Service, *Stalin: A Biography*, Houndmills, Basingstoke: Macmillan, 2004, p. 132; Eugene Lyons, *Stalin: Czar of all the Russians*, New York: J. B. Lippincott, 1940, p. 287; Stephen Kotkin, *Stalin: Paradoxes of Power, 1878–1928*, New York: Penguin Press, 2014, p. 424.

6 Kotkin, *Stalin: Paradoxes of Power*, p. 534.

7 Fernand Corcos, *Une visite à la Russie nouvelle*, Paris: Editions Montaigne, 1930, pp. 404–5; Benno Ennker, 'The Origins and Intentions of the Lenin Cult' in Ian D. Thatcher (ed.), *Regime and Society in Twentieth-Century Russia*, Houndmills, Basingstoke: Macmillan Press, 1999, pp. 125–6.

8 Alexei Yurchak, 'Bodies of Lenin: The Hidden Science of Communist Sovereignty', *Representations*, no. 129 (Winter 2015), pp. 116–57; Béraud, *Ce que j'ai vu à Moscou*, p. 45.

9 Kotkin, *Stalin*, p. 543; Robert H. McNeal, *Stalin: Man and Rule*, New York: New York University Press, 1988, pp. 90–93.

10 Service, *Stalin*, pp. 223–4.

11 For instance RGASPI, 17 Oct. 1925, 558-11-1158, doc. 59, p. 77.

12 'Stalin's Word', *Time* magazine, 27 April 1925.

13 Kotkin, *Stalin*, p. 648.

14 Eugene Lyons, *Assignment in Utopia*, London: George G. Harrap, 1938, p. 173; Service, *Stalin*, p. 259.

15 Alexander Trachtenberg, *The History of May Day*, New York: International Pamphlets, 1931.

16 Lyons, *Assignment in Utopia*, pp. 102–3.

17 Service, *Stalin*, pp. 265–7.

18 Lyons, *Assignment in Utopia*, pp. 206–7; Pravda, in a special issue on the Stalin Jubilee published on 21 December 1929, hailed Stalin as the 'true inheritor' of Marx and Lenin and the 'leader' of the proletarian party: RGASPI, 558-11-1352, 21 Dec. 1929, doc. 8; see also Jeffrey Brooks, *Thank You, Comrade Stalin!: Soviet Public Culture from Revolution to Cold War*, Princeton: Princeton University Press, 2000, pp. 60–61.

19 RGASPI, 558-11-1352, doc. 1, 19 Dec. 1929; see also 'Stalin', *The Life of Stalin: A Symposium*, London: Modern Books Limited, 1930, pp. 12–14.

20 Lazar Kaganovich, 'Stalin and the Party'; Sergo Ordzhonikidze, 'The "Diehard" Bolshvik', both reproduced in *The Life of Stalin*, pp. 40 and 87–9.

21 Lyons, *Assignment in Utopia*, pp. 265–6; on posters in 1929 see James L. Heizer, 'The Cult of Stalin, 1929–1939', doctoral dissertation, University of Kentucky, 1977, p. 55 quoted in Sarah Davies, *Popular Opinion in Stalin's Russia: Terror, Propaganda and Dissent, 1934–1941*, Cambridge: Cambridge University Press, 1997, p. 147.

22 The expression 'victor with a grudge' comes from Stephen Kotkin's astute analysis in *Stalin*, pp. 474 and 591; Kotkin, however, does not believe that the Testament was genuinely the work of Lenin.

23 Leon Trotsky, *My Life*, New York: Charles Scribner, 1930, pp. 309, 378 and 398.

24 Avel Yenukidze, 'Leaves from my Reminiscences' in *The Life of Stalin*, pp. 90–96.

25 Lyons, *Assignment in Utopia*, pp. 381–91; 'Russia: Stalin Laughs!', *Time* magazine, 1 Dec. 1930.

26 'Soso was Good', *Time* magazine, 8 Dec. 1930.

27 See Stanley Weintraub, 'GBS and the Despots', *Times Literary Supplement*, 22 Aug. 2011.

28 Emil Ludwig, *Nine Etched from Life*, New York: Robert McBride, p. 348; the vetting of Barbusse is recounted by Michael David-Fox, *Showcasing the Great Experiment: Cultural Diplomacy and Western Visitors to the Soviet Union, 1921–1941*, Oxford: Oxford University

Press, 2011, pp. 231–2, as well as Jan Plamper, *The Stalin Cult: A Study in the Alchemy of Power*, New Haven, CT: Yale University Press, 2012, p. 133; neither mention the financial transactions that took place, which can be found in RGASPI, 558-11-699, 12 Oct. 1933, doc. 6, pp. 53–4; André Gide, 'Retouches à mon "Retour de l'URSS"' in *Souvenirs et Voyages*, Paris: Gallimard, 2001, pp. 803–71, quoted in Andrew Sobanet, 'Henri Barbusse, Official Biographer of Joseph Stalin', *French Cultural Studies*, 24, no. 4 (Nov. 2013), p. 368; on other foreign writers approached by Stalin for a biography, see Roy Medvedev, 'New Pages from the Political Biography of Stalin' in Robert C. Tucker (ed.), *Stalinism: Essays in Historical Interpretation*, New Brunswick, NJ: Transaction, p. 207, note 9.

29 Henri Barbusse, *Stalin: A New World seen through One Man*, London: John Lane, 1935, pp. viii and 291.

30 On this, see, among others, David-Fox, *Showcasing the Great Experiment*.

31 Emil Ludwig, *Three Portraits: Hitler, Mussolini, Stalin*, New York: Longmans, Green and Co., 1940, p. 104.

32 Lyons, *Assignment in Utopia*, pp. 340–42.

33 The statues were noted by Corcos, *Une Visite à la Russie Nouvelle*, p. 117, and in the countryside by Malcolm Muggeridge, box 2, Hoover Institution Archives, 'Russia, 16.9.1932-29.1.1933', p. 125.

34 Service, *Stalin*, pp. 312–13 and 360.

35 Richard Pipes, *Communism: A History of the Intellectual and Political Movement*, London: Phoenix Press, p. 66.

36 On 'little Stalins' see Malte Rolf, 'Working towards the Centre: Leader Cults and Spatial Politics' in Apor Balázs, Jan C. Behrends, Polly Jones and E. A. Rees (eds), *The Leader Cult in Communist Dictatorships: Stalin and the Eastern Bloc*, Houndmills, Basingstoke: Palgrave Macmillan, 2004, p. 152; E. A. Rees, 'Leader Cults: Varieties, Preconditions and Functions' in Balázs et al., *The Leader Cult in Communist Dictatorships*, p. 10; Sheila Fitzpatrick, *Everyday Stalinism. Ordinary Life in Extraordinary Times: Soviet Russia in the 1930s*, Oxford: Oxford University Press, 1999, pp. 30–31; Rumiantsev called Stalin a genius in February 1934, see *XVII s'ezd Vsesojuznoj Kommunisticheskoj Partii, 26 janvarja – 10 fevralja 1934*, Moscow: Partizdat, 1934, p. 143; on his cult see Jörg Baberowski,

Scorched Earth: Stalin's Reign of Terror, New Haven, CT: Yale University Press, 2016, pp. 224–7.

37 Larissa Vasilieva, *Kremlin Wives*, New York: Arcade Publishing, 1992, pp. 122–4.

38 Brooks, *Thank You, Comrade Stalin!*, p. 106; John Brown, *I Saw for Myself*, London: Selwyn and Blount, 1935, p. 260.

39 Malte Rolf, 'A Hall of Mirrors: Sovietizing Culture under Stalinism', *Slavic Review*, 68, no. 3 (Fall 2009), p. 601.

40 Lyons, *Stalin*, p. 215.

41 Rolf, 'A Hall of Mirrors', p. 610; Anita Pisch, 'The Personality Cult of Stalin in Soviet Posters, 1929–1953: Archetypes, Inventions and Fabrications', doctoral dissertation, Australian National University, 2014, p. 135.

42 Brooks, *Thank You, Comrade Stalin!*, pp. 69–77; Pisch, 'The Personality Cult of Stalin in Soviet Posters', p. 69.

43 The encounter between Avdeenko and Mekhlis is in Davies, *Popular Opinion in Stalin's Russia*, p. 149; the broadcast is reported in Eugene Lyons, 'Dictators into Gods', *American Mercury*, March 1939, p. 268.

44 Lyons, 'Dictators into Gods', p. 269.

45 Nadezhda Mandelstam, *Hope against Hope: A Memoir*, New York: Atheneum, 1983, p. 420; RGASPI, 558-11-1479, doc. 36, pp. 54–6.

46 Simon Sebag Montefiore, *Stalin: The Court of the Red Tsar*, New York: Knopf, 2004, p. 164; *SSSR. Sezd Sovetov (chrezvychajnyj) (8). Stenograficheskij otchet, 25 nojabrja – 5 dekabrja 1936 g.*, Moscow: CIK SSSR, 1936, p. 208; Sergo Ordzhonikidze, *Izbrannye stat'i i rechi, 1918–1937*, Moscow: Ogiz, 1945, p. 240.

47 David Brandenberger, 'Stalin as Symbol: A Case Study of the Personality Cult and its Construction' in Sarah Davies and James Harris (eds), *Stalin: A New History*, Cambridge: Cambridge University Press, 2005, pp. 249–70; see also the classic David King, *The Commissar Vanishes: The Falsification of Photographs and Art in Stalin's Russia*, New York: Metropolitan Books, 1997.

48 Kees Boterbloem, *The Life and Times of Andrei Zhdanov, 1896–1948*, Montreal: McGill-Queen's Press, 2004, pp. 176–7 and 215.

49 RGASPI, 558-11-1354, 20 Nov. 1939, pp. 29–34; all the letters are in document 21.

50 The request from the Museum of the Revolution is in RGASPI, 558-11-1354, 29 July 1940, document 15, the list of gifts put on display in document 15.

51 'Foreign Statesmen Greet Stalin on 60th Birthday', *Moscow News*, 1 Jan. 1940.

52 Andrew Nagorski, *The Greatest Battle: Stalin, Hitler, and the Desperate Struggle for Moscow that Changed the Course of World War II*, New York: Simon & Schuster, 2008, pp. 16–17.

53 Service, *Stalin*, p. 403; see also David Glantz, *Stumbling Colossus: The Red Army on the Eve of World War*, Lawrence, KA: University Press of Kansas, 1998.

54 Service, *Stalin*, p. 409.

55 Anna Louise Strong, quoting a report from Erskine Caldwell in her *The Soviets Expected It*, New York: The Dial Press, 1942, p. 39; Alexander Werth, *Russia at War, 1941–1945: A History*, New York: Skyhorse Publishing, 2011, p. 165.

56 Victoria E. Bonnell, *Iconography of Power: Soviet Political Posters Under Lenin and Stalin*, Berkeley, CA: University of California Press, 1998, p. 252; Service, *Stalin*, p. 451; Richard E. Lauterbach, *These Are the Russians*, New York: Harper, 1944, p. 101.

57 Werth, *Russia at War*, p. 595; John Barber, 'The Image of Stalin in Soviet Propaganda and Public Opinion during World War 2' in John Garrard and Carol Garrard (eds), *World War 2 and the Soviet People*, New York: St Martin's Press, 1990, p. 43.

58 Plamper, *The Stalin Cult*, p. 54.

59 Michael Neiberg, *Potsdam: The End of World War II and the Remaking of Europe*, New York: Basic Books, 2015, p. 58; Paul Hollander, *Political Pilgrims: Western Intellectuals in Search of the Good Society*, London: Routledge, 2017, p. 1; Kimberly Hupp, ' "Uncle Joe": What Americans thought of Joseph Stalin before and after World War II', doctoral dissertation, University of Toledo, 2009.

60 Mandelstam, *Hope against Hope*, p. 345.

61 Casualty figures in Timothy C. Dowling (ed.), *Russia at War: From the Mongol Conquest to Afghanistan, Chechnya, and Beyond*, Santa Barbara, CA: ABC-Clio, vol. 1, 2015, p. 172; Richard Overy, *Russia's War: A History of the Soviet Effort: 1941–1945*, Harmondsworth: Penguin Books, 1997, p. 291; Catherine Merridale, *Ivan's War: The Red Army 1939–45*, London: Faber and Faber, 2005, p. 3.

62 Werth, *Russia at War*, p. 369.

63 Merridale, *Ivan's War*, pp. 67, 117–18 and 136; Beevor, *The Fall of Berlin 1945*, p. 424.

64 Beevor, *The Fall of Berlin 1945*, p. 107.

65 Isaac Deutscher, *Stalin: A Political Biography*, New York: Vintage Books, 1949, p. 466; Beevor, *The Fall of Berlin 1945*, pp. 425–6.

66 Service, *Stalin*, p. 543; Brandenburg, 'Stalin as Symbol', pp. 265–70; *Iosif Vissarionovich Stalin. Kratkaya biografiya*, Moscow: OGIZ, 1947, pp. 182–222.

67 Service, *Stalin*, pp. 508 and 564.

68 Anne Applebaum, *Iron Curtain: The Crushing of Eastern Europe, 1944–1956*, New York: Doubleday, 2012; Jan C. Behrends, 'Exporting the Leader: The Stalin Cult in Poland and East Germany (1944/45–1956)' in Balázs et al., *The Leader Cult in Communist Dictatorships*, pp. 161–78.

69 'Mr. Stalin 70 Today, World Peace Prizes Inaugurated', *The Times*, 21 Dec. 1949, p. 4; 'Flags And Lights For Mr. Stalin Birthday Scenes in Moscow', *The Times*, 22 Dec. 1949, p. 4.

70 RGASPI, 558-4-596, 1950; see also McNeal, *Stalin*, pp. 291–2.

71 RGASPI, 558-11-1379, doc. 2 and 4; see also list dated 22 April 1950 in RGASPI, 558-11-1420; RGASPI, 558-4-596, 1950.

72 Service, *Stalin*, p. 548; Overy, *Russia's War*, pp. 288 and 302; Roy Medvedev, *Let History Judge: The Origins and Consequences of Stalinism*, New York: Knopf, 1972, p. 508.

73 Harrison E. Salisbury, 'The Days of Stalin's Death', *New York Times*, 17 April 1983; Brooks, *Thank You, Comrade Stalin!*, p. 237.

CHAPTER 4 MAO ZEDONG

1 On Mao's trip to Moscow, see Paul Wingrove, 'Mao in Moscow, 1949–50: Some New Archival Evidence', *Journal of Communist Studies and Transition Politics*, 11, no. 4 (Dec. 1995), pp. 309–34; David Wolff, '"One Finger's Worth of Historical Events": New Russian and Chinese Evidence on the Sino-Soviet Alliance and Split, 1948–1959', *Cold War International History Project Bulletin*, Working Paper no. 30 (Aug. 2002), pp. 1–74; Sergey Radchenko and David Wolff, 'To the Summit via Proxy-Summits: New Evidence from Soviet and Chinese Archives on Mao's Long March to Moscow,

1949', *Cold War International History Project Bulletin*, no. 16 (Winter 2008), pp. 105–82.

2 *New York Times*, 15 May 1927.

3 Mao Zedong, 'Report on an Investigation of the Peasant Movement In Hunan', March 1927, *Selected Works of Mao Zedong*, Beijing: Foreign Languages Press, 1965, vol. 1, pp. 23–4.

4 Alexander V. Pantsov and Steven I. Levine, *Mao: The Real Story*, New York: Simon & Schuster, 2012, pp. 206, 242 and 248.

5 Mao Zedong, 'On Tactics against Japanese Imperialism', 27 Dec. 1935, translated in Stuart Schram, *Mao's Road To Power: Revolutionary Writings, 1912–49*, Armonk, NY: M. E. Sharpe, 1999, vol. 5, p. 92.

6 Alvin D. Coox, *Nomonhan: Japan Against Russia 1939*, Palo Alto, CA: Stanford University Press, 1988, p. 93.

7 Yang Kuisong, *Mao Zedong yu Mosike de enen yuanyuan* (Mao and Moscow), Nanchang: Jiangxi renmin chubanshe, 1999, p. 21; Pantsov and Levine, *Mao*, p. 293.

8 Jung Chang and Jon Halliday, *Mao: The Unknown Story*, London: Jonathan Cape, 2005, p. 192.

9 Edgar Snow, *Red Star over China: The Classic Account of the Birth of Chinese Communism*, New York: Grove Press, 1994, p. 92.

10 Lee Feigon, *Mao: A Reinterpretation*, Chicago: Ivan R. Dee, 2002, pp. 67–9.

11 Feigon, *Mao*, p. 67; Robert M. Farnsworth, *From Vagabond to Journalist: Edgar Snow in Asia, 1928–1941*, Columbia, MO: University of Missouri Press, 1996, p. 222.

12 Pantsov and Levine, *Mao*, p. 296.

13 Jay Taylor, *The Generalissimo: Chiang Kai-shek and the Struggle for Modern China*, Cambridge, MA: Harvard University Press, 2009, p. 169.

14 Pantsov and Levine, *Mao*, p. 324.

15 RGASPI, 17-170-128a, Georgii Dimitrov, Report to Stalin on the Sixth Plenum of the Central Committee of the CCP, 21 April 1939, pp. 1–3; see also report by Dmitrii Manuilsky on pp. 14–43.

16 Pantsov and Levine, *Mao*, p. 331; Arthur A. Cohen, *The Communism of Mao Tse-tung*, Chicago: University of Chicago Press, 1964, pp. 93–5.

17 Gao Hua, *Hong taiyang shi zenyang shengqi de. Yan'an zhengfeng yundong de lailong qumai* (How did the red sun rise over Yan'an?

A history of the Rectification Movement), Hong Kong: Chinese University Press, 2000, p. 580.

18 Gao, *Hong taiyang shi zenyang shengqi de*, p. 530; see also Chen Yung-fa, *Yan'an de yinying* (Yan'an's Shadow), Taipei: Institute of Modern History, Academia Sinica, 1990.

19 Gao, *Hong taiyang shi zenyang shengqi de*, p. 593.

20 Gao Wenqian, *Zhou Enlai: The Last Perfect Revolutionary*, New York: PublicAffairs, 2007, p. 88.

21 Raymond F. Wylie, *The Emergence of Maoism: Mao Tse-tung, Ch'en Po-ta, and the Search for Chinese Theory, 1935–1945*, Palo Alto, CA: Stanford University Press, 1980, pp. 205–6; Gao, *Hong taiyang shi zenyang shengqi de*, pp. 607–9; Li Jihua, 'Dui Mao Zedong geren chongbai de zisheng' (The propagation of Mao's cult of personality), *Yanhuang chunqiu*, no. 3 (March 2010), pp. 40–45; Theodore H. White and Annalee Jacoby, *Thunder out of China*, London: Victor Gollanz, 1947, p. 217.

22 PRO, FO 371/35777, 1 Feb. 1943, p. 21.

23 Stuart R. Schram, 'Party Leader or True Ruler? Foundations and Significance of Mao Zedong's Personal Power' in Stuart R. Schram (ed.), *Foundations and Limits of State Power in China*, London: School of Oriental and African Studies, 1987, p. 213.

24 Frank Dikötter, *The Tragedy of Liberation: A History of the Chinese Revolution, 1945–1957*, London: Bloomsbury, 2013, pp. 16–17.

25 Dikötter, *The Tragedy of Liberation*, pp. 3 and 22–3.

26 PRO, FO 371/92192, 20 Nov. 1950, p. 19; Robert Guillain, 'China under the Red Flag' in Otto B. Van der Sprenkel, Robert Guillain and Michael Lindsay (eds), *New China: Three Views*, London: Turnstile Press, 1950, pp. 91–2; on rules in the display of portraits see, for instance, SMA, 9 Sept. 1952, A22-2-74, pp. 6–7; 29 Dec. 1951, B1-2-3620, p. 61; Hung Chang-tai, 'Mao's Parades: State Spectacles in China in the 1950s', *China Quarterly*, no. 190 (June 2007), pp. 411–31.

27 Dikötter, *The Tragedy of Liberation*, pp. 134–7.

28 Ibid., p. 83.

29 Ibid., pp. 47–8.

30 Ibid., pp. 99–100.

31 Ibid., p. 190; William Kinmond, *No Dogs in China: A Report on China Today*, New York: Thomas Nelson, 1957, pp. 192–4.

32 John Gitting, 'Monster at the Beach', *Guardian*, 10 April 2004.

33 The classic work on this subject is Cohen, *The Communism of Mao Tse-tung*; the author was ostracised, of course, as learned professors from Harvard University wrote learned books about the 'Sinification of Marxism'.

34 Valentin Chu, *The Inside Story of Communist China: Ta Ta, Tan Tan*, London: Allen & Unwin, 1964, p. 228.

35 See Richard Curt Kraus, *Brushes with Power: Modern Politics and the Chinese Art of Calligraphy*, Berkeley, CA: University of California Press, 1991.

36 Chow Ching-wen, *Ten Years of Storm: The True Story of the Communist Regime in China*, New York: Holt, Rinehart and Winston, 1960, p. 81.

37 Dikötter, *The Tragedy of Liberation*, p. 227.

38 William Taubman, *Khrushchev: The Man and his Era*, London, Free Press, 2003, pp. 271–2.

39 Dikötter, *The Tragedy of Liberation*, pp. 275–6.

40 Pang Xianzhi and Jin Chongji (eds), *Mao Zedong zhuan, 1949–1976* (A biography of Mao Zedong, 1949–1976), Beijing: Zhongyang wenxian chubanshe, 2003, p. 534; Li Zhisui, *The Private Life of Chairman Mao: The Memoirs of Mao's Personal Physician*, New York: Random House, 1994, pp. 182–4.

41 Dikötter, *The Tragedy of Liberation*, p. 291.

42 GSPA, Mao's speech on 10 March 1958 at Chengdu, 91-18-495, p. 211.

43 Li Rui, *Dayuejin qin liji* (A witness account of the Great Leap Forward), Haikou: Nanfang chubanshe, 1999, vol. 2, p. 288.

44 Frank Dikötter, *Mao's Great Famine: The History of China's Most Devastating Catastrophe, 1958–1962*, London: Bloomsbury, 2010, p. 20.

45 Ibid., pp. 22–3.

46 Li Rui, *Lushan huiyi shilu* (A true record of the Lushan plenum), Hong Kong: Tiandi tushu youxian gongsi, 2nd edn, 2009, pp. 232 and 389–90; Li, *The Private Life of Chairman Mao*, p. 381.

47 Li, *Lushan huiyi shilu*, p. 232.

48 Gao, *Zhou Enlai*, pp. 187–8; Liu Tong, 'Jieshi Zhongnanhai gaoceng zhengzhi de yiba yaoshi: Lin Biao biji de hengli yu yanjiu' (A key to understanding high politics in Zhongnanhai: Sorting out and studying Lin Biao's notes), paper presented at the International Conference on Chinese War and Revolution in the Twentieth Century, Shanghai Communications University, 8–9 Nov. 2008.

49 Dikötter, *Mao's Great Famine*, p. 102.

50 Ibid., pp. 116–23.

51 See Frank Dikötter, *The Cultural Revolution: A People's History, 1962–1976*, London: Bloomsbury, 2016, p. 12.

52 *The People's Daily*, 7 Feb. 1963, quoted in Cohen, *The Communism of Mao Tse-tung*, p. 203.

53 David Milton and Nancy D. Milton, *The Wind Will Not Subside: Years in Revolutionary China, 1964–1969*, New York: Pantheon Books, 1976, pp. 63–5; see also Jacques Marcuse, *The Peking Papers: Leaves from the Notebook of a China Correspondent*, London: Arthur Barker, 1968, pp. 235–46.

54 Lu Hong, *Junbao neibu xiaoxi: 'Wenge' qinli shilu* (An Insider's Story of the PLA Daily), Hong Kong, Shidai guoji chubanshe, 2006, pp. 14–17; Daniel Leese, *Mao Cult: Rhetoric and Ritual in China's Cultural Revolution*, Cambridge: Cambridge University Press, 2011, pp. 111–13.

55 Li, *The Private Life of Chairman Mao*, p. 412; Lynn T. White III, *Policies of Chaos: The Organizational Causes of Violence in China's Cultural Revolution*, Princeton: Princeton University Press, 1989, pp. 194–5, 206, 214–16.

56 Letter by D. K. Timms, 6 Oct. 1964, FO 371/175973; see also Laszlo Ladany, *The Communist Party of China and Marxism, 1921–1985: A Self-Portrait*, London: Hurst, 1988, p. 273.

57 Dikötter, *The Cultural Revolution*, p. xi.

58 Ibid., pp. 71–4.

59 Ibid., pp. 107–9.

60 Chang Jung, *Wild Swans: Three Daughters of China*, Clearwater, FL: Touchstone, 2003, p. 413.

61 Dikötter, *The Cultural Revolution*, p. 89.

62 PRO, FO 371-186983, Leonard Appleyard to John Benson, 'Manifestations of the Mao Cult', 28 Sept. 1966.

63 Louis Barcata, *China in the Throes of the Cultural Revolution: An Eye Witness Report*, New York: Hart Publishing, 1968, p. 48.

64 SMA, 11 Dec. 1967, B167-3-21, pp. 70–3; NMA, Instructions from the Centre, 5 April and 12 July 1967, 5038-2-107, pp. 2 and 58–9.

65 HBPA, Directive from the Ministry of Trade, 30 Aug. 1966, 999-4-761, p. 149.

66 SMA, 2 May 1967, B182-2-8, pp. 5–8.

67 Helen Wang, *Chairman Mao Badges: Symbols and Slogans of the Cultural Revolution*, London: British Museum, 2008, p. 21.

68 PRO, FCO 21/41, Donald C. Hopson, 'Letter from Beijing', 7 Oct. 1967.

69 For instance Pamela Tan, *The Chinese Factor: An Australian Chinese Woman's Life in China from 1950 to 1979*, Dural, New South Wales: Roseberg, 2008, p. 131.

70 PRO, FCO 21/19, Percy Cradock, 'Letter from Peking', 3 June 1968.

71 SMA, B103-4-1, 11 July 1967, pp. 1–3; B98-5-100, 9 Dec. 1969, pp. 10–11; B109-4-80, 1 Aug. 1968, p. 31; on statues in Shanghai, one should read Jin Dalu, *Feichang yu zhengchang: Shanghai 'wenge' shiqi de shehui bianqian* (The extraordinary and the ordinary: Social change in Shanghai during the Cultural Revolution), Shanghai: Shanghai cishu chubanshe, 2011, vol. 2, pp. 198–228.

72 Dikötter, *The Cultural Revolution*, pp. 240–41.

73 'Zhongyang zhuan'an shencha xiaozu "guanyu pantu, neijian, gongzei Liu Shaoqi zuixing de shencha baogao" ji "pantu, neijian, gongzei Liu Shaoqi zuizheng"' (Report on Liu Shaoqi by the Central Case Examination Group), 18 Oct. 1968, Cultural Revolution Database; with a few minor changes, I have used the translation in Milton and Milton, *The Wind Will Not Subside*, pp. 335–9; on the composition of the congress, see Roderick MacFarquhar and Michael Schoenhals, *Mao's Last Revolution*, Cambridge, MA: Harvard University Press, 2006, pp. 292–3.

74 GDPA, 296-A2.1-25, Report on Shanghai, 7 March 1973, pp. 189–98; PRO, FCO 21/962, Michael J. Richardson, 'Naming of Streets', 26 Jan. 1972.

75 Chang and Halliday, *Mao*, p. 583.

76 Chang, *Wild Swans*, p. 651.

77 Jean Hong, interview, 7 Nov. 2012, Hong Kong; Rowena Xiaoqing He, 'Reading Havel in Beijing', *Wall Street Journal*, 29 Dec. 2011.

78 Ai Xiaoming interviewed by Zhang Tiezhi, 22 Dec. 2010, Guangzhou.

79 Wu Guoping interviewed by Dong Guoqiang, 1 Dec. 2013, Zongyang county, Anhui.

CHAPTER 5 KIM IL-SUNG

1 Robert A. Scalapino and Chong-sik Lee, *Communism in Korea*. Part I: *The Movement*, Berkeley, CA: University of California Press, 1972, pp. 324–5; Lim Un, *The Founding of a Dynasty in North Korea: An Authentic Biography of Kim Il-song*, Tokyo: Jiyu-sha, 1982, p. 149.

2 Hongkoo Han, 'Wounded Nationalism: The Minsaengdan Incident and Kim Il-sung in Eastern Manchuria', University of Washington, doctoral disertation, 1999, p. 347.

3 Han, 'Wounded Nationalism', pp. 365–7; Scalapino and Lee, *Communism in Korea*, pp. 202–3; Dae-sook Suh, *Kim Il-sung: The North Korean Leader*, New York: Columbia University Press, 1988, pp. 37–47.

4 Charles Armstrong, *The North Korean Revolution: 1945–50*, Ithaca, NY: Cornell University Press, 2002, chapter 2.

5 Lim, *The Founding of a Dynasty in North Korea*, p. 152.

6 Bradley K. Martin, *Under the Loving Care of the Fatherly Leader: North Korea and the Kim Dynasty*, New York: Thomas Dunne Books, 2004, p. 53; Armstrong, *The North Korean Revolution*, p. 223; John N. Washburn, 'Russia Looks at Northern Korea', *Pacific Affairs*, 20, no. 2 (June 1947), p. 160.

7 Armstrong, *The North Korean Revolution*, p. 150; the estimate of one million is in Byoung-Lo Philo Kim, *Two Koreas in Development: A Comparative Study of Principles and Strategies of Capitalist and Communist Third World Development*, quoted in Martin, *Under the Loving Care of the Fatherly Leader*, p. 56.

8 David Allen Hatch, 'The Cult of Personality of Kim Il-Song: Functional Analysis of a State Myth', doctoral dissertation, Washington, DC: The American University, 1986, pp. 106–9.

9 Benoit Berthelier, 'Symbolic Truth: Epic, Legends, and the Making of the Baekdusan Generals', 17 May 2013, Sino-NK.

10 Hatch, 'The Cult of Personality of Kim Il-Song', pp. 83 and 104.

11 Chen Jian, *China's Road to the Korean War*, New York: Columbia University Press, 1996, p. 110; Sergei N. Goncharov, John W. Lewis and Xue Litai, *Uncertain Partners: Stalin, Mao, and the Korean War*, Stanford: Stanford University Press, 1993, pp. 142–5.

12 Max Hastings, *The Korean War*, New York: Simon & Schuster, 1987, p. 53; Hatch, 'The Cult of Personality of Kim Il-Song', p. 153.

13 Suh, *Kim Il-sung*, pp. 123–6; Lim, *The Founding of a Dynasty in North Korea*, p. 215.

14 Hatch, 'The Cult of Personality of Kim Il-Song', pp. 159–60.

15 Scalapino and Lee, *Communism in Korea*, pp. 428–9.

16 Andrei Lankov, *The Real North Korea: Life and Politics in the Failed Stalinist Utopia*, Oxford: Oxford University Press, 2013, pp. 37–9.

17 Blaine Harden, *The Great Leader and the Fighter Pilot: A True Story About the Birth of Tyranny in North Korea*, New York: Penguin Books, 2016, pp. 6–7; Suh, *Kim Il-sung*, pp. 127–30; Andrei Lankov, *From Stalin to Kim Il Sung: The Formation of North Korea, 1945–1960*, New Brunswick, NJ: Rutgers University Press, 2002, pp. 95–6.

18 See MfAA, A 5631, Information Report from Embassy, 23 March 1955, pp. 63–4.

19 MfAA, A 5631, Information Report from Embassy, 23 March 1955, p. 54; RGANI, 5-28-411, Diary of Ambassador V. I. Ivanov, 21 March 1956, pp. 165–8; a rock encased in glass is mentioned in Horst Kurnitzky, *Chollima Korea: A Visit in the Year 23*, Lulu Press Inc., 2006 (first published in 1972), p. 19.

20 Hatch, 'The Cult of Personality of Kim Il-Song', pp. 172–5; Hunter, *Kim Il-song's North Korea*, p. 13.

21 Hatch, 'The Cult of Personality of Kim Il-Song', pp. 176–80.

22 RGANI, 5-28-410, pp. 233–5; this document has been translated by Gary Goldberg in 'New Evidence on North Korea in 1956', *Cold War International History Project Bulletin*, no. 16 (Fall 2007/Winter 2008), pp. 492–4.

23 RGANI, 5-28-412, 30 May 1956, pp. 190–96; this document has also been translated by Gary Goldberg in 'New Evidence on North Korea in 1956', *Cold War International History Project Bulletin*, no. 16 (Fall 2007/Winter 2008), p. 471; on this incident, see Andrei Lankov, *Crisis in North Korea: The Failure of De-Stalinization, 1956*, Honolulu: University of Hawai'i Press, 2005; Balázs Szalontai, *Kim Il Sung in the Khrushchev Era: Soviet-DPRK Relations and the Roots of North Korean Despotism, 1953–1964*, Stanford, CA: Stanford University Press, 2006.

24 Lankov, *Crisis in North Korea*, p. 154.

25 Ibid., pp. 152–4.

26 Curiously, there are hardly any explicit acknowledgements in the secondary literature that the *songbun* system was based on the one devised under Mao; for an exception, see Judy Sun and Greg Wang, 'Human Resource Development in China and North Korea' in Thomas N. Garavan, Alma M. McCarthy and Michael J. Morley (eds), *Global Human Resource Development: Regional and Country Perspectives*, London: Routledge, 2016, p. 92; on the persecutions, see Lankov, *Crisis in North Korea*, p. 164.

27 Lankov, *Crisis in North Korea*, p. 182.

28 RGANI, 5-28-314, Letter from S. Suzdalev, Ambassador of the Soviet Union, to N. T. Fedorenko, 23 March 1955, pp. 13–15; RGANI, 5-28-412, 10 May 1956, Report of conversation of I. Biakov, First Secretary of the Soviet Embassy, with director of Museum of the History of the Revolutionary Struggle of the Korean People, pp. 249–52; BArch, DY30 IV 2/2.035/137, Information Bulletin, 14 March 1961, p. 72.

29 Suh, *Kim Il-sung*, pp. 168–71.

30 BArch, DY30 IV 2/2.035/137, Information Bulletin, 14 March 1961, pp. 72–3 and 79; see also Hatch, 'The Cult of Personality of Kim Il-Song', pp. 183–92; on his withdrawal from public life, see Suh, *Kim Il-sung*, p. 187.

31 MfAA, A 7137, Information on National Day, 16 Sept. 1963, pp. 45–9.

32 On the December 1955 speech, one should read Brian R. Myers, 'The Watershed that Wasn't: Re-Evaluating Kim Il-sung's "Juche Speech" of 1955', *Acta Koreana*, 9, no. 1 (Jan. 2006), pp. 89–115.

33 James F. Person, 'North Korea's chuch'e philosophy' in Michael J. Seth, *Routledge Handbook of Modern Korean History*, London: Routledge, 2016, pp. 705–98.

34 MfAA, C 1088/70, Ingeborg Göthel, Report on Information, 29 July 1966, p. 100.

35 Person, 'North Korea's chuch'e philosophy', pp. 725–67; MfAA, G-A 344, 10 Nov. 1967, Letter from Embassy, pp. 1–7, notes how the cult increased with the purges.

36 MfAA, C 1092/70, Information Report from Embassy, 19 Aug. 1968, pp. 19–20; PRO, FCO 51/80, 'North Korea in 1968', 3 July 1969, p. 13; FCO 21-307, 'Kim Il-sung, the "Prefabricated Hero"', 3 June 1967.

37 Suh, *Kim Il-sung*, p. 197; PRO, FCO 51/80, 'North Korea in 1968', 3 July 1969, p. 13.

38 MfAA, C 1088/70, Ingeborg Göthel, Report on May Day, 5 May 1967, pp. 55–8.

39 MfAA, C 1088/70, Hermann, Information Report from the Embassy, 5 Jan. 1968, pp. 76–7 as well as Ingeborg Göthel, Report on Information, 3 Nov. 1967, pp. 16–17; Ingeborg Göthel, Information Report from Embassy, 22 Sept. 1967, pp. 18–19; C 1023/73, Information Report from Embassy, 22 May 1968, pp. 98–9; on dedicated study rooms, see also Rinn-Sup Shinn et al., *Area Handbook for North Korea*, Washington: U.S. Government Printing Office, 1969, p. 276.

40 MfAA, C 1088/70, Ingeborg Göthel, Report on May Day, 5 May 1967, pp. 55–8; Ingeborg Göthel, Report on Information, 3 Nov. 1967, pp. 16–17.

41 Suh, *Kim Il-sung*, pp. 231–4.

42 MfAA, G-A 347, Barthel, Report on Discussion with Samoilov, 17 May 1972, pp. 16–18; see also Suh, *Kim Il-sung*, p. 242.

43 'Talk to the Officials of the Propaganda and Agitation Department of the Central Committee of the Workers'', 29 October 1971, document from the Korean Friendship Association website retrieved on 15 January 2016; Suh, *Kim Il-sung*, p. 319.

44 Harrison E. Salisbury, *To Peking and Beyond: A Report On The New Asia*, New York: Quadrangle Books, 1973, p. 207; Suh, *Kim Il-sung*, p. 319.

45 MfAA, C 6877, 6 March 1972, pp. 76–7; MfAA, G-A 347, Letter from Embassy, 11 Jan. 1972, p. 14.

46 Salisbury, *To Peking and Beyond*, pp. 208–9; see also Suh, *Kim Il-sung*, pp. 316–17; both mention 240,000 square metres for the museum's overall surface, which seems unlikely for ninety-two rooms; the figure of 50,000 square metres comes from Helen-Louise Hunter, *Kim Il-song's North Korea*, Westport, CT: Praeger Publishers, 1999, p. 23.

47 MfAA, C 6877, 6 March 1972, pp. 76–7; Sonia Ryang, *Writing Selves in Diaspora: Ethnography of Autobiographics of Korean Women in Japan and the United States*, Lanham, MD: Lexington Books, 2008, p. 88.

48 Salisbury, *To Peking and Beyond*, pp. 208–9; Suh, *Kim Il-sung*, pp. 316–19.

49 SMA, B158-2-365, 20 Dec. 1971, pp. 107–111 and B163-4-317, 1 Dec. 1971, pp. 134–5; for an overview of badges in later years, see Andrei Lankov, *North of the DMZ: Essays on Daily Life in North Korea*, Jefferson, NC: McFarland, 2007, pp. 7–9.

50 Suh, *Kim Il-sung*, pp. 270–71.

51 MfAA, C 6877, Information Bulletin, 28 April 1972, pp. 66–7.

52 Salisbury, *To Peking and Beyond*, pp. 196–7 and 204–5.

53 Ibid., pp. 214 and 219.

54 MfAA, C 315/78, 8 April 1970, pp. 155–8.

55 Suh, *Kim Il-sung*, p. 262.

56 Lim, *The Founding of a Dynasty in North Korea*, p. 269; Suh, *Kim Il-sung*, pp. 267–8.

57 Suh, *Kim Il-sung*, pp. 267–8.

58 Philippe Grangereau, *Au pays du grand mensonge. Voyage en Corée*, Paris: Payot, 2003, pp. 134–7; Hunter, *Kim Il-song's North Korea*, p. 22.

59 C 6926, Kirsch, Letter from Embassy, 21 Nov. 1975, pp. 1–3.

60 Suh, *Kim Il-sung*, pp. 278–82.

61 Hans Maretzki, *Kim-ismus in Nordkorea: Analyse des letzten DDR-Botschafters in Pjöngjang*, Böblingen: Anika Tykve Verlag, 1991, pp. 34 and 55; Lankov, *North of the DMZ*, pp. 40–41.

62 Don Oberdorfer, *The Two Koreas: A Contemporary History*, Reading, MA: Addison-Wesley, 1997, pp. 341–2; Barbara Demick, *Nothing to Envy: Ordinary Lives in North Korea*, New York: Spiegel and Grau, 2009, pp. 100–101.

CHAPTER 6 DUVALIER

1 On the early history of Haiti, see Philippe Girard, *Haiti: The Tumultuous History – From Pearl of the Caribbean to Broken Nation*, New York: St Martin's Press, 2010.

2 Eric H. Cushway, 'The Ideology of François Duvalier', MA dissertation, University of Alberta, 1976, pp. 79 and 96–7; Martin Munro, *Tropical Apocalypse: Haiti and the Caribbean End*, Charlottesville, VA: University of Virginia Press, 2015, p. 36.

3 John Marquis, *Papa Doc: Portrait of a Haitian Tyrant 1907–1971*, Kingston: LMH Publishing Limited, 2007, p. 92.

4 Paul Christopher Johnson, 'Secretism and the Apotheosis of Duvalier', *Journal of the American Academy of Religion*, 74, no. 2 (June 2006), p. 428; Cushway, 'The Ideology of François Duvalier', pp. 78–83.

5 François Duvalier, *Guide des 'Oeuvres Essentielles' du Docteur François Duvalier*, Port-au-Prince: Henri Deschamps, 1967, p. 58.

6 Trevor Armbrister, 'Is There Any Hope for Haiti?', *Saturday Evening Post*, 236, no. 23 (15 June 1963), p. 80; see also Bleecker Dee, 'Duvalier's Haiti: A Case Study of National Disintegration', doctoral dissertation, University of Florida, 1967, p. 70.

7 NARA, RG 59, Box 3090, Gerald A. Drew, 'Political Situation in Haiti', 3 Aug. 1957.

8 Bernard Diederich, *The Price of Blood: History of Repression and Rebellion in Haiti Under Dr. François Duvalier, 1957–1961*, Princeton, NJ: Markus Wiener, 2011, pp. 17–18.

9 NARA, RG 59, Box 3090, Gerald A. Drew, 'Political Situation in Haiti', 3 Aug. 1957.

10 Mats Lundahl, 'Papa Doc: Innovator in the Predatory State', *Scandia*, 50, no. 1 (1984), p. 48.

11 MAE, 96QO/24, Lucien Félix, 'Conférence de presse de Duvalier', 4 Oct. 1957; MAE, 96QO/24, Lucien Félix, 'Un mois de pouvoir du président Duvalier', 22 Nov. 1957; NARA, RG 59, Box 3090, 'Harassment of Haitian Labor Leaders', 10 Jan. 1958; Virgil P. Randolph, 'Haitian Political Situation', 30 Jan. 1958.

12 *Haiti Sun*, 24 Dec. 1957, p. 11; Louis E. Lomax, 'Afro Man Chased out of Haiti', *Baltimore Afro-American*, 15 Oct. 1957; Stephen Jay Berman, 'Duvalier and the Press', MA in Journalism, University of Southern California, 1974, p. 28.

13 NARA, RG 59, Box 3090, Virgil P. Randolph, 'Haitian Political Situation', 30 Jan. 1958; Louis E. Lomax, 'Afro Man Chased out of Haiti', *Baltimore Afro-American*, 15 Oct. 1957.

14 MAE, 96QO/24, Lucien Félix, 'Un mois de pouvoir du président Duvalier', 22 Nov. 1957; NARA, RG 59, Box 3090, 'Harassment of Haitian Labor Leaders', 10 Jan. 1958; Virgil P. Randolph, 'Haitian Political Situation', 30 Jan. 1958.

15 MAE, 96QO/25, Lucien Félix, telegram, 13 March 1958; NARA, RG 59, Box 3090, Virgil P. Randolph, 'Haitian Political Situation', 30 Jan. 1958.

16 NARA, RG 59, Box 3092, Virgil P. Randolph, 'Joint Weeka No. 32', 6 Aug. 1958; MAE, 96QO/25, 'Lucien Félix, 'Le coup de main du 29 juillet 1958', 31 July 1958.

17 Robert D. Heinl and Nancy Gordon Heinl, *Written in Blood: The Story of the Haitian People, 1492–1995*, Lanham, MD: University Press of America, 1998, p. 572; Robert I. Rotberg, *Haiti: The Politics of Squalor*, Boston: Houghton Mifflin, 1971, pp. 215–16.

18 MAE, 96QO/25, Lucien Félix, 'La nouvelle constitution de la République d'Haiti', 17 April 1958; Lundahl, 'Papa Doc', p. 60.

19 Elizabeth Abbott, *Haiti: The Duvaliers and Their Legacy*, New York: McGraw-Hill, 1988, pp. 91–2.

20 Bernard Diederich and Al Burt, *Papa Doc: Haiti and its Dictator*, London: Bodley Head, 1969, p. 139; Rotberg, *Haiti*, p. 218.

21 Lundahl, 'Papa Doc', p. 60.

22 MAE, 96QO/25, Lucien Félix, 'La situation politique et économique en Haiti', 3 Feb. 1959; 'Voyage du Président', 18 March 1959.

23 NARA, RG 59, Box 3092, 'Joint Weeka No. 22', 5 June 1959; NARA, RG 59, Box 3093, Gerald A. Drew 'Embtel 423', 3 June 1959; Rotberg, *Haiti*, p. 218.

24 NARA, RG 59, Box 3093, Gerald A. Drew, 'President François Duvalier Resumes Active Duty', 7 July 1959.

25 NARA, RG 59, Box 3091, Philip P. Williams, 'Executive-Legislative Relations', 23 Sept. 1959; Rotberg, *Haiti*, pp. 220–21.

26 NARA, RG 59 Box 7, Caspar D. Green, 'Memorandum', United States Operations Mission, 13 May 1960.

27 MAE, 96QO/26, 'Evolution vers l'extrémisme de gauche', 9 Aug. 1960; also Charles le Genissel, 'Arrestation de M. Clément Barbot', 6 Aug. 1960; NARA, RG 59, Box 1633, Letter to Secretary of State from Haitian Ambassador, 15 July 1960; 'Civilian Militia Palace Parade', *Haiti Sun*, 7 Dec. 1960, pp. 1 and 20.

28 MAE, 96QO/26, 'Bulletin Mensuel d'Information', 13 April 1961; NARA, RG 59, Box 1633, Letter to Secretary of State from Haitian Ambassador, Charles Wm Thomas, 'Haiti Re-Elects President', 9 May 1961.

29 NARA, RG 59, Box 1633, David. R Thomson, 'Political Events in Haiti', 21 May 1961.

30 MAE, 96QO/26, Charles le Genissel, 'Prestation de serment du docteur Duvalier', 25 May 1961; NARA, RG 59, Box 1634, Ambassy Port-au-Prince, 'Joint Weeka No. 21', 26 May 1961.

31 NARA, RG 59, Box 3922, 'Joint Weeka No. 29', 20 July 1963; Berman, 'Duvalier and the Press', p. 57.

32 Dee, 'Duvalier's Haiti', pp. 154–7; Diederich, *Papa Doc*, pp. 216–17; Berman, 'Duvalier and the Press', p. 62.

33 MAE, 96QO/27, Charles le Genissel, 'Mesures exceptionelles', 29 Aug. 1963; NARA, RG 59, Box 3922, 'Joint Weeka No. 38', 22 Sept. 1963.

34 Rotberg, *Haiti*, p. 233; NARA, RG 59, Box 3923, Norman E. Warner, 'Duvalier Speech on September 30, 1963', 8 Oct. 1963; *Hispanic American Report*, vol. 16, no. 8 (Sept. 1963), p. 869; NARA, RG 59, Box 1634, 'Joint Weekas No. 24 and 29', 16 June and 21 July 1961.

35 MAE, 96QO/54, 'Présidence à vie', 13 April 1964; Dee, 'Duvalier's Haiti', pp. 177–8.

36 NARA, RG 59, Box 2262, 'Joint Weeka No. 26', 26 June 1964; NARA, RG 59, Box 2263, 'Build-Up Begins for May 22 Celebrations', 20 May 1964.

37 Jean Fourcand, *Catéchisme de la révolution*, Port-au-Prince: Imprimerie de l'Etat, 1964, p. 17.

38 NARA, RG 59, Box 2262, 'Joint Weeka No. 38', 18 Sept. 1964.

39 Rotberg, *Haiti*, pp. 239–42.

40 Richard West, 'Haiti: Hell on Earth', *New Statesman*, 29 April 1966, translation into French in MAE, 96QO/54, 'Articles et documents', 12–19 Aug. 1966; 'Crushing a Country', *Time* magazine, 27 Aug. 1965; starvation reports in NARA, RG 59, Box 2263, 'Joint Weeka No. 46', 12 Nov. 1965.

41 Rotberg, *Haiti*, p. 243; Millery Polyné, *From Douglass to Duvalier: U. S. African Americans, Haiti, and Pan Americanism, 1870–1964*, Gainesville, FL: University of Florida Press, 2010, p. 190.

42 Rotberg, *Haiti*, p. 344; Michel Soukar, *Un général parle: Entretien avec un Chef d'état-major sous François Duvalier*, Port-au-Prince: Le Natal, 1987, p. 56.

43 NARA, RG 59, Box 2263, 'Joint Weeka No. 25', 20 June 1965.

44 NARA, RG 59, Box 2263, 'Joint Weeka No. 46', 12 Nov. 1965.

45 Rotberg, *Haiti*, p. 247; NARA, RG 59, Box 2263, 'Joint Weeka No. 16', 24 April 1966.

46 NARA, RG 59, Box 2263, 'Joint Weeka No. 16', 24 April 1966; Confidential telegram to Department of State, 26 April 1966.

47 NARA, RG 59, Box 2263, 'Joint Weeka No. 24', 19 June 1966.

48 NARA, RG 59, Box 2263, 'Alleged Statement by Haile Sellasie', 8 May 1966.

49 NARA, RG 59, Box 2263, Confidential telegram to Department of State, 9 June 1966; 'Duvalier October 26 Speech', 18 Dec. 1966.

50 NARA, RG 59, Box 2263, 'Joint Weeka No. 30', 31 July 1966; 'Joint Weeka No. 36', 9 Sept. 1966.

51 NARA, RG 59, Box 2263, 'Joint Weeka No. 30', 31 July 1966; 'Confidential Report', 2 Sept. 1966; NARA, RG 59, Box 2172, 'Joint Weeka No. 43', 29 Oct. 1967.

52 NARA, RG 59, Box 2263, 'Joint Weeka No. 30', 31 July 1966; 'Confidential Report', 2 Sept. 1966.

53 NARA, RG 59, Box 2172, 'Joint Weeka No. 15', 16 April 1967; 'The Birthday Blowout', *Time* magazine, 28 April 1967.

54 Abbott, *Haiti*, p. 144; 'Coming to a Boil', *Time* magazine, 25 Aug. 1967.

55 NARA, RG 59, Box 2172, 'Joint Weeka No. 25', 25 June 1967; see also, Abbott, *Haiti*, p. 145.

56 NARA, RG 59, Box 2172, 'Joint Weeka No. 11', 19 March 1967; NARA, RG 59, Box 2172, 'Joint Weeka No. 37', 24 Sept. 1967; NARA, RG 59 Box 5, 'Haiti', 26 Sept. 1967.

57 NARA, RG 59, Box 2173, 'Duvalier Speaks Extemporaneously Again', 5 Nov. 1967; 'Joint Weeka No. 37', 24 Sept. 1967.

58 On radio see NARA, RG 59, Box 2172, 'Joint Weeka No. 2', 14 Jan. 1968.

59 Rotberg, *Haiti*, pp. 350–66.

60 NARA, RG 59, Box 2172, 'Trip Report: Northwest Department of Haiti', 29 Dec. 1968.

61 Rotberg, *Haiti*, p. 235.

62 MAE, 96QO/56, Philippe Koening, 'La rébellion du 24 avril', 10 June 1970; 'Action anti-communiste', 30 April 1969; Abbott, *Haiti*, p. 152; Marquis, *Papa Doc*, p. 264.

63 MAE, 96QO/73, Philippe Koenig, 'Haiti après la mort du Président François Duvalier', 28 April 1971; NARA, RG 59, Box 2346, 'Political/Economic Summary No. 3', 21 Feb. 1971; 'Political/Economic Summary No. 8', 8 May 1971.

CHAPTER 7 CEAUŞESCU

1 'Obituary: Anca Petrescu', *Daily Telegraph*, 1 Nov. 2013; Robert Bevan, *The Destruction of Memory: Architecture at War*, London: Reaktion Books, 2006, pp. 127–31.

2 John Sweeney, *The Life and Evil Times of Nicolae Ceauşescu*, London: Hutchinson, 1991, pp. 44–51.

3 Dennis Deletant, *Communist Terror in Romania: Gheorghiu-Dej and the Police State, 1948–1965*, New York: St Martin's Press, 1999.

4 Alice Mocanescu, 'Surviving 1956: Gheorghe Gheorghiu-Dej and the "Cult of Personality" in Romania' in Apor Balázs, Jan C. Behrends, Polly Jones and E. A. Rees (eds), *The Leader Cult in Communist Dictatorships: Stalin and the Eastern Bloc*, Houndmills, Basingstoke: Palgrave Macmillan, 2004, p. 256; 'Rumania: Want amid Plenty', *Time* magazine, 8 June 1962.

5 Mary Ellen Fisher, *Ceaușescu: A Study in Political Leadership*, Boulder, CO: Lynne Rienner Publishers, 1989, pp. 49–52; Vladimir Tismaneanu, *Stalinism for All Seasons: A Political History of Romanian Communism*, Berkeley, CA: University of California Press, 2003, p. 176.

6 Fisher, *Ceaușescu*, p. 69.

7 MAE, 201QO/167, Jean-Louis Pons, '50eme anniversaire de Mr. Ceausescu', 30 Jan. 1968.

8 Fisher, *Ceaușescu*, pp. 133–9.

9 Ibid., pp. 143–5.

10 Sweeney, *The Life and Evil Times of Nicolae Ceausescu*, p. 95.

11 Strictly speaking, one other leader remained from the Gheorghiu Dej Politburo, namely Emil Bodnaras, but he was sick and did not attend the congress; Fisher, *Ceaușescu*, pp. 154–7.

12 Fisher, *Ceaușescu*, pp. 92–3; OSA, 300-8-3-5811, 'Nicolae Ceausescu and the Politics of Leadership', 29 March 1973, pp. 16–18.

13 ANR, 2574-72-1971, Minutes of the Executive Committee (Politburo) meeting, 25 June 1971, p. 11.

14 Ibid.

15 Ibid., pp. 45–6; OSA, 300-8-47-188-23, Rumanian Situation Report, 13 July 1971, pp. 9–11.

16 Fisher, *Ceaușescu*, p. 126.

17 OSA, 300-8-47-188-23, Rumanian Situation Report, 13 July 1971, pp. 9–11; the reference to a 'New Man' is from party secretary Popescu; see OSA, 300-8-47-188-24, Rumanian Situation Report, 20 July 1971, p. 13.

18 The row between Ceaușescu and Iliescu is mentioned in Sweeney, *The Life and Evil Times of Nicolae Ceausescu*, p. 102.

19 Michel-Pierre Hamelet, *Nicolae Ceausescu: Présentation, choix de textes, aperçu historique, documents photographiques*, Paris: Seghers, 1971.

20 ANR, 2898-19-1976, List of books on Nicolae Ceaușescu published abroad, 4 March 1976, pp. 1–6; OSA, 300-8-47-201-3, 'Situation Report', 9 Feb. 1978, p. 9.

21 ANR, 2898-10-1973, Note of the Foreign Relations Section, 28 May 1973, pp. 12–13.

22 The exact amount was 7.5 million lire; see ANR, 2898-21-1971, Note of the Foreign Relations Section of the Central Committee, 4 Sept. 1971, p. 102; see also Günther Heyden, Report on a visit to

the Romanian Institute for Historical and Social-Political Studies, 27 Sept. 1971, DY 30/IVA 2/20/357, pp. 377–8.

23 OSA, 300-8-3-5811, 'Nicolae Ceausescu and the Politics of Leadership', 29 March 1973, pp. 3–15.

24 ANR, 2574-31-1974, Transcript of the Executive Committee (Politburo) of the Central Committee meeting, 27 March 1974, p. 50–59.

25 Sweeney, *The Life and Evil Times of Nicolae Ceausescu*, p. 105.

26 Fisher, *Ceauşescu*, pp. 184–5 and 212–13; Anneli Ute Gabanyi, *The Ceauşescu Cult: Propaganda and Power Policy in Communist Romania*, Bucharest: The Romanian Cultural Foundation Publishing House, 2000, pp. 17–18; Thomas J. Keil, *Romania's Tortured Road toward Modernity*, New York: Columbia University Press, 2006, p. 301.

27 ANR, 2898-19-1976, List of books on Nicolae Ceauşescu published abroad, 4 March 1976, pp. 1–6.

28 OSA, 300-8-3-5850, 'Ceausescu's Ideological Role is Strengthened', 29 July 1976, pp. 1–9.

29 Ibid., p. 7.

30 OSA, 300-8-47-201-3, 'Situation Report', 9 Feb. 1978, p. 2.

31 OSA, 300-8-47-201-3, 'Situation Report', 9 Feb. 1978, p. 3; PRO, FCO 28/3444, R. A. Burns, 'President Ceauşescu's 60th Birthday', 8 Feb. 1978, pp. 4–5.

32 OSA, 300-8-47-201-3, 'Situation Report', 9 Feb. 1978, pp. 6–10.

33 PRO, FCO 28/3407, R. L. Secondé, 'President Ceausescu of Romania: A Summary', 24 April 1978, pp. 4–5; Sweeney, *The Life and Evil Times of Nicolae Ceausescu*, pp. 111–20.

34 Pacepa went on to write a damning memoir of the Ceauşescu regime, entitled *Red Horizons: The True Story of Nicolae and Elena Ceausescus' Crimes, Lifestyle, and Corruption*, Washington, DC: Regnery Publishing, 1990.

35 ANR, 2898-28-1977, Inventories of foreign medals and decorations awarded to Elena and Nicolae Ceauşescu, 21 Nov. 1977, pp. 1–16.

36 The East Germans described the Pirvulescu affair in BArch, DY 30/IV 2/2.035/52, 23 Nov. 1979, pp. 2–7; see also Fisher, *Ceauşescu*, p. 240.

37 Jonathan Eyal, 'Why Romania Could Not Avoid Bloodshed' in Gwyn Prins (ed.), *Spring in Winter: The 1989 Revolutions*, Manchester: Manchester University Press, 1990, pp. 149–50.

38 OSA, 300-8-47-204-10, 'Situation Report', 22 July 1980, pp. 2–5; MAE, 1929INVA/4629, Pierre Cerles, Ambassador's Report, 22 Dec. 1980.

39 MAE, 1929INVA/4630, 'Situation en Roumanie', 20 Dec. 1980.

40 Sweeney, *The Life and Evil Times of Nicolae Ceausescu*, pp. 130–33.

41 OSA, 300-8-3-5914, Anneli Maier, 'Anniversary of the 1965 RCP Congress', 11 Aug. 1982, pp. 1–4.

42 BArch, DY 30/11599, June 1982, pp. 87–9.

43 MAE, 1930INVA/5471, Michel Rougagnou, 'Célébration du vingtième anniversaire', 23 July 1985.

44 ANR, 2898-80-1984, Rules for displaying the official portrait of Nicolae Ceauşescu, 7 March 1984, pp. 1–4; ANR, 2989-21-1984, Note on the new ABECEDAR, 1984, p. 8.

45 ANR, 2898-32-1985, Report on special programmes dedicated to the sixty-fifth anniversary of the foundation of the communist party, 1985, pp. 1–4.

46 David Binder, 'The Cult of Ceausescu', *New York Times*, 30 Nov. 1986.

47 ANR, 2898-36-1984, Transcript of a meeting between Nicolae Ceauşescu and representatives of the Union of Visual Artist, 18 Sept. 1984, pp. 2–6.

48 Lucian Boia, *Romania: Borderland of Europe*, London: Reaktion Books, 2001, pp. 288–90.

49 Gabriel Ronay, 'Romania Plans Village Blitz', *Sunday Times*, 23 May 1988; OSA, 300-8-47-212-11, 'The Rural Resettlement Plan', 16 Sept. 1988, p. 13.

50 Binder, 'The Cult of Ceausescu'.

51 MAE, 1930INVA/5471, Michel Rougagnou, 'Célébration du vingtième anniversaire', 23 July 1985; Sweeney, *The Life and Evil Times of Nicolae Ceausescu*, pp. 157–8.

52 Sweeney, *The Life and Evil Times of Nicolae Ceausescu*, p. 158.

53 The numbers are from MAE, 1930INVA/5471, Michel Rougagnou, 'La vie du parti dans l'entreprise', 6 Oct. 1983.

54 MAE, 1930INVA/4630, Pierre Cerles, 'Le communisme à la roumaine', 24 May 1978.

55 OSA, 300-8-47-211-1, 'Ceausescu Rejects Soviet-Style Reform', 6 Feb. 1980, pp. 3–6.

56 Sweeney, *The Life and Evil Times of Nicolae Ceausescu*, pp. 172–4.

57 MAE, 1935INVA/6478, Jean-Marie Le Breton, 'Campagne d'élections', 16 Nov. 1989.
58 Peter Siani-Davies, *The Romanian Revolution of December 1989*, Ithaca, NY: Cornell University Press, 2007, pp. 81–2; Emma Graham-Harrison, '"I'm Still Nervous", Says Soldier who Shot Nicolae Ceausescu', *Guardian*, 7 Dec. 2014.

CHAPTER 8 MENGISTU

1 Estelle Sohier, 'Politiques de l'image et pouvoir royal en Éthiopie de Menilek II à Haylä Sellasé (1880–1936)', doctoral dissertation, University of Paris 1, 2007, pp. 159–69.
2 PRO, FCO 31/1829, Willie Morris, 'Annual Review for 1974', 6 Feb. 1975.
3 Bahru Zewde, *A History of Modern Ethiopia*, London: James Currey, 2001, p. 234.
4 PRO, FCO 31/1829, Willie Morris, 'Annual Review for 1974', 6 Feb. 1975.
5 Ibid.
6 Richard J. Reid, *Frontiers of Violence in North-East Africa: Genealogies of Conflict since c.1800*, Oxford: Oxford University Press, 2011, p. 174; Christopher Clapham, *Transformation and Continuity in Revolutionary Ethiopia*, Cambridge: Cambridge University Press, 1988, p. 41.
7 Shambel Tesfaye Reste Mekonnen, *Misikirnet be Derg Abalat* (Testimonies of Derg members), Addis Ababa, 2007, p. 164; PRO, FCO 31/2093, D. M. Day, 'Mengistu', 15 June 1977.
8 *Ethiopian Herald*, 21 Dec. 1974 and 30 Jan. 1975; Paul B. Henze, *Layers of Time: A History of Ethiopia*, London: Hurst, 2000, p. 290; Andargatchew Tiruneh, *The Ethiopian Revolution 1974–87*, Cambridge: Cambridge University Press, 1993, pp. 102–3.
9 Begashaw Gobaw Tashu, *Yecoloel Mengistu Haile Maryam ena Yederggemenawoch* (Secrets of Mengistu Haile Mariam and the Derg), Addis Ababa: Far East Trading, 2008, p. 220.
10 Babile Tola, *To Kill a Generation: The Red Terror in Ethiopia*, Washington, DC: Free Ethiopia Press, 1989, pp. 38–9; PRO, FCO 31-2098, 'Annual Review for 1976', 3 Jan. 1977.
11 *Ethiopian Herald*, 29 Sept. 1976; PRO, FCO 31/2098, 'Annual Review for 1976', 3 Jan. 1977; Henze, *Layers of Time*, p. 291.

12 Eshetu Wendemu Hailesselasie, *Heiwot Be Mengistu Betemengist* (Life at the palace during Mengistu's time), Addis Ababa: Zed Printing House, 2010, pp. 81–90.

13 *Ethiopian Herald*, 5 Feb. 1977.

14 Feseha Desta, *Abyotuna Tezetaye* (My reminiscences of the revolution), Addis Ababa: Tsehay Asatami Derejet, 2008, p. 80; Geset Techane (pen name Zenebe Feleke), *Neber* (Was), Addis Ababa: Hetemet Alfa Asatamewoch, 2007, p. 238; Baalu Girma, *Oromay* (The end), Addis Ababa: Mankusa Asatami, 1983, pp. 21 and 50.

15 Fekreselasie Wegderes, *Egnana Abyotu* (We and the Revolution), Addis Ababa: Tsehay Akefafay Derejet, 2006, pp. 75–6; Baalu, *Oromay*, pp. 24 and 50–54.

16 *Ethiopian Herald*, 5 Feb. 1977; Begashaw, *Yecoloel Mengistu Haile Maryam*, p. 291.

17 Marina and David Ottaway, *Ethiopia: Empire in Revolution*, New York: Africana Publishing, 1978, pp. 142–6; Judith Ashakih, *Gift of Incense: A Story of Love and Revolution in Ethiopia*, Trenton, NJ: Red Sea Press, 2005, p. 290; Stéphane Courtois et al. (eds), *The Black Book of Communism: Crimes, Terror, Repression*, Cambridge, MA: Harvard University Press, 1999, p. 691.

18 'Farewell to American Arms', *Time* magazine, 9 May 1977.

19 David A. Korn, *Ethiopia, the United States and the Soviet Union*, Carbondale, IL: Southern Illinois University Press, 1986, pp. 28–9.

20 NARA, RG 59, 1978STATE106159, 26 April 1978.

21 PRO, FCO 31-2251, C. M. Carruthers, 'Leading Personalities of Ethiopia', 19 May 1978; NARA, RG 59, 1978ADDIS02129, 11 May 1978.

22 NARA, RG 59, 1979ADDIS01388, 19 April 1979; Donald L. Donham, 'Revolution and Modernity in Maale: Ethiopia, 1974 to 1987', *Comparative Studies in Society and History*, 34, no. 1 (Jan. 1992), p. 43.

23 Paul Henze archives, Hoover Institution, box 71, 'A Communist Ethiopia?', 1981.

24 NARA, RG 59, 1979ADDIS01388, 19 April 1979.

25 Shambel, *Misikirnet be Derg Abalat*, p. 327.

26 Habtamu Alebachew, *Ye Kesar Enba* (Tears of Cesar), Addis Ababa: Far East Trading Publishing, 2007, pp. 122, 142–3, 145 and 150.

27 Dawit Wolde Giorgis, *Red Tears: War, Famine and Revolution in Ethiopia*, Trenton, NJ: Red Sea Press, 1989, p. 58; BArch, DY 30/IV 2/2.035/127, Report on Propaganda, 4 April 1978, pp. 253–6; Baalu

wrote the critical memoir entitled *Oromay*, used elsewhere in this chapter, and vanished in 1984, presumably killed.

28 Dawit Shifaw, *The Diary of Terror: Ethiopia 1974 to 1991*, Bloomington, IN: Trafford Publishing, 2012, p. 72; Begashaw, *Yecoloel Mengistu Haile Maryam ena Yederggemenawoch*, p. 378.

29 Paul Henze archives, Hoover Institution, box 68, 'Revolution Day', 12 Sept. 1977, pp. 16–17; the fines are mentioned in PRO, FCO 31-2093, D. M. Day, 'Mengistu', 15 June 1977; see also Giorgis, *Red Tears*, p. 59.

30 MAE, 326QONT/28, Pierre Nolet, 'Chronique mensuelle', 11 Dec. 1979; Habtamu, *Ye Kesar Enba*, p. 122.

31 MAE, 326QONT/28, 'Note: Situation intérieure de l'Ethiopie', 27 Feb. 1981.

32 Clapham, *Transformation and Continuity in Revolutionary Ethiopia*, pp. 70–77.

33 Ibid., p. 77.

34 François Jean, *Éthiopie: Du bon usage de la famine*, Paris: Médecins Sans Frontières, 1986, pp. 21–5; Harold G. Marcus, *A History of Ethiopia*, Berkeley, CA: University of California Press, 1994, pp. 204–5.

35 BArch, DY 30/11498, 6 May 1982, p. 12; BArch, DY 30/27158, 3 Dec. 1982, p. 3; PRO, FCO 31-3895, D. C. B. Beaumont, 'Meeting of EC Ambassadors', 23 Sept. 1983.

36 *Ethiopian Herald*, 6 and 26 July 1984.

37 Henze, *Layers of Time*, pp. 306–7; Paul Henze archives, Hoover Institution, box 72, 'Communist Ethiopia: Is it Succeeding?', Jan. 1985; Giorgis, *Red Tears*, p. 135, mentions 'hundreds' of North Koreans; see also p. 59 for the trip to North Korea in 1982.

38 Paul Henze archives, Hoover Institution, box 71, 'A Communist Ethiopia?', 1981; Korn, *Ethiopia, the United States and the Soviet Union*, pp. 122–3.

39 *Ethiopian Herald*, 4 and 7 Sept. 1984; the biography is mentioned in Giorgis, *Red Tears*, p. 172.

40 Korn, *Ethiopia, the United States and the Soviet Union*, pp. 122–3.

41 'Ethiopians Mark 10th Anniversary of Socialist Revolution', *United Press International*, 12 Sept. 1984; *Ethiopian Herald*, 16 Sept. 1984.

42 MfAA, C 1852, Travel Report, April 1978, p. 58; Donham, 'Revolution and Modernity in Maale', p. 29.

43 Korn, *Ethiopia, the United States and the Soviet Union*, pp. 123–4.

44 Henze, *Layers of Time*, p. 307; Paul Henze archives, Hoover Institution, box 72, 'Communist Ethiopia: Is it Succeeding?', Jan. 1985; box 73, 'Exploiting Famine and Capitalizing on Western Generosity', March 1986, p. 91; Korn, *Ethiopia, the United States and the Soviet Union*, pp. 124–6.

45 Laurence Binet (ed.), *Famine et transferts forcés de populations en Ethiopie 1984–1986*, Paris: Médecins Sans Frontières, 2013; Alex de Waal, 'Is the Era of Great Famines Over?', *New York Times*, 8 May 2016.

46 Gebru Tareke, *The Ethiopian Revolution: War in the Horn of Africa*, New Haven, CT: Yale University Press, 2009, pp. 218–61.

47 Charles Mitchell, ' "Operation Red Star": Soviet Union, Libya back Ethiopia in Eritrean War', 20 March 1982, UPI; Messay Kebede, *Ideology and Elite Conflicts: Autopsy of the Ethiopian Revolution*, Lanham, MD: Lexington Books, 2011, pp. 307–24.

48 Alex de Waal, *Evil Days: Thirty Years of War and Famine in Ethiopia*, New York: Human Rights Watch, 1991, pp. 302–7.

49 Henze, *Layers of Time*, pp. 327–9.

50 Paul Henze archives, Hoover Institution, box 68, 'Travel Diary, 1991 June'.

AFTERWORD

1 Elleni Centime Zeleke, 'Addis Ababa as Modernist Ruin', *Callaloo*, 33, no. 1 (Spring 2010), p. 125.

2 'How Kim Jong Un Builds his Personality Cult', *The Economist*, 8 June 2017.

3 Joseph Willits, 'The Cult of Bashar al-Assad', *Guardian*, 1 July 2011.

4 Kadri Gursel, 'The Cult of Erdogan', *Al-Monitor*, 6 Aug. 2014.

5 Tom Phillips, 'Xi Jinping: Does China Truly Love "Big Daddy Xi" – or Fear Him?', *Guardian*, 19 Sept. 2015.

6 Rowan Callick, 'No Turning Back the Tide on Xi Jinping Personality Cult', *Australian*, 25 Nov. 2017; Viola Zhou, ' "Into the Brains" of China's Children: Xi Jinping's "Thought" to Become Compulsory School Topic', *South China Morning Post*, 23 Oct. 2017; Jamil Anderlini, 'Under Xi Jinping, China is Turning Back to Dictatorship', *Financial Times*, 11 Oct. 2017.

Acknowledgements

A very faint idea of this project goes back to my first year as an undergraduate student in 1981, when I came across 'La fabrication d'un charisme', a riveting article on Stalin's cult written before its time by my teacher Bronisław Baczko at the University of Geneva. Professor Baczko was a pioneer in cultural history, and I would like to acknowledge, belatedly, that his body of work has shaped my approach to history to a much greater extent than I realised at the time.

Writing about the cult of personality can be a risky business. Every historian of Mussolini is deeply indebted to Camillo Berneri, who published an illuminating study entitled *Mussolini Grande Attore* (Mussolini the Great Actor) in 1934, only to be killed by a squad of communists in Spain three years later, probably on the orders of Stalin. Great dictators often attract great writers, and one of the pleasures in working on these tyrants is to be in the company of so many gifted scholars, whether they wrote at the time or with hindsight. My debt to them is indicated, however inadequately, in the footnotes.

I spent many a week in archives across Europe, but would not have been able to make sense of the documents in the Arhivele Naționale ale României in Bucharest without the help of Ștefan Bosomitu, a researcher with unparalleled knowledge of the Ceaușescu files. In Addis Ababa, Eyob Girma read patiently through dozens of memoirs in Amharic, while Jen Seung Yeon Lee helped with propaganda material from North Korea. A seemingly infinite amount of material on twentieth-century war, revolution and peace can be found at the Hoover Institution, and the staff in both the library and the archives were unstinting with their help.

Robert Peckham rekindled my interest in the history of image and power by lending me a copy of Peter Burke's *The Fabrication of Louis XIV*. A number of people have read and commented on draft versions, especially Peter Baehr, Gail Burrowes, Christopher Hutton, Peter and Gabriele Kennedy, Françoise Koolen, Andrei Lankov, Norman Naimark, Robert Peckham, Priscilla Roberts, Robert Service, Facil Tesfaye and Vladimir Tismaneanu. Others were generous in sharing stories and sources, in particular Paul S. Cha, Mihai Croitor, Brian Farrell, Sander Gilman, Paul Gregory, Paul Hollander, Jean Hung, Mark Kramer, Michelle Kung, James Person, Amir Weiner and Arne Westad.

I am indebted to my publishers, namely Michael Fishwick in London and Anton Mueller in New York, and my copy editor Richard Collins, as well as Marigold Atkey, Chloe Foster, Genista Tate-Alexander, Francesca Sturiale and Lilidh Kendrick at Bloomsbury. I would like to convey my gratitude to my literary agent Andrew Wylie in New York and Sarah Chalfant in London. I thank my wife Gail Burrowes, as always, with love.

Hong Kong, December 2018

Index

Note on the Author

Frank Dikötter is Chair Professor of Humanities at the University of Hong Kong and Senior Fellow at the Hoover Institution. His books have changed the way historians view China, from the classic *The Discourse of Race in Modern China* to his award-winning People's Trilogy documenting the lives of ordinary people under Mao. He is married and lives in Hong Kong.

Note on the Type

The text of this book is set Adobe Garamond. It is one of several versions of Garamond based on the designs of Claude Garamond. It is thought that Garamond based his font on Bembo, cut in 1495 by Francesco Griffo in collaboration with the Italian printer Aldus Manutius. Garamond types were first used in books printed in Paris around 1532. Many of the present-day versions of this type are based on the *Typi Academiae* of Jean Jannon cut in Sedan in 1615.

Claude Garamond was born in Paris in 1480. He learned how to cut type from his father and by the age of fifteen he was able to fashion steel punches the size of a pica with great precision. At the age of sixty he was commissioned by King Francis I to design a Greek alphabet, and for this he was given the honourable title of royal type founder. He died in 1561.